General Sharon's war against multi-billion

For three months, th captured the natio major newspapers and magazines reported on it in great detail. It received front-page attention because it pitted one of the world's great media empires against the free world's greatest general, Israel's flamboyant contender for the Prime Minister's seat vs. the arrogant *Time* conglomerate.

During the trial, Dov Aharoni spent time in the courtroom and met with many of the key principals in the case. As the weeks passed by, he began to dig deeper into the background issues which figured so prominently in the legal battle: Israel's 1982 incursion into Lebanon, the killings in Sabra and Shatilla, and *Time* magazine's abysmal record of Middle East coverage since the creation of the State of Israel in 1948. After the trial, he pored through thousands of pages of documents (the transcript of the trial alone was over 4,000 pages) in the process of writing the first major study of the case to be published anywhere in the world.

An important piece of new and original scholarship on the celebrated case, *General Sharon's War Against Time Magazine* also makes for dramatic and gripping reading, as this fast-paced account brings the reader into the battlefields of Lebanon and the New York courtroom, face-to-face with the issues and personalities of this historic event.

GENERAL
SHARON'S
WAR
AGAINST
TIME MAGAZINE
HIS TRIAL AND VINDICATION

**STEIMATZKY
SHAPOLSKY**

NEW YORK • JERUSALEM • TEL AVIV

0-933-50300-8 $4.95

**Featuring Original
Courtroom Sketches
and Photographs**

By Dov Aharoni

A Steimatzky and Shapolsky Book
Published by Steimatzky, N.Y.

For any additional information, contact Steimatzky, Inc., 152 E. 65th Street, New York, NY 10021.

Typesetting by A Lot of Type and Graphics Too, Inc., New York City, NY
Cover design by A Lot of Type and Graphics Too, Inc., New York City, NY

1st Edition, April 1985

ISBN 0-933-50300-8 $4.95

About the Author

Dov Aharoni (Fisch) is a prominent American Jewish author and thinker, and he has held a number of important leadership posts within that community. He has served as a member of the American Zionist Federation's executive committee, as an honorary board member of his city's United Jewish Appeal, and as the national executive director of the Herut Zionists of America. In this last capacity, he worked closely with leading Israeli Cabinet ministers and Knesset members.

A columnist for the *Jewish Press* and a member of three editorial boards, Dov Aharoni (Fisch) has published in *Midstream, American Jewish History,* and other scholarly journals. His most recent book, *Jews for Nothing,* was the subject of widespread critical acclaim for its hard-hitting and creative analysis of the American Jewish community.

After receiving his undergraduate degree in political science from Columbia University, Dov Aharoni (Fisch) was awarded his master's degree in Jewish history at Yeshiva University, where he was also ordained a rabbi in 1981. He is married to the former Linda Yellin of Aurora, Illinois and has three daughters: Yael, Kineret-Yardena, and Ayelet-Geula.

Dedication

For My Grandparents
"Bubbe Rosie & Zeyde Izzy"
Whose Commitment to Torah
and the Jewish People
Has Served as a
Life-Long Inspiration

Table of Contents

Preface

When the New York jury deliberating in the Southern District returned its final decision in the case of *Ariel Sharon v. Time,* it was clear that a major milestone of American libel law had been achieved. Judge Abraham Sofaer's process of breaking up the verdicts into three separate decisions enabled Minister Ariel Sharon to win a stunning victory in the battle, even though he technically failed to secure a formal "libel" verdict.

In two months, he and his attorneys, led by Milton Gould, proved that *Time* magazine had published a defamation rooted in falsehood. He established, moreover, something extraordinary: an amplification by the jury, pounding in its message, sharply denouncing the negligence and carelessness manifested by *Time* magazine in this sordid matter.

Yet, *Time* attempted to arrogantly project itself as some kind of "winner," citing the baseball metaphor: you're not out until they get the third strike.

What eluded *Time* was that defamation and falsity—the first two strikes—had been amplified by the jury to also include "negligence" and "carelessness." Even using the baseball metaphor, *Time* had struck out—and deservedly so.

This book comes on the heels of *Ariel Sharon v. Time Inc.* in the hope that the public will have an opportunity to gain an insight into what may have been the most profound first-amendment case in many years . . . and a powerful courtroom drama, at that. Its principals are people of influence right now, and the results of this trial are certain to have serious implications both at home and in the State of Israel, where Minister Ariel Sharon returns a man vindicated.

I would like to thank David Prebor for assistance he rendered in research for this book. The staff at the Zionist Archives prepared materials faster than they could be requested. And Brenda Cameron proved a godsend, making important documents available.

Ian Shapolsky, in supporting the idea behind this book, and in encouraging its preparation, has my deepest thanks. I am likewise deeply grateful to Harry Taubenfeld for his extraordinary support of the cause of Jewish rights and his efforts to encourage me in that path. And I owe a special debt to Jerry Strober, whose humanity and understanding cleared a major obstacle along the road to this book's realization.

For Charles Shapiro, I have few words to adequately express my thanks. As editor, as proofreader, and in so many ways, he deserves much of the credit for this book.

To Yael, Kineret, and Ayelet—I can't say much yet; they aren't old enough to read this. But I thank G-d for them.

And, last, to Linda. You have been wonderful. On to Samaria!

I
Vindication

It was a bitter winter's day. Inside the courtroom, a tense atmosphere prevailed. It was evident on the faces of spectators and principals alike, as the jury of six filed into their reserved box for one last verdict.

They had already found *Time* magazine guilty of publishing defamatory material which had charged that Israeli Minister Ariel Sharon had "consciously intended" that Lebanese Christian forces would massacre civilians. Defamation was a heavy rap, indeed, for one of the world's most respected newsweeklies to bear.

Only two days later, the same jury had returned with their second verdict: *Time*'s report that Sharon had discussed the issue of revenge with the Lebanese Christians was outright false.

False. The most damaging adjective in the business.

Now, there was one last decision to announce: would Sharon, having proven that he was grievously wronged, be able to collect the $50,000,000 in damages he sought?

Were he a private citizen, he would already have been on the way to the bank. But American libel law imposes a stricter standard for public officials. Not only must the prominent personality prove defamation and falsehood, but he must also prove malice. He must, somehow, enter the reporter's mind, expose it to the jury, and convince everyone that the defamation was done with a reckless disregard for the truth.

□   □   □   □   □

The jury entered the courtroom. There was 27-year-old Patricia DeLoatch, a marketing specialist for AT&T. Lydia Burdick, with a master's degree in clinical psychology, was unemployed at the time. Ingrid Tineo, a Dominican native now living in Manhattan, was working in personnel for Young & Rubicam. Patricia Young, 49, was an executive secretary, while 64-year-old Spencer James was a retired Con Edison supervisor.

As the jury settled into their assigned seats one last time, foreman Richard Peter Zug, the IBM computer programmer, stood up to read the jury's final verdict.

The courtroom was packed. Overpacked. Even if the tension were not so thick, the air would still be in short supply. Spectators jammed the seats and the aisles, while security officers barred others from entering. Yet, from Judge Abraham D. Sofaer down to the last spectator in the last seat in the room, there was an overpowering silence. Silence.

Time's attorneys and defense team held their breaths for good reason. One more losing decision, and the magazine would be out a huge fortune. More importantly, while insurance coverage would save the magazine's fiscal neck, it would not restore a tarnished reputation.

In Sharon's corner, the tension was of a different kind. He had won his points. He had proven his facts. But malice? Ah, malice. The Fifty-Million-Dollar Question.

Foreman Zug informed the judge that the jury had reached its verdict:

"Has plaintiff proved by clear and convincing evidence that a person or persons at Time Inc. responsible for either reporting, writing, editing or publishing the paragraph at issue did so with actual malice in that he, she, or they knew, at the time of publishing any statement we have found was false and defamatory, that the defamatory statement was false or had serious doubts as to its truth?

□   □   □   □   □

"To that question the answer is no. . . ."

The silence was broken by a humming buzz about to erupt. *Time's* staff and defense team began to break into the smiles which had been denied by cold sweat only moments before. They were ready to celebrate. But celebration was not on the jury's mind.

Zug went on, beyond the judge's original charge, to read one of the most remarkable statements in American libel history. Transcending precedent, he reported that the jury could not leave this case with a simple verdict of "No." There was something more it had to say.

"We find that certain *Time* employees, particularly

correspondent David Halevy, acted negligently and carelessly in reporting and verifying the information which ultimately found its way into the published paragraph of interest in this case."

□   □   □   □   □

In thirty-four words, the six men and women who represented all of America, reading the words of that disputed article as any typical reader would, put on record a stunning condemnation of *Time* magazine, denying the journal its last chance at vindication.

As Ariel Sharon began to rise from his seat, it was clear to every person in the room that the judgment rendered could have only one meaning.

□   □   □   □   □

Sharon, hero of so many battles and wars on the stormy fronts of the Middle East's danger zones, had won his greatest victory.

He had eradicated the blood libel. He had exonerated his name and that of his people.

He had proven to the spectators, to the jury, and to the American public that *Time* magazine had been guilty of one of journalism's worst botch-ups of the century.

Sharon had won.

II

From Kfar Malal

to the Knesset

For Ariel ("Arik") Sharon, the road from the battle fronts of Israel to a New York court room was an extraordinary trek of six thousand miles. It was also one of the most difficult journeys and consuming ordeals he had ever encountered.

□ □ □ □ □

The personal saga of Ariel Sharon goes back to the days of Mandatory Palestine, before the State of Israel had gained its independence from the British. His family had been among those perspicacious pioneers who emigrated to Palestine well before the Holocaust.

The road from persecution in Europe to liberation in Zion was not an easy one. In 1922, faced with a reality of hopelessness, Sharon's parents—then they were the Scheinermans—emigrated to Palestine (a term then used by Britain to denote the lands today called "Israel" and

"Jordan"). They came with no possessions, no money— nothing. Only dreams.

Theirs were the dreams of so many Jewish pioneers who settled the land during those hard years of economic uncertainty and political insecurity. They had little to lose—the next two decades in Poland would attest to the clear-headedness of their move. Nonetheless, life was harsh and uncompromising for the young idealists who hoped to redeem the Holy Land with the labor of their hands.

Despite the difficulties, the Scheinermans took to far- ming in the tiny village of Kfar Malal located in the Sharon region of the land. Only the year before, during the savage 1921 Arab riots, this very community had suf- fered a terrible massacre. Men, women, and children had been murdered, and the moshav had been overrun. Now, the Jewish National Fund was reconstructing Kfar Malal, and the Scheinermans were among the brave volunteers for the dangerous project.

Seven years later, the Arabs would come raiding once again, as part of a national wave of terror which saw, among other outrages, the wanton slaughter of sixty young rabbinical students at a seminary in Hebron. But this time, Kfar Malal did not fall. The settlers resisted the marauders and secured the area from further attack. The *moshav* (community settlement) of Kfar Malal stands to this day.

Ariel Sharon was born the year before those terrible 1929 riots. At the time, the land of Israel was not in full bloom, and those families who had chosen to work the land faced extreme poverty. While in Europe, Ariel's mother had been training for a different life: she was just one year away from completing her medical studies. But fate took her on a different course. She would not become that doctor.

Despite the material deprivation, Sharon's boyhood was culturally very rich. His father, when not tilling the soil, painted and played the violin. His mother taught him the values of sacrifice and determination. And she set an example to follow. To this day, Sharon still speaks of the bare-footed mother of his childhood. When she had to traverse the rugged terrain, she would place a piece of leather beneath each foot and bind it onto her leg with rope. Those were the formative years of his life.

The family lived in a hut, which they had to share with the animals being raised on the farm. The family dwelled in one room; the cows and the mule in the other.

By the time he was eight years old, young Ariel was already working on the farm, attending diligently to his chores before going off to school. Like the village, the school was poor and struggling. Often, the lack of space and facilities required that three different grades of children crowd together in a single classroom.

Even as the children of those years went to school and assumed the burdens of farm work, they also had to learn about self-defense. With Arab terrorists attacking Jewish villages in another rage of pogroms between 1936 and 1939, Ariel Sharon and his contemporaries grew up quickly, seeing first-hand the consequences of Jewish powerlessness.

After finishing grade school, Sharon went on to high school in Tel Aviv. He continued to live on the family farm, working two hours each morning, after which he would travel two more hours to school. At the end of the school day, he would return home — another two hours — to work on the farm until dusk. And then he sat down to do his homework.

After graduating high school in 1945, he joined the Jewish settlement police force and played an active part in their defense work. But he wanted to study at college, and he began his courses in the agriculture department at the Hebrew University in 1947.

Once again, his life was reordered by Arab armies. When the United Nations General Assembly voted its resolution recognizing the State of Israel, the Arab world declared a *jihad* (holy war) to eliminate the Jewish State. On December 12, 1947 Ariel Sharon was called into service.

The Israeli War of Independence was the small nation's most perilous and costly armed struggle. At the outset of the war, Sharon held the rank of corporal, but his natural military ability gained him the attention of his superiors. He quickly rose to sergeant and then was named a platoon commander at the remarkably young age of 20.

Fighting in the central region, Sharon's unit was assigned to fight one of the most gruesome battles of the war. They were to capture the infamous Latrun police fortress which, heavily fortified and set high on a hill, controlled the Jerusalem highway. Leading his forces with the

Israeli motto *"Acharai!"* ("After me!"), he was badly
wounded during the assault. Sustaining severe wounds in
his left leg and his stomach, he spent many months in the
hospital. As a result, he never finished officers' school.
He would later say: "I earned my officer's rank on the
battlefield."

The following year, Sharon was named the commander of a special reconnaissance unit. After attending
Battalion Commander School, he was appointed intelligence officer of the central command. He moved to
the northern command the following year. By age 22, he
had reached the rank of major.

It was at this time that Sharon began to make a lasting
impact on the future of military strategy of the Israeli
army by advancing his bold concepts of military strategy.
The *New York Times*, referring to this period in his life,
called him "Israel's pioneer tactician and battlefront leader
in retaliatory guerrilla warfare." It was then that he first
advocated the concept of behind-the-line raids, a strategy
which would gain him lasting fame two decades later during the Yom Kippur War.

He took a leave from the army, hoping to utilize a brief
period of peace to pursue the college studies he had been
denied earlier. For two years he studied history and Oriental studies at Hebrew University. But, then, the demands
of the nation's security once more took him away from his
books.

Across the river to Israel's east, terrorist outrages were
being organized, as marauders entered Israel's borders
from Jordan and committed attrocities against Jews. The

young nation of Israel was at wit's end: what to do?

Ariel Sharon, the young military tactician with daring ideas, was called upon to take charge of "Unit 101," an extraordinary commando group, in 1953. Their mission: to secure the borders by stamping out the terror . . . even if it meant going into enemy territory to hit the terror at its source. For the government of Israeli Prime Minister David Ben-Gurion, besieged by Arab armies attacking both overtly and covertly, there was no choice but to fight for survival.

Sharon assembled a top-notch unit which staged a series of dramatic reprisal raids, aiming their attacks at the source of the terror. And the sources were many. From 1950-1956 alone, 967 people were killed by Arab terrorists, a paralyzing figure. The favorite target of these killers was Israeli civilians, with a preference for unarmed women and children.

Sharon's Unit 101 struck back into the heart of enemy territory, eradicating the terror from Israel's borders, and securing the country's lines. Considering how much Unit 101 did for the young country, it is remarkable that the whole force numbered just 45 fighters.

The success of his commando group led to a new commission for Major Sharon. He was appointed commander of Israel's paratroops.

Enthusiastically assuming the new challenge, he welded the paratroopers into a powerful force which continued the defense against terrorism. In 1954 he was badly wounded in the left leg, battling Arab guerrillas invading from the Gaza District, which was then under Egyptian occupation. For his efforts and successes, he was soon promoted to a new rank: Lieutenant-Colonel, commander of the Parachute Brigade.

During the 1956 war in the Sinai, Sharon gained a reputation as a defiant field commander, when he argued spiritedly with his superiors over how far to push his paratroop battalion through the desert. His troops ultimately penetrated much farther than General Moshe Dayan had ordered. In the course of the battle his men secured the Mitla Pass, sustaining heavy casualties. On November 5 the Egyptian command post was taken, and Sharon's Parachute Brigade went on to reach Sharm-el-Sheikh. The straits that had been closed by the Egyptians could now be opened.

At the war's end, Sharon went to Kimberly Staff College in England. When he returned to Israel, he was named one of the heads of the Training Command of the Israeli Army. He was next named to command an armored tank brigade. In 1964, he was appointed Head of Staff, Northern Command, and two years later named director of the Training Command.

It was at about this time that this warrior, this man of tanks and parachutes, this leader of commandos decided to study law. His diligence and dedication to his studies saw him earn his law degree from Tel Aviv University at the age of 40.

Modern Jewish history, changed by the rise of Israel in 1948, was elevated to a new dimension in the face of the 1967 Six-Day War. Threatened on three fronts, the State of Israel engaged Egypt in the south, Jordan in the east, and Syria in the north in a desperate struggle for survival. Early reports coming from the front included frenzied Arab claims that the Israelis had been dealt severe blows. Throughout the world, people shuddered at the time of the war's outbreak: Could the glimmering spark of Israel be extinguished so soon? Was this to be Israel's last war?

The fear and sorrow were turned to hope and euphoria, as the true battle results emerged. The State of Israel had survived the most concentrated threat yet made to her survival. The ancient Jewish capital city of Jerusalem had been united under Israeli sovereignty for the first time in two thousand years. The Biblical prophecies of a Jewish return to the ancient sites of Jewish history were realized before a stunned world's eyes as the Israeli Defense Forces marched into Jordanian-occupied Judea and Samaria and liberated the cities of Hebron, Shechem, and Shiloh.

□   □   □   □   □

Less glamorous were the awesome battles which shaped up in the south, in the Sinai desert. There, the troops fought without the intensity of world attention and without the drama of the international spotlight. But the fighting was difficult, and the defense in the south against Egypt represented one of the greatest challenges of the war.

Commanding an armored division, with infantry and paratroops, Sharon's Tank Corps breached Egyptian positions in Northern and Central Sinai, retracing the steps of his battles during the 1956 Sinai Compaign.

□   □   □   □   □

The euphoria of the 1967 victory quickly abated, as the Israelis found themselves at arms with Egypt once again. During the War of Attrition, one of Israel's most painful conflicts despite its relative historical anonymity in the West, Sharon was named General Operations Commander of the Southern Command. His men held the lines. He argued, once again, that a flexible defense based on mobile defense units would be far preferable to a static line. Although he did not win the complete agreement of the Israeli Defense Forces general staff, he did gain partial support for his advocacy of deep-penetration commando raids. Given the opportunity, he personally led some of the daring thrusts behind enemy lines. He is remembered throughout Israel, to this day, as the "Pacifier of the Gaza District" for the role he played in wiping out the terrorist enclaves which had festered in Gaza, endangering the Israeli population.

Despite his legendary military record, he remained a highly controversial personality within the I.D.F. framework, and it was made clear to him in quiet meetings that the doors for future advancement were shut. Having attained the rank of General, he expressed his interest in a future opportunity to serve as the Israeli Defense Forces Chief of Staff.

He received his answer. No way. You are not part of the Labor Party machinery.

□   □   □   □   □

To understand Sharon, one must understand Israel's

political fabric. While the country has more than twenty political parties contending against each other in any particular election, the nation is really divided into three political blocs: the socialist Labor Alignment, the centrist-conservative Likud coalition, and the religious parties.

In Israel, elections are held every four years for the 120 seats in the country's parliament, the *Knesset*. To effectively rule the country, a union of parties must join together after election day so that parties controlling 61 or more seats agree to vote together, assuring their new government a working parliamentary majority.

From 1948-1977, for all of Israel's first three decades, the Labor Alignment out-polled the Likud (which then went by other names). Together with the votes of the religious bloc, Labor was able to rule Israel.

In time it became evident that the road to political survival lay in the Labor constellation. Thus, many conservatives and most centrists with political aspirations also joined Labor. They may not have supported all of Labor's policies or goals, but they recognized that there was only one game in town: the Labor game.

There were many talented personalities in various walks of life who refused to compromise their consciences during these first thirty years of Israel's history. They remained adherents of the Likud or the religious parties. By doing so, they often won great respect for their principled behavior. They also found the door to social and political advancement locked shut when their talents elevated them beyond the rank-and-file.

Among those whose careers were stymied by the petty

politics of a country whose Labor Party won every election from 1948-1977 were Generals Ezer Weizman and Ariel Sharon. Both had proven military skills and talents which would have earned them even greater promotions and opportunities had they been aligned with the ruling class. But their ideals led them towards the Likud, and they were not interested in compromising those beliefs in capitalism and in a more Jewish direction for Israel than the socialists in Labor desired.

In the aftermath of the War of Attrition, General Ariel Sharon had all the makings of a future Israeli Chief-of-Staff, except for one pronounced deficiency: he was not affiliated with Labor.

With the door to future military advancement locked tight, Gen. Sharon decided to retire from active duty in the latter part of 1973. He would pursue a career in politics and would try to achieve in the political arena the same dramatic attainments which had been his on the battlefield.

He formally joined the Israeli Liberal Party. The hallmark of the party's platform is its advocacy of a capitalistic economic system, along the lines of that practiced in the United States. Israel, however, had been ruled for three decades by the Labor parties which advocated a system of socialism that was tempered by basic Western democratic values, so the call for American-style capitalism was virtually revolutionary.

General Sharon, now a civilian political figure, determined that the Labor parties could be beaten only if the opposition parties would unite together in a formidable bloc. He approached leaders of many of Israel's twenty-plus parties, arguing that the differences separating them from other parties did not justify the continued splintering which relegated them to the political wilderness.

Incredibly, the general of the battlefield proved to be a remarkable diplomat and negotiator. Despite the incredible odds against him and the scorn of his opponents who jeered at his "impossible" undertaking, Ariel Sharon succeeded in winning over a number of prominent political leaders and parties, who agreed with his premise that petty differences had to be put aside for the greater good of the nation. The results of his efforts were crowned with success with the announcement that a number of major parties would join together under the umbrella title: "Likud" (literally, "Coalition").

Aimed at winning election on a platform advocating a return to capitalist economic principles and a policy of advocating Jewish rights to settle in the historic Jewish communities of Judea and Samaria, the Likud experiment shaped up as Labor's most formidable challenge in thirty years.

But the 1973 election year was not to be like any previous one. President Anwar Sadat of Egypt had other plans.

□   □   □   □   □

On the holiest day of the Jewish calendar—Yom Kippur, an awe-filled occasion when Jews spend the entire day in solemn prayer in synagogue and abstain from food and drink for 25 hours—the Egyptian army launched an invasion in the Sinai, crossing the Suez Canal.

The army of Israel was taken completely by surprise. Soldiers stationed along the Suez Canal were assigned to maintain the so-called "Bar-Lev line" (named after a former Israeli chief-of-staff) in the Sinai. This "line" had been established by those who advocated the value of a stationary defense formation and the soldiers defending it were sitting ducks for Egyptian gunners. They never knew what hit them. As the Egyptian army penetrated into the desert, in an operation coordinated with Syria which made similar thrusts into Israel's north, the people of Israel frantically mobilized for war.

Calls went out through the synagogues. Emergency mobilization orders were broadcst on radio. And every possible method was undertaken to convert a civilian population into a national army as fast as possible—and faster than that.

When Anwar Sadat's troops were sighted and the call for national mobilization went out, Ariel Sharon—politician—returned to active duty and became Major General Ariel Sharon once again. He reported to his division in the Sinai.

▫   ▫   ▫   ▫   ▫

The Yom Kippur War, which would ultimately become the scene of Sharon's greatest victories and glory, was his most frustrating encounter. From the outset, Sharon viewed the conflict in a light completely different from that of his superiors, arguing that the war could be won in hours. The Chief-of-Staff, David Elazar, did not see it that way. General Haim Bar-Lev did not see it that way. In fact, virtually no one in the Israeli military command saw it Sharon's way. The accepted viewpoint was that Sadat had taken Israel by surprise, administered a heavy clobbering, and was on a roll. The common wisdom which emerged as the battle plan for Israel was to step back, retreat, regroup.

Sharon was deeply frustrated by the rest of the army's refusal to see things his way. He believed that the Egyptians were not so invulnerable. Their fighting skills and training were really not so advanced. Yes, Israel had suffered a terrible initial blow, the product of surprise and a lack of readiness across-the-board. But now we are mobilized, argued Sharon. Now we are ready. Now we can wipe them out.

Sharon persevered through the early stages of the war, as one recommendation after another was ignored. In the face of his critics, who repeatedly claimed over the years that Sharon had a tendency to manifest insubordination, his behavior during the Yom Kippur War marked exemplary conduct and irrefutable proof that he was a disciplined officer. Despite his deep-felt sense that the general staff had turned a potential victory into a national disaster, he maintained his professional standards throughout the struggle, arguing potently for his views—and then accepting his obligation to follow the final staff policy.

When the Yom Kippur War seemed at its most bleak, with the Egyptians penetrated deep into Israeli-held territory in the Sinai, the world was suddenly stunned by the reports emanating from the front that, somehow, Major Gen. Ariel Sharon had led his division across the Suez Canal into Egypt. The reaction was stupefication.

With Sharon's bridgehead secured, the tide of the battle changed markedly. The Egyptian spirits and morale suddenly tumbled, and the march of Egypt was halted. In a few days' time, the Israeli Defense Forces succeeded in surrounding Egypt's Third Army, and the real possibility suddenly loomed that thousands of Egyptian soldiers might be slaughtered in hours if the Sadat government did not retreat.

The world was now aware of Israel's incredible victory—in the face of early setbacks. The Yom Kippur War's achievements were unquestionably Israel's greatest victories in her quarter-century of independent statehood. But, now, the world forced a settlement on Israel which required her to leave Egypt, to end the encirclement of the Egyptian Third Army, and to ultimately cede the Sinai Peninsula to Egyptian authority.

(A few years later, when Sadat visited Jerusalem during the process which led to Camp David, he met with Sharon in person. He told Sharon: "During the 1973 War, I wanted so much to capture you when you were on the west bank of the Suez in Egyptian territory—though I would have preferred capturing you in the Sinai . . . ")

(Sharon replied: "Mr. President, today you have a greater opportunity than we could ever have hoped for before. Today, you can capture me as a friend.")

□   □   □   □   □

In the aftermath of the Yom Kippur War, the Israeli public demanded an investigation into the war and its results. The Agranat Commission's findings implicated many prominent Israeli officers and officials. From Chief-of-Staff David Elazar on down, the Israeli army, its officers, and its policies came in for heavy criticism. Ariel Sharon, himself the object of many charges, emerged not only exonerated but vindicated. He was the unquestioned hero of the war, and in many circles a slogan was heard for the first time: "Arik, King of Israel!" Pictures of Sharon's heavily bandaged head, the result of a serious wound sustained in the heat of battle during the Yom Kippur War, became a favorite poster around the country.

□   □   □   □   □

In the aftermath of the Yom Kippur War, the Israeli electorate went to the polls to elect its new Knesset parliament and national leadership. Reflective of thirty years' undefeated successes at the polls, the discredited Labor government of Golda Meir nevertheless won another victory.

But Yom Kippur and Arik Sharon had done their damage. The new Likud marked a turning-point in the organization of a spirited opposition to Labor policies, and continued revelations in the aftermath of the 1973 War further damaged Labor's image. Especially devastating were findings that the Egyptian "surprise attack" had not been all that surprising after all. Far from being caught off-guard, Israel's top brass knew an Egyptian first-strike was coming, and an actual meeting was held in which strategy around that strike was discusssed. In the face of pleas from David Elazar for a "green light" to pre-empt the Egyptian attack with a prior strike, Prime Minister Golda Meir took the firm position that Israel must not strike first. She maintained that Israel had to consider her world-wide political image, and it was vital that the world see that Sadat and Egypt had launched the war, not Israel. Accordingly, she ordered that there be no Israeli preemptive raid, and that Israel absorb the full brunt of an Egyptian assault. Thus, the Israeli soldiers on the Sinai front, the sitting ducks who were mowed down by Egypt in the first days of the war, were Golda Meir's sacrifices on an altar of public opinion.

Perhaps dispassionate observers, reflecting years later, would determine that Golda acted wisely. Maybe not. But, for those who had been touched by death or severe injury during the Yom Kippur War — and Israel is a small country, where casualties are felt by all — there emerged a sense that "it is time for a change."

In the 1977 Israeli general elections, the Likud coalition swept to its first-ever electoral victory. Menachem Begin became Prime Minister of Israel, and Ariel Sharon was named Minister of Agriculture.

To Sharon's enemies, his ministry was the subject of open sneering. "Minister of Tomatoes," heckled one opponent. But Sharon well understood the significance of his new post.

As Israeli Minister of Agriculture, he used his influence and ministry to master-mind a massive expansion of Jewish communities throughout the regions of Judea and Samaria, rescued from Jordanian occupation in 1967. Working closely with Prime Minister Begin, Sharon emerged as a major voice and force in Israeli public life, and as one of the counry's most powerful political leaders.

In one of his most memorable experiences during the

years in which he served as Minister of Agriculture, Sharon visited Egypt for the purpose of sharing with the Sadat government insights into Israeli agricultural know-how. In the aftermath of efforts to create a peace between Israel and Egypt, the Israelis wanted very much to share their secrets of combating hunger, of making deserts bloom with abundance. To further this objective, Sharon traveled to Egypt, where he met with Sadat. He was then asked to survey Egypt's terrain to get a better sense of the situation on the land. Into the Egyptian jet he went, and the plane took of for the mundane survey of the land. In the plane itself, Agriculture Minister Sharon conversed with the two young Egyptian pilots. In time he learned from them that they had each served in the Sinai during the Yom Kippur War, flying sorties for the Egyptian air force. Sharon marveled at the thought that the three of them could now be aloft in the skies of Egypt, jointly planning a process which would result in the cultivation of Egypt's dry lands.

The human side of Ariel Sharon, the profile the public rarely sees, is evidenced by his experiences with Sadat and the Egyptian pilots during peace time. This extremely complex figure does not always project the intensely human dimension of his personality. But it is there.

He has known personal tragedy and great pain. While ostensibly impervious to war, he has met with deep grief in his personal life. His first wife, mother of his first child, was killed in an automobile accident in 1962, leaving behind their five-year-old son. That boy was killed as a youngster in the mid-1960's when he was accidentally shot to death by another boy who was handling a pistol. In 1964, Sharon married his first wife's sister, Lily. He has had two sons with her, the first now serving as an Israeli army paratrooper.

Together, they manage the family's 1000-acre farm near Ashkelon, where they grow wheat, cotton, and citrus crops—and raise riding horses as a hobby.

The District Attorney of Manhatttan in New York City, Robert Morgenthau, is one of those who knows Sharon well and has visited him on the farm. He paid his first visit in 1979, right after Israel had come to terms with Egypt. Morgenthau's wife was with him.

"We saw the great pleasure that he took in the land and growing of his oranges and the grapefruit, wheat, melons, sheep, and we stayed in touch with him whenever he has come to this country . . . ."

"He has an excellent reputation not only, of course, as a military genius but also as a man of honesty, integrity, and forthrightness . . . ."

Bayard Rustin, the preeminent Black American leader, first met Sharon in 1973. In addition to regarding him as "an important and creative military general, obviously a major political figure, [and] a great patriot of the State of Israel," Rustin also adds that he sees Sharon as "a humanitarian."

It is that aspect of Sharon—his humanitarianism—which is most important to consider in light of his paradoxical role as a military leader, often assigned the unpleasant task of ferreting out terrorists who hide among civilian populations. In Israel's thirty-six-year struggle to exist in a sea of Arab hostility and rejection, she has been plagued by the morally wrenching challenges posed by Arab terrorists who use civilians as strategic weapons in their war against Israeli survival.

How does one fight an enemy who places his weapons in apartment houses, in hospitals, and in schools? How does one battle the murderer who hides behind a woman's skirt, who holds a baby in his arm as a shield as he attacks, who stations his main headquarters and fighting units in the heart of civilian neighborhoods?

For Sharon, the problem is difficult; the solution, however, can only be one.

"We were brought up. . . . It goes along our religion, it goes with our culture, it comes as our education. And that is the important, highly important, the most important thing was always human life. . . . Those moral values that refer to human life were basic elements in the education that we gave, that we got ourselves [as] children, that we gave to our children, that we gave to our soldiers and armed forces since we formed the Israeli Defense Forces when the State of Israel was established. . . ."

"I would like you to know that, for these moral values that brought us to take all the measures in order to avoid casualties among civilian populations, we paid with blood — our blood — a very precious price and very high price. . . ."

"It's a natural thing when you take care of your own civilians. You go to war in order to defend your people. I speak about measures and steps taken in order to avoid casualties among Arab civilian populations...."

"Palestinians are like other civilians. They are human beings like other Arab civilians.... We live together, and we will have to live together in peaceful coexistence...."

"Also soldiers.... We took care of enemy wounded soldiers as no one ever did in the Middle East..."

□   □   □   □   □

In 1981 Prime Minister Menachem Begin and his Likud slate won reelection for another term in office. In the new government Ariel Sharon was promoted to the portfolio of Minister of Defense. He had come a long way.

III

Operation Peace for Galilee

The great paradox of modern Israel is that it has emerged as a modern Athens, despite the need to maintain a footing more reminiscent of ancient Sparta. Israel is a broadly cultured Western society with a full range of diversions, including operas, ballet troupes, a world-class symphony orchestra, and theater companies.

More than twenty political parties debate ideas openly and freely, and they may all stand before the national electorate and lay claim to Western man's most precious possession: his vote. Newspapers abound — in various languages, representing opposing viewpoints.

And, yet, this strange oasis of sanity and Western civilization must take cognizance of its place in the Middle East. Surrounded by tyrannies and dictatorships, most of which are ruled over by butchers and megalomaniacs, Israel has been forced to fight for its life.

When not under coordinated attack by a number of allied Arab armies, the Israeli populace faces the cruel reality of Arab terrorism—even during "peacetime." This terror comes courtesy of a terrorist outfit known as the "P.L.O."

The P.L.O. was founded in 1964—when the Gaza District was in Arab hands (Egypt). When Judea and Samaria ("the West Bank") were in Arab hands (Jordan). Yet, the P.L.O. of 1964 and 1965 and 1966 did not aim their voluminous armed attacks against Egyptian or Jordanian occupation of "Palestine." They could not care less about controlling the Gaza or Judea-Samaria. Their targets were the cities in pre-1967 Israel: Tel Aviv, Jaffa, Haifa. The flag of the P.L.O. includes on it the map of "Palestine"—and that map does not contemplate the Gaza District or the regions of Judea and Samaria. The flag—and the map on it—are of the State of Israel.

That is the "Palestine" coveted by the P.L.O. The State of Israel.

□   □   □   □   □

In pursuit of their effort to drive the Jews of Israel into the Mediterranean Sea (the slogan was coined by P.L.O. founding chairman Ahmed Shukairy), the band has adopted a covenant and a policy of terror aimed at realizing the dream of a *Judenrein* Middle East. It is worthwhile to consider aspects of the P.L.O. charter:

ARTICLE 9. Armed struggle is the only way to liberate Palestine and is therefore a strategy and not tactics
. . .

ARTICLE 15. The liberation of Palestine, from an

Arab viewpoint, is a national duty to repulse the Zion-ist . . . and to eliminate the Zionist presence from Palestine . . .

ARTICLE 19. The partitioning of Palestine in 1947 and the establishment of Israel are fundamentally null and void . . .

ARTICLE 21. The Palestinian Arab people, in ex-pressing itself through the armed Palestinian revolution, rejects every solution that is a substitute for a complete liberation of Palestine . . .

ARTICLE 23. The demands of security and peace . . . oblige all states . . . to consider Zionism an illegitimate movement and to prohibit its existence and activity.

These are the words of the P.L.O., the band of terror-ists who would displace the Jewish State from the face of this earth if only given the opportunity to actualize their "covenant." One looks at the words and marvels at the brazenness of their positions: they advocate a Hitler-like position aimed at the physical extermination of Israel. Zionism is illegitimate and illegal. Israel is null and void. The Zionist presence must be eliminated. No solution short of *complete* "liberation" (i.e., dismemberment of Israel) will be considered.

And, until the world gives in to their demands, there can only be armed struggle — no other course.

□   □   □   □   □

To give a more potent meaning to their threatening words, the P.L.O. has staged a series of murderous raids and terrorist actions over the past decade, endangering the lives of not only Israelis but also Jews who live outside of Israel — and, increasingly, targeting non-Jews, too. And, in keeping with the P.L.O.'s time-honored tradition, their victims are invariably civilians — preferably unarmed women and children.

There has probably never been a combat force as corrupt and unprincipled as this "Palestine Liberation Organization." Its tactics and strategies are unique in the history of warfare. Unlike civilized societies which place a premium on protecting their civilian populations, the P.L.O. goes to every length to bring its violence into the heart of its civilian centers. It bases its main terror headquarters in the heart of population centers. Its armed camps are established in residential neighborhoods. It places heavy artillery equipment and arms in hospitals, in mosques and churches, in schools, and in apartment buildings. It recruits children to join the fight, and its own men often carry babies in their arms during street fighting to shield themselves.

Their contempt for civilians, then, cuts across racial and religious grounds. They will hijack civilian airliners and threaten the passengers' lives. They will blow up school buildings, as they did in Maalot, and they will go to civilian centers like Kiryat Shmoneh, where they will throw children out of windows.

But they are an equal-opportunity employer. For every outrage against Jews throughout the world, they are eager to sacrifice the lives of Arab civilians, too.

      □   □   □   □   □

When the Jordanian government decided to throw the P.L.O. out of their country in 1970, the terrorists set up shop in Southern Lebanon. In doing so, they took the Arab world's only peaceful land with a modicum of democracy, and they set it on the road to hell.

At first the Southern Lebanese population ignored the P.L.O. invaders, as Arafat's men aimed their thrusts against the Israeli population. Lebanon shares its southern border with Israel's Galilee region. And, for years, the Galilee rocked under P.L.O. artillery bombardment, peppered by Soviet-supplied Katyusha rockets. And, for color, the P.L.O. paid occasional visits across the border.

They murdered babies and old men in Kiryat Shmoneh in April, 1974 – and they killed students in a Maalot school building the following month. They attacked Kibbutz Misgav Am, where they went for the children once again. They attacked a tourist bus of civilians traveling along the Tel Aviv-Haifa coastal road. They murdered a young American woman taking photographs on an Israeli beach. They reveled in the opportunity to inflict whatever outrages were within their grasps.

Outside of Israel they commandeered airliners and held hostage citizens from virtually every Western country. They murdered eleven members of the Israeli Olympic team during the 1972 Munich Olympic games. They killed a party of 26 pilgrims arriving from Puerto Rico. They spilled blood with impunity.

□   □   □   □   □

All this – and more – they achieved from the safety and security of south Lebanon, an area difficult to patrol under the best of circumstances. But Lebanon represented something other than the best of circumstances. Itself a hopelessly divided country, its central government was barely able to run the country, much less secure its borders. A crazy patchwork of variegated interest-groups, religious factions, and ethnic minorities, Lebanon barely held together into the 1970's. Just consider the incredible constitutional agreement which various Lebanese parties had been following in apportioning national power since 1943.

By law, Lebanon's President must always be a Maronite Christian. Its Prime Minister must be a Sunni Moslem. The Speaker of its parliament must be a Shi'ite Moslem. And its Defense Minister must be a Druze. That is the law. Shi'ites can't be presidents; Sunnis can't be defense ministers. And if, after enough massacres, there remains only one Druze left in Lebanon—well, he gets to be Defense Minister.

Quite a system . . .

But no other system could work in a country split sixteen ways. There are twelve distinct Christian sects in Lebanon, the main one being the Maronites, who came to the country in the eighth century. The Druze, believers in an offshot of Islam, arrived in the eleventh century after being driven out of Egypt. Shi'ite Moslems are of the sect made famous by Iran's elder statesman, the Ayatollah Khomeini. And the Sunnis are a more mainstream Moslem set. To the casual observer, there is an understandable tendency to forget the Lebanese Armenians, Kurds, Nestorian Assyrians, and Greek Orthodox Christians.

□   □   □   □   □

The influx of Palestinians into Lebanon, in the aftermath of Hussein's decision to evict them from Jordan, added a new ingredient to the unstable mix: half a million displaced persons whose main political entity—the P.L.O.—thrives on instability.

A civil war erupted in Lebanon, finally, in 1975. Actually, it was anything but civil. Moslems fought Christians. Leftists fought Rightists. Christians blew up Christians. Moslems blew up Moslems.

In time, Lebanon eroded from the only hopeful spot on the Arab map into one more hell. And the very word "hell" took on a new meaning in the face of the P.L.O. presence in the country. Because of the weakness of Lebanon's central government, the P.L.O. was able to create its own country—"Fatahland"—in the south. And, throughout the surrounding environs, it seized a control of the region which made it the virtual government of the South. It maintained an army, a police force, a "judicial system," and all the other trappings of power and subjugation. This "government" ruled not only in isolated towns and villages but also in such population centers as Damur, Sidon, Tyre, and West Beirut.

Thus, for example, Dr. Ramsey Shabb's country estate in the hills east of Sidon became P.L.O. territory. The terrorists set up rocket launchers in his orange groves and stacked crates of ammunition nearby. His barns were turned into armories, while his estate filled up with explosives, ammunition, fuel drums, jeeps, trucks, 130-millimeter artillery pieces, and other P.L.O. accoutrements. Dr. Shabb could do nothing about it. He preferred to live.

His mother had a nearby garden. The P.L.O. cut the

flowers away. When she asked a ten-year-old boy to leave the garden alone, he replied: "We'll blow up your house." Cute kid.

In the Maronite village of Lebaa, the P.L.O. rented a country house. After turning the building into a restaurant and casino, they informed the owners that they would no longer pay the rent. The building was not the property of the P.L.O. Indeed, theft was a common practice of the P.L.O. in Lebanon. They would take whatever merchandise they wanted . . . without paying for it. And, if one demanded payment, they would be shot. A case in point:

One afternoon in 1979 the P.L.O. entered the Khalde home of Zouhair Ladki, a 25-year-old Moslem. They ordered the family out of the house; when the Palestine liberators departed, the family returned to learn that they had stolen jewelry, television sets, a hi-fi set, and some rugs.

The P.L.O. had a number of car-theft rings throughout the country. At P.L.O. road checkpoints, drivers of expensive cars would be ordered out from their automobiles, and the P.L.O. would seize the property. Their theft of farm produce had even more severe consequences putting many Lebanese farmers completely out of business.

They even intimidated the democratically elected officials of Lebanon's villages and towns. In Tyre they intimidated the entire city council into stepping down from office. In Nabtiye, the Lebanese provincial governor, Adnan Ibrahim, was stripped of all practical authority. He later told David Shipler of the *New York Times:* "I worked, but with such difficulty . . . I worked without having power. They did not want the police here. We were never free to say what we thought. We were not allowed to hang the picture of the President of the republic during the Palestinian occupation . . ."

The bad got worse as the P.L.O. began importing terrorists from outside the Arab world and training terrorists to play mercenary roles in the great popular struggle of the Palestinian people. Soon, paid fighters came to Lebanon from Bangladesh, Sri Lanka, Pakistan, and sundry parts of North Africa. These people were crude in demeanor and even less understanding of the Lebanese people than were the P.L.O. terrorists.

David Shipler, in his landmark account of this period, writes of the contempt the P.L.O. had for its own civilians' safety:

"But the P.L.O. was not on a campaign to win friends among the Lebanese. Its thrust was military. The huge sums of money the P.L.O. received from Saudi Arabia and other Arab countries seems to have been spent primarily on weapons and ammunition, which were placed strategically in densely populated civilian areas in the hope that this would either deter Israeli attacks or exact a price from Israel in world opinion for killing civilians.

"Towns and camps were turned into vast armories as crates of ammunition were stacked in underground shelters, and anti-aircraft guns were emplaced in schoolyards, among apartment houses, next to churches and hospitals . . ."

It is in the context of Shipler's searching report that two residential neighborhoods deserve special consideration. Just on the perimeter of West Beirut, the P.L.O. maintained some of its main command posts in the two communities of Shatilla and Sabra. While P.L.O. propangandists and media-experts called Sabra and Shatilla "refugee camps," they were anything but that. They were two built-up neighborhoods with substantial populations. It has been estimated that the community of Sabra had a population of 30,000, and Shatilla's population was similar.

These two Palestinian neighborhoods were well developed and included multi-story dwellings and other accomodations which made them attractive to Palestinian residents.

The P.L.O., as a strategic policy, decided to protect its major operations in Lebanon by locating key headquarters and training centers there. Moreover, they pre-positioned some of their heaviest, most sophisticated weapons in Shatilla and Sabra. Literally, hundreds of tons of weapons were stored in these two residential neighborhoods by late 1982. Usually, the weapons were stored in school buildings or near hospitals. The purpose was obvious: the Israelis, a highly moral and ethical army, would be effectively handcuffed by the dilemma posed: to eradicate the terror at the expense of civilian life, or not?

Secure in their plan, the P.L.O. next constructed a massive network of underground tunnels connecting these two suburbs with West Beirut proper. In the tunnels, they stored enormous caches of weapons and munitions. The tunnels served two purposes. First, they allowed the P.L.O. "guerrillas" a rapid and easy escape route from Shatilla and Sabra in the event of difficult fighting; in such a way, the P.L.O. "fighters" would be able to save themselves without facing a substantial onslaught from invading forces. Of course, this plan would leave their own civilians unprotected. That did not concern the P.L.O., which does not regard the fate of its own civilians to be any more important than the fate of others' civilians.

A second advantage of the tunnel network linking Shatilla and Sabra with West Beirut was that it enabled the P.L.O. to preposition huge stocks of weapons in the safety of the underground tunnels—thereby avoiding their dection, and providing an ample supply of weapons' stocks in the event of heavy fighting in West Beirut proper.

As the P.L.O. steadily converted the Shatilla and Sabra neighborhoods into virtual bases for terrorist activities, the P.L.O. acted in clear contravention of a 1977 international Protocol which had been adopted in an international conference aimed at expanding the famous 1949 Geneva Conventions. Article 51 (7) of the Protocol reads:

> The presence of movements of the civilian population or individual civilians shall not be used to render certain points or areas immune from military operations, in particular in attempts to shield military objectives from attacks or to shield, favor or impede military operations. The Parties to the conflict shall not direct the movement of the civilian population or individual civilians in order to attempt to shield military objectives from attacks or to shield military operations.

Article 58 goes on to say that "the Parties to the conflict shall, to the maximum extent feasible, (a) ... endeavor to remove the civilian population, individual civilians and civilian objects under their control from the vicinity of military objectives; (b) avoid locating military objectives within or near densely populated areas," etc.

These conventions were clearly violated by the P.L.O. in its own military strategy aimed at compromising Israel's moral base.

In time, the P.L.O. brass became increasingly brazen in their preference for the Shatilla and Sabra suburbs as sites for military-related purposes. On August 21, 1982 the *Times* of London reported that "members of the Italian Red Brigades and the West German Baader-Meinhoff Gang were trained at the so-called 'European base' at the Shatilla refugee camp in Beirut. . ." While Shatilla hardly looks like a "refugee camp"—it is a built-up neighborhood—the *Times* report underscored a new development not widely reported before then.

In time, Shatilla was uncovered as the center for world terror. Even as its Palestinian residents went about their daily routines, refusing to protest the P.L.O.'s militarization of their neighborhood, Arafat was constructing in the heart of the community an unparalleled international terror center. When the full dimensions of Shatilla's purposes were finally uncovered in late 1982, it was found to have served as the training base for terrorists from throughout the world. Among those who had enjoyed the training and hospility of the Shatilla "refugee camp" were: the Italian Red Brigades, the Baader-Meinhoff Gang, the Irish Republican Army's communist wing, Indians, and Pakistanis.

In all, some 2,300 terrorists from throughout the world trained at Shatilla and at other "Palestine Liberation" bases between 1980 and 1981. The following other terror groups participated at one P.L.O. training base or another during this period:

Red Help (Holland)
BENTA (Spain)
FLNC (Corsica)
International Workers (Portugal)
Action Directe (France)
Front for the Liberation of Oman (Oman)
Frolinat (Chad)
Eritrean Liberation Front (Ethiopia)
Vanguarda popular Revolucionaria (Brazil)
Montoneros (Argentina)
Columbia Guerrila Group (Colombia)
MIR (Chile)
Sandinistas (Nicaragua)
MR-13 (Guatemala)
ELN (Bolivia)
Tupamaros (Uruguay)
The Carlos Network (Venezuela)

The standard terrorism course at the Shatilla "refugee camp" would run 45 days and consisted of classes in demolition, small arms operation, karate, and military tactics. In November 1981 a delegation of the British Communist Party visited the base. They were led there by the Party secretary.

The unbridled P.L.O. domination of southern Lebanon, consolidated by their establishment of a state-within-a-state, left no shortage of deep scars. The P.L.O. forcibly conscripted young boys—as young as twelve—and kidnapped many from parents who attempted to shield their children from the barbaric draft. (This policy once again reflected the terrorists' cynical contempt for the indigenous Palestinian population which they were ostensibly "liberating." By endangering the children's lives, Arafat's strategists well understood that they would, on the other hand, be posing the Israelis with a terrible burden: the conscious decision to shoot at children.)

P.L.O. road checkpoints stopped cars to search for youngsters who had avoided their imposed draft. Sister Alisse Araigi, headmistress of a Maronite school in Nabatiye, told David Shipler: "Families came to us and asked for certificates that children were sick and couldn't be drafted."

The *New York Times'* Shipler reported that there was "tentative evidence that the P.L.O. used the United Nations Relief and Works Agency, which cares for Palestinians and receives 25 percent of its budget from the United States, as a kind of civil service to enforce and carry out its draft military training program." Shipler cited the anti-Jewish curriculum taught in agency schools, and he pointed to the Siblin teachers' training school, east of Sidon, a where the dormitories were full of military uniforms and the storerooms full of ammunition. He quoted 25-year-old Youssef Sayed, who revealved that students who do not fulfill their P.L.O. military service are denied entry in the U.N.R.W.A. school. An employee of the U.N. agancy, listening to Sayed, nodded in agreement.

     □   □   □   □   □

Beyond exploiting Lebanon's children, the P.L.O. raped the land itself. East of Sidon, a deep tunnel was bored into the side of a mountain, and it was so tightly packed with grenades, rockets, artillery shells, missiles, explosives, and small-arms ammunition that only a narrow corridor remained for people to walk in.

Even the ancient Roman ruins in Tyre, preserved and reconstructed by Lebanese archaeologists, were expropriated by the P.L.O., which converted the site into a base and barred Lebanese tourists from entering.

□   □   □   □   □

Shipler also tells of the heart-wrenching story of the imam of a local village, Ali Bader el-Din, whose town came under P.L.O. domination. After studying for twelve years at the Shi'ite religious centers of Iraq, the imam returned to his hometown unaware of the deeper implications of the new P.L.O. control. He refused to bend to P.L.O. pressures to incorporate their preferred themes into his sermons. One morning during the Ramadan season, he was shot through the head on his way to the mosque.

Yasser Arafat, hearing of the incident and concerned about the potential unrest it might cause, traveled to the village and sat down with the imam's grieving young boy. He looked at the ten-year-old youth and told him, "The Zionists killed your father." Arafat pulled out his Czechoslovak-made pistol and gave it to the boy, saying, "We consider your father a hero of the Palestinian revolution. When you grow up, use this to take revenge."

The boy's brother, disgusted, turned over the gun to the Israeli army.

□   □   □   □   □

At a nearby village another Islamic leader, Sheik Mohammed al-Masri, refused to capitulate to the P.L.O.

They responded by raping and murdering his fifteen-year-old daughter.

Yunis Noufal, a 73-year-old Maronite Christian, lives in Sidon. Speaking to an American congressman, he told of the night when two P.L.O. terrorists broke into his home, tied up his wife and him, and then stole all their life-savings and valuables. Nothing was left. Noufal reported the incident to the police. The police looked pained, but shrugged their shoulders. "There was no justice here," explained Noufal. "The P.L.O. did whatever they wanted."

□   □   □   □   □

John Nasser, a Maronite priest, recalled the October 19, 1976 massacre in the small village of Heishi. "A thousand armed terrorists attacked our village that day. They burst into houses and rounded up all the people of the village, putting us in a church. Sixty-five people were left outside. We heard shooting but could not move, as the terrorists threatened to kill us if we did."

For two days the villagers were held inside the church. When they were finally permitted to leave, they beheld a grisly sight: sixty-five bodies of men, women, and children lay dead in a pool of coagulated blood. "I want to cry out to the world," beseeches Nasser.

Georges Haddad, the Roman Catholic Archbishop of Tyre, told Western journalists that a group had invaded the community and crucified seven Christians during the civil-war fighting in 1976.

In the Moslem village of Ansar, near Nabatiye, Palestinian thugs entered the area in 1980, then proceeded to the home of the local sheikh who had opposed them. They tied up the man and his wife, then raped and murdered their daughter.

In Nabatiye itself, the P.L.O. seized a Christian school, kidnapping two of the nuns who were beaten and raped. From 1975-1982, the P.L.O. completely dominated the school compound, allowing the nuns and school children use of the basement area only.

□   □   □   □   □

This was the hell which the P.L.O. made of Lebanon during its decade of power there. Because the government based in Beirut was weak and splintered, there was no salvation which would come from within.

At this same time, the P.L.O. expanded their use of their Lebanon base into a staging area for artillery attacks against Israel's northern border settlements in the Galilee. In addition to the individual terrorist outrages which challenged the very sovereignty of Israel, the nightly bombardments of homes in the Galilee made life impossible for Israel's northern residents. There were periods when entire communities in the Galilee were subjected to such extended and intense bombings that whole neighborhoods had to relocate into underground bomb shelters. The situation became untenable. No sovereign state, no government can tolerate such a state of affairs indefinitely.

In the wake of the P.L.O.'s 1978 attack against the tourist bus on the coastal highway between Haifa and Tel Aviv, the Israel Defense Force launched "Operation Stone of Wisdom," a carefully calculated entry into southern Lebanon, for the purpose of searching out and destroying the P.L.O. bases. Prime Minister Begin, in declaring the operation, vowed to "sever the arm of iniquity. We shall do what has to be done. Gone forever are the days when Jewish blood could be shed with impunity. The shedders of innocent blood shall not go unpunished."

Israel's forces attacked the terrorist installations and created a security belt south of the Litani River. As the Israelis advanced further inland, they found themselves welcomed as liberators by the repressed populations which had been subjected to the unremitting terror of P.L.O. dominance for years.

But external pressures forced Israel to retreat, and the United Nations sent in its own "peace-keeping" force, U.N.I.F.I.L. Thus, Israel's successful destruction and flushing-out of the P.L.O. terrorist infrastructure in Lebanon, terminated by U.N. Security Council resolution 425 which established U.N.I.F.I.L., left the Israelis hopeful that life in the north could return to normal.

Those hopes were not to be realized.

No sooner did the Israelis turn over their positions to the United Nations forces then the P.L.O. began to re-appear. A mixture of U.N.I.F.I.L. incompetence, and selected instances of complicity with the P.L.O.[Israeli checkpoints caught a number of U.N.I.F.I.L. soldiers red-handed] saw Israel's achievements dissipate rapidly. In a short matter of time, the full force of P.L.O. terror had returned. Shelling, heavy shelling, of the Galilee resumed.

Arafat was back.

In the aftermath of Israel's 1978 incursion, marked by early success but culminating in a disappointing restoration of the status quo, two significant personalities appeared on the scene. These two men would play major roles in the next phase of Israel's war against P.L.O. terror.

In April, 1978 General Rafael ("Raful") Eitan was named the new chief-of-staff of the Israeli Defense Forces. Raful, a proud and iron-willed leader—a soldier's soldier with firm ideas about the need for a steadfast Israeli defense policy marked by military alertness and a commitment to guaranteeing permanent Israeli retention of the Jewish communities established in Judea and Samaria—fit in well with the Likud government's way of thinking. He was a perfect complement to the political lead set by Prime Minister Menachem Begin.

The second change of personnel took place in August, 1981 when the newly reelected Likud government decided to assign the Defense Ministry portfolio to Major General Ariel Sharon. Sharon had served in the previous government as the Agriculture Minister who, in effect, was the grand architect of the Likud's program to populate the regions of Judea and Samaria with as many Jewish communities as could be established in the period of four years. His assignment successfully completed, he was promoted to the Defense Ministry in the second Begin government. Together with Begin and Eitan, Sharon forcefully advocated an aggressive foreign policy and argued for military action against the P.L.O.

Both of these military figures—although technically, Sharon was serving in a civilian capacity now—were reinforced in their opinions by the objective realities evident in the aftermath of Israel's 1978 operation.

Back in Lebanon, meanwhile, chaos took on a new meaning as a full-scale civil war broke out. By 1980, reliable observers were speaking of the civil war's devastating human cost: 100,000 dead and nearly 300,000 wounded. The numbers are worst than of staggering. They are beyond comprehension. Exacerbating matters was Syria's increasing foothold in Lebanon, under the guise of serving as a peace-keeper. In its five years in Lebanon, Syria had made and broken alliances with various factions in the conflict, cynically playing off party against party, all the while strengthening her own position in the country. Whatever Syria had accomplished by her five-year presence in Lebanon, it had surely not been peace.

In early July, 1981 the P.L.O. launched a new assault on Israel's northern communities, subjecting them to a terrible bombardment. Using their 130-millimeter artillery and their Soviet-supplied 120-millimeter Katyusha rocket launchers in a brutal, devastating ten-day onslaught, the terrorists drove 60,000 Jews below ground level, back to the bomb shelters they had said "good-bye" to only two years earlier. Indeed, the tension for many proved so unbearable that a wholesale exodus of Israelis from the Galilee began. For a short time, some observers in Israel wondered whether Israel's very sovereignty in the Galilee was at stake.

Raful Eitan pleaded with Begin for a "green light" to go into Lebanon, this time as far north as Sidon, to administer an even more telling blow against Arafat's murderers than had been dealt the P.L.O. in 1978. But American mediator Philip Habib arrived on the scene and pressed Israel into accepting a cease-fire with Arafat; Israel gained no other concessions. For many in Israel, the accord was simply inadequate to assure the security of Israel's northern regions. But Israel signed the accord. For her part, she would live by its word with the same conviction that she had abided by previous contracts like Camp David.

The P.L.O., however, did not keep its covenant with Habib. Arafat's Gang had a more compelling covenant before it — the P.L.O. charter. Initially, the P.L.O. maintained a quiet external posture. As the world would learn later, these were not days of peaceful tranquility; this was a period of unprecedented arms stockpiling. In essence, the P.L.O. chose to utilize the initial breathing period which came on the heels of the accord to acquire hundreds of tons of weapons. While there is no way to know for certain how much the P.L.O. had accumulated, the Israeli Defense Forces were to uncover the following stores a year later:

> 540 weapons depots (140 of them in West Beirut)
> 4330 truckloads of supplies
> 62 rocket launchers
> 1320 armored vehicles
> 1352 anti-tank weapons
> 82 fixed artillery pieces
> 215 mortars
> 196 anti-aircraft weapons
> 33,303 small arms
> 5,630 *tons of* ammunition

Again, no one can know what the P.L.O. really had in total. The figures cited here only reflect that which the

Israeli Defense Forces ultimately uncovered during their inspections of the Shatilla and Sabra underground tunnels, the school yards and hospitals, the apartment complexes and the mosques. The P.L.O. thuggery which saw them amass a huge arsenal—and then protect it by placing it in the heart of the acquiescing Palestinian civilian population—will go down as one of the most infamous acts in modern warfare.

Interestingly, the markings on these weapons indicated a wide variety of suppliers: Syria, Libya, North Korea, the Soviet Union. Even more fascinating was the revelation that the P.L.O. stocks included large amounts of American-made weapons. Since the United States does not supply them with anything, much less weapons of destruction, the question may well be asked: Where did the P.L.O. get American weapons from? Presumably, Israel was not the secret supplier. . . .

Then whodunnit?

It was not long before all eyes fell on the "moderate" Saudi Arabians, the P.L.O.'s major financier.

And a damn good arms supplier, too.

With all these weapons—including T34 and T55 tanks, tens of thousands of carbines, grenade lauchers, and submachine guns—it became apparent that the P.L.O. had plans for something much bigger than it had ever done before.

The P.L.O. was planning an armed invasion of Israel.

Even as the P.L.O. systematically worked at storing an incredible array of weapons, they itched, once again, for some terror action. Accordingly, they revealed a novel interpretation of their cease-fire agreement with Israel: the agreement only binds the P.L.O. from attacking Israel proper; there is nothing in the accords which forbids attacks on Jewish targets throughout the world. Likewise, the P.L.O. regards it permissible to attack Israelis and their interests anywhere in the world, so long as it is outside of Israel.

By the following summer, the P.L.O. had put its new interpretation to good use. 289 individual terrorist acts and related incidents took place in the year of the accord, between July 24, 1981 and June 6, 1982. The last straw came on June 3, 1982 when a Palestinian terror squad shot Shlomo Argov, Israel's ambassador to London. The following day, the Israeli air force retaliated by launching a coordinated attack against a major Arafat arms depot, located in the Beirut sports stadium.

The P.L.O. responded late June 4 by bombarding Israel's northern communities in a 24-hour torrential downpouring of rockets and shells. More than 1,000 shells hit sections all over the Galilee during that awesome attack. An additional 500 katyusha rockets were sent raining down on 23 Israeli towns.

For Defense Minister Sharon and Chief-of-Staff Eitan, the die was cast. Prime Minister Begin agreed: "We must put all settlements in the Galilee out or reach of terrorist artillery . . . and repulse the terrorists so that all the inhabitants of Galilee should be delivered from the constant threat to their lives."

Operation Peace for Galilee — Israel's determined struggle to bring security to her north and to destroy the infrastructure of the P.L.O.—had begun.

□ □ □ □ □

In truth, the 1982 war was like no war Israel had previously fought. In military terms, the battles were among Israel's most successful, recalling the Hundred Hours Campaign of 1956 and the 1967 Six-Day War. Israel's battle plan operated brilliantly. Objectives were attained rapidly and flawlessly. Cities were liberated from the P.L.O. terror. The ancient Beaufort Castle, a strategic site overlooking so much of Israel's northern terrain that it served as a tailor-made P.L.O. launching ground, came under Israeli control. The march northward along the Mediterranean coastal plane, past Tyre and Sidon and Damur—all the way to the foot of Beirut—went as well as military tacticians could have hoped. The Israeli navy quickly established itself at sea, while the air force made military history by devastating the Syrian air force in direct dog fights and in countering the ground threat posed by S.A.M. missile batteries, the likes of which had severely hampered Israel during the early stages of the 1973 Yom Kippur War. In time, Israel downed 89 Syrian fighter aircraft, sustaining nary a loss—and, in the bargain, the Israelis wiped out nineteeen surface-to-air missile batteries, stunning the Syrians.

Even the Soviet Union's highly coveted T-72 tank, reputed to be impenetrable, bit the dust in the face of superior Israeli strategy and weaponry.

Step by step, on land, on sea, and in the air, the Israelis scored an absolutely stunning military success, the likes of which she had never known before.

In a month's time, the Syrians were retreating in fear, unable to fathom the wholesale collapse of their entire air defense and offense. The Soviets had been devastated by the awesome failure of their weapons to match the Israeli counterparts, which had been American-supplied and often subsequently upgraded by Israeli military experts.

Arafat, reeling from shock in the face of his men's appalling retreat from the security of Fatahland, contemplated his options. The Lebanese themselves came out to celebrate Israel's achievements in ousting from their towns and villages the despised P.L.O. In every city, town, and village the Israelis traversed, they encountered welcoming committees which offered the soldiers everything from tea to flowers. The images recalled scenes of Americans liberating France four decades earlier.

Israel, it appeared, had struck the final blow against her tormentors, stopping the terror.

But life is never simple. Especially not for the Israelis.

In this strange war, Israel—victorious on the battlefield—suffered a new kind of defeat virtually unrecorded in the annals of war. She lost the war in the media.

Arafat's strategy of planting his weapons and bases in high-concentration civilian populations paid off. American cameramen seeking dramatic footage, American photographers seeking all the pathos possible in a 5x7 glossy, aimed their lenses at Israel.

There were pictures of bombed-out mosques and churches. Captions somehow neglected to note that P.L.O. arms caches had been stored there.

There were bombed-out apartment buildings. Captions neglected to site the presence of P.L.O. anti-aircraft gunners operating from the roofs or P.L.O. strategy zones operating out of the basements.

There were pictures of hospitals attacked. The photos somehow never carried tag-lines noting the P.L.O. presence in the buildings, the P.L.O. seizure of such buildings.

There were the wounded twelve-year-old boys. No descriptions appeared identifying them as active, drafted and trained P.L.O. fighters, usually assigned the role of firing rocket-propelled grenades.

There were devastated school yards. By-lines did not recall the P.L.O. heavy artillery which had filled the yards.

There was a U.P.I. photograph of an East Beirut child whose arms had reportedly been blown off by an errant Israeli shell. President Ronald Reagan had a copy of that photo on his desk; it symbolized the war to him. Later, when it was affirmatively learned that the child in the photograph did, in fact, have both arms — and the injury he had sustained came as a result of an errant Palestinian shell fired into the predominantly Christian enclave of East Beirut — it was too late. The damage had been done.

Perhaps the single greatest tragedy of the early struggle for public understanding was the Big Lie that Israel's initial thrust into Beirut had been so wanton that she had killed 10,000 people and sent 600,000 into homeless oblivion. Throughout the Western world, the media reported the figures: 10,000 dead and 600,000 homeless.

Even though all of southern Lebanon had a maximum population of only 510,000 before the war's inauguration.

How could 600,000 people have been scattered from

their homes if there were only 510,000 people present to begin with? The answer was simple, almost predictable. The initial reports had come from the highly impartial "Palestinian Red Crescent Society," ostensibly an agency as professional and non-partisan as is our own national Red Cross. And why should the Palestinian Red Crescent give false numbers? A good question. Perhaps the answer would have been better evident if more reporters had taken the trouble to ask that question of the society's head and chief spokesman.

Dr. Fathi Arafat. Yasser's brother. Publisher of statistics.

Indeed, in time it became evident that the casualty figure was not 10,000 — a Big Lie — but fewer than 400. And the number of homeless was not 600,000 but a figure one-twentieth of that Big Lie. And, to compound the comedy of errors, many of the newly "homeless" were merely individuals and families who had used the Israeli incursion as an opporutnity to return to the homes they had abandoned during the years of the P.L.O. terror. With the terrorists subdued, it was now safe to return home — and be recorded as "homeless" in the process.

□   □   □   □   □

The television networks' evening news reports featured correspondents standing on the scene of "devastated" cities. But others who subsequently visited the sites found that the cities had not been devastated after all. Yes, one block may have seen brutal fighting. Perhaps two or three blocks. But whole cities razed off the map?

Absurd.

Yes, there was the reporter who stood at Damur and spoke of it being a once-thriving town, now rubble. And he was correct. Damur was turned to rubble. But the razing of Damur and the massacre of its Christian population had long preceded the Israeli military incursion; Damur was wiped out by the P.L.O. during the mid-1970's during the earlier phases of the Lebanese civil war.

There was the case of the reporter who stood alongside a Christian church, which had been bombed into smithereens. He spoke of Israel's heavy bombings, of Israeli-imposed damage. Only the most alert observers watching the report could notice that, in fact, there was grass growing alongside the demolished church. How could an Israeli aerial bombing—albeit highly accurate and surgically targeted—demolish a church into Kingdom Come without in the slightest way impairing the grass growing on both sides of the building? The answer was, of course, simple—for those who cared to hear it. The church had been yet another victim of P.L.O. savagery during the years of the Lebanese civil war, when the P.L.O. dominated that region. But, while the church was never restored, the grass had plenty of time to grow back over the years.

There were pictures of Yasser Arafat, who had actually led his people to another infamous defeat—the most infamous yet—smiling, kissing babies as though he were joining the list of personalities who had announced their candidacy for the Democratic Presidential nomination.

□   □   □   □   □

The victory Israel had won on the battlefield slipped through her fingers, as she lost the campaign for public opinion. Lost in the reportage were the extraordinary regulations imposed on all Israeli officers and soldiers to scrupulously avoid civilian casualties. Soldiers were ordered to withhold fire in civilian locations. Planned assaults on civilian areas — so chosen because the P.L.O. had cynically holed-up in precisely those areas to confound the Israelis — were carefully delayed. The Israeli's forfeited the important tactical advantages of surprise in an extraordinary effort to evacuate unarmed civilians from the battle theater. Air attacks were coordinated with a stress on the surgical strike, in order to minimize non-combatant casualties. Pilots were actually instructed to return to base without delivering their assigned payload if aerial conditions made it impossible to accurately and precisely attack the designated — and only the designated — target.

Brigadier-General Amos Yaron, commander of the West Beirut sector, described the extent to which Israel had sought to avoid civilian casualties — and the extent to which the P.L.O. circumvented those efforts. Orders were given to troops entering towns, villages, and other civilian areas where the terrorists had deliberately based themselves, to avoid harming non-combatants. As a corollary, a regulation was added: no shots are to be fired at any building from which laundry is hanging to dry. After all, what better external evidence is there that a building is inhabited by civilian non-combatants than the presence of hanging laundry?

The soldiers of the army scrupulously followed this order. And then it happened: slowly, slowly, but surely, the P.L.O. began to catch on. Soon, all buildings began to sport hanging laundry, as though it had supplanted the cedar tree as Lebanon's national symbol. And, now, with fire coming at Israeli troops from buildings covered with an abundance of hanging laundry, new questions arose: what do we do?

□　　□　　□　　□　　□

There were cases of Israeli soldiers who died because they hesitated, they flinched, as Arab terrorists ran and fired at them while holding babies in their arms for cover.

It was a strange and different kind of war from anything Israel had every known before.

□　　□　　□　　□　　□

Special announcements were made on radio to evacuate non-combatants. On June 9, 1982, Announcement # 10 was read on the radio to the inhabitants of Sidon:

> I.D.F. forces are about to complete removing the remnants of trapped Palestinian terrorist nests in your city. The I.D.F. is doing its utmost in order to avoid injuring the civilian population in the city, but will uproot anyone holding arms. The fate of the trapped terrorists has already been sealed, after their commanders abandoned them.
>
> Residents of Sidon: your brother residents of Tyre hearkened to I.D.F. calls and evacuated their town in order to enable the elimination of terrorist nests in that city. Residents of Tyre have been returning to their homes since last night and are better protected and more secure than at any time. Residents of Sidon, the I.D.F. will enable you to return safely to your

homes as soon as possible.

You have been warned. Remember: your lives are in your own hands.

On June 27, the Israeli air force risked anti-aircraft fire and spent the day dropping leaflets to the civilians of West Beirut. The leaflets said:

TO THE INHABITANTS

The I.D.F. continues its battle against the terrorists and has not yet brought to bear its full force. But the I.D.F. has no wish to harm innocent civilians and those who do not wage war against it. You, living in Beirut, take advantage of the ceasefire and save yourself. You have the following choices:

A. Cross I.D.F. lines to the east . . .

B. Go northward, in the direction of Tripoli . . .

◻   ◻   ◻   ◻   ◻

During the course of the war, special Israeli Civilian Assistance Units (C.A.U.) went into operation in major Lebanese urban areas, as Israel liberated villages, towns, and cities from P.L.O. occupation. As reports spread throughout the country of Israeli troops driving out the P.L.O. and returning the Lebanese communities to their residents, a vast wave of Lebanese citizens streamed south, from the havens in which they were taking refuge back to the homes they had fled during the P.L.O. reign of terror. Nearly 100,000 people returned to southern Lebanon.

The massive influx taxed the already-strained resources of these areas, where local economies had been severely paralyzed as a result of the decade-long civil war. As of the second day of Operation Peace for Galilee,

Israeli C.A.U.'s were already at work, restoring daily Lebanese life to normal, acting in coordination and cooperation with the duly elected municipal authorities. Vital public services—hospitals, police, water, and electricity—were restored, and assistance was given in reconstructing local commerce. Supplies of goods were procured. Several hundred Lebanese civilians were helped to Israeli hospitals, which had special equipment not available on the scene, such as dialysis machines and the like. In fact, captured P.L.O. terrorists and Syrian soldiers were accorded the same humane treatment. the Israeli Magen David Adom (equivalent to the Red Cross) dispatched twenty ambulances, bloodbanks, mobile operating units, medical teams, and equipment. Ultimately, most of these supplies went unused because the situation proved to be much better than expected.

A survey carried out by the Chief Medical Officer of the International Committee of the Red Cross in Geneva concluded that the situation was "under control" and that there was, therefore, no need for the importation of blood and plasma. They also found the local hospitals to be in good condition, and the Israeli Ministry of Health buttressed their operations by offering all forms of aid.

Israeli C.A.U.'s also arrived with stores of foodstuffs and water, and distributed such supplies where needed. The Israel Electric Corporation, working in conjunction with the Israeli Defense Forces and the local authorities, helped the Lebanese repair the Tyre power station. Likewise, damaged water-supply systems were restored by *Mekorot,* the Israel Water Authority.

In one of their strangest tasks, Israeli Civilian Assistance Units combed the countryside, helping communities relocate judges and magistrates who had fled during the reign-of-terror. After a seven-year cessation of justice, Lebanese judges once again sat on their benches, adjudicating in accordance with official Lebanese law.

▫   ▫   ▫   ▫   ▫

How tragic it was that misinformation filtered to the West as it did! Consider the achievements of Operation Peace for Galilee:

- Eradication of the P.L.O. state-within-a-state.
- Restoration of cities, towns, and villages to the people of Lebanon.
- Disbanding of the international terror network run by the P.L.O. at Shatilla and other sites.
- Seizure of the huge P.L.O. arsenal.
- Restoration of tranquility and normalcy to the Galilee, where residents could finally, for the first time in a decade, learn the joys of living without constant fear of bombardment.
- Destruction of the most advanced Soviet weapons systems available, pointing out to the world the superiority of American-made equipment and thereby strengthening America's strategic position in terms of international alliances.

In the face of these attainments it was not surprising to read accounts of Ariel Sharon's increased popularity, especially in the Galilee. One *New York Times* account, published at the end of the war's main thrust, was titled: " 'Sharon, King of Israel,' Sephardic Town Chants." Reporting from Kiryat Malachi, James Feron wrote:

The banner across the stage Wednesday night read, "Kiryat Malachi Welcomes the Volunteers"—Americans who had come to Israel to help the war effort—but the shouting, foot-stamping and applause in the packed community hall was for someone else, Ariel Sharon...

There were more than 500 residents in the steamy hall. Many of the men were bearded and wore skullcaps. It was a Sephardic audience, and possibly their biggest night in years. They applauded the Americans, sat patiently through the tributes, and waited for Arik...

One especially popular moment [came] when Haviv Alon, the director of the community hall, came to the microphone with his two-year-old son folded into an arm.

"Since Judah Maccabee, there has been no hero like Ariel Sharon," he said. "And so, two years ago, when my son was born, I named him Sharon." There were cheers and, later, there was a similar announcement: a child born that evening in Kiryat Malachi had been named Ariel..."

So, Ariel Sharon, the man who had risen to become Defense Minister of Israel, after petty opponents had denied him the Chief-of-Staff role ten years earlier, had emerged from the War in Lebanon a knight in shining armor.

Or did he?

IV
Begin (rhymes with...)

During the autumn months of 1982, as the Israeli Defense Forces scored stunning achievements in their Operation Peace for Galilee, it was clear that their victories were being tarnished by the images appearing in the world press. In the struggle for public understanding and enlightened world opinion's approbation, Israel was not doing as well.

But, while many newsmedia endeavored to do their best to get at an objective reading of what was going on — the *New York Times,* for example, did publish David Shipler's incredible, gripping exposé of the P.L.O. terror machine's repression of Lebanon — one publication stood apart from the crowd. In reportage, in opinion, in every way it was clear that Israel's sharpest enemy in the world press was America's largest newsweekly.

Time magazine.

In a sense, one would expect Time Inc. to be beyond the pettiness of it all. A huge corporation with annual sales in the billions of dollars, Time Inc. is ranked in the top 300 American corporations by *Forbes*. They publish not only *Time* magazine but also *Fortune, Sports Illustrated, Money, People,* and *Life.* Time Inc. is the largest private landholder in the state of Texas, and their Temple-Eastex subsidiary owns timberland in that state which covers more area than all of Rhode Island. In addition to owning the *Washington Star* and Little, Brown publishers, Time Inc. also owns the Book-of-the Month Club, which claims one million members. They own Home Box Office. They make films.

They make money.

Founded in 1923 by Henry Luce, the corporation's most famous publication, *Time* magazine, has always been identified with America's capitalist system and the related values which were at the core of Luce's own beliefs. Deeply conservative and imbued with a strong Protestant faith, Luce used his weekly news magazine to shape America's values. He played a vigorous role at *Time's* helm until his death in 1967. In light of his orientation, one would have presumed that *Time's* Middle East editorial policy would be fiercely supportive of Israel—a unique bastion of Western-style freedom in a place of the world ill-disposed to such values. Indeed, the strong pro-Americanism which marked Israel since her founding stands in sharp contrast to the Soviet alliances shared by Syria, Iraq, and Libya— among other Arab countries.

Yet, somehow, *Time* never made the connection. And,

in the aftermath of Luce's passing from the scene, bad turned to worse.

□   □   □   □   □

Ironically, *Time's* earliest invective against Israel — going back to Israel's very founding period — was aimed most sharply against the Israeli party which advocated American-style capitalism, Herut. The Party leader, Menachem Begin, bore every blow possible form *Time's* thesaurus of insults.

In July, 1948 a Time report referred to "sharp-eyed Menachem Begin" and his "force of bully boys." Describing the Israeli parliamentarian's role in Israel's pre-state days, the article published a series of inaccuracies including one major defamation against him, claiming that he had once "deserted" the Polish Army, an assertion sharply criticized by Begin's biographers who recall his refusal to join the Israeli underground until he had obtained an honorable discharge from Poland's armed forces.

Begin, too busy establishing his Party in Israel, did not have the time or interest to sue *Time* for libel. Accordingly, the lie stands unchallenged as historical "fact."

In the August 16 issue that year, *Time* was at it again, equating the Begin Zionist philosophy — known as "Revisionism"— with gangsterism. On January 24, 1949 *Time* discussed Israel's first national elections and described the Herut Party as "Israel's newest and potentially most dangerous party." The following month, on February 28, Herut was deprecated as "ultra-nationalist."

Nor did *Time* reserve its invective for Begin. No less a figure than David Ben-Gurion was labeled "pugnacious" when the then-prime minister declared Jerusalem to be Israel's capital.

Over the ensuing years, the approach continued, with Ben-Gurion absorbing other adjectives. ("Defiant" was an especially popular one.) On one occasion, an Israeli commando raid undertaken in response to a series of Arab terrorist attacks, which had left 421 Israelis killed or wounded in three years, was described as an attack "in the Mosaic tradition of an eye for an eye."

If *Time's* coverage of Israel was problematic during Israel's early years, it became downright vicious by the late 1970's. In one case, an article describing the ills of South Africa's *apartheid* system referred to South Africa's Prime Minister John Vorster and his firm views. It then went from descriptive to nasty, describing him as "showing an intransigence that recalls Golda Meir . . . " In a world of Kadafis, Idi Amins, and countless other dictators and intransigents, *Time* saw the Israeli Prime Minister as the most appropriate symbol of human intransigence.

The anti-Israel prejudice had descended to the gutter only a few short weeks earlier, when the Israeli electorate chose Menachem Begin to be Prime Minister of Israel. In a May 30, 1977 cover story entitled "Israel: Trouble in the Promised Land/Triumph of a Super Hawk" an angry account of Begin's democratic victory featured a special insert profiling him. In the box, titled "Kind . . . Honest . . . Dangerous," the author of the piece wrote:

> His first name means "comforter." Menachem Begin (rhymes with Fagin) has been anything but that to his numerous antagonists.

William Safire, writing of that contribution to American poetry, described the not-so-subtle Fagin equation as a "classic ethnic slur." And well it was. Fagin, the vile Dickens character who corrupted children and forced them into lives of crime, was — of all things — a miserly, old Jew. The image of the hook-nosed Fagin, leading his gang of children-thieves in a life of crime until he was finally captured and hanged in public, has long been a source of deep anguish to the Jewish people. It is a heinous stereotype, a relic of an earlier period in Western culture.

But *Time* magazine brought Fagin back to life, using his name to help readers pronounce "Begin." As if Ronald Reagan (also rhymes with Fagin) were not adequately well known in the United States. As if *Time* readers, on an earlier occasion, had been treated to the same rhyme when Reagan emerged as a major American political figure. (They were not.) As though *Time* prints such guides to pronunciation as standard policy.

The imagery was clear. For those who missed the implication, *Time* later referred to Begin's "rabid" rhetoric — just to get the messgage across.

Letter writers from throughout the United States swamped the magazine with protests. *Time* was gracious enough to print three representative statements. Peter Almagor of Toronto called the entire article "a disgrace. In the only democratic election in the Middle East, the people of Israel elected a man and his party . . . and *Time* talks about Trouble in the Promised Land."

Van Lewis Caplan of New York City wrote: "Your cheap attack on Menachem Begin was an assault on Israel and every Jew." And Rabbi Zalmon M. Stein wrote from Leominister, Massachusetts that "I find it in extremely poor taste—whatever your opinion of Mr. Begin—to use the name 'Fagin' to show people how Mr. Begin's name is pronounced. Since Fagin was Dickens' infamous caricature of a Jew, I can only assume that your magazine wished to make an unfavorable implication."

Incredibly, *Time* did not respond to the letter, nor did it apologize to its readers. It would not be *Time's* last refusal to apologize for an editorial indiscretion. Indeed, *Time* almost seemed to thrive on its newly earned infamy.

Only two months later, *Time* published an article (October 3) entitled "How to Lean on Israel." As a public service to its readers, it had amassed a series of suggestions for American government leaders interested in squeezing the Jewish State. Accompanied by a drawing of Uncle Sam squishing a Jewish Star-of-David into the ground with his index finger, the article offered all kinds of ideas, many of which would probably have hurt America, too, in the long run. *Time* suggested that America could remain silent during certain United Nations debates, and it even recommended a possible U.S. pull-out from a desalinization project in Tel Aviv. The article was mean-spirited, and it included uncomplimentary references to "the Jewish lobby," whatever that is.

If Begin rhymed with "Fagin," *Time* was beginning to rhyme with "slime."

In July, 1978, *Time* ran an article on Menachem

Begin's first year in office. The analysis, timed to coincide with the first anniversary of his election, was predictably titled: Begin: "Beyond the Pale." Unprovoked by any particular Begin action or policy statement, the *Time* article nevertheless assaulted him ferociously:

"It was just a year ago that the former guerrilla leader and ultranationalist Menachem Begin came to power—and all the worst fears, and more, of his critics have since come to pass. More than any other man, Begin has set back the chances for peace in the Middle East. He has proved inflexible, myopic, hard-lining and probably deceptive. . . .

"During his twelve months in power, Begin has emerged as a mystic, a legalist, a man totally insensitive to any problems beyond those of Jewish Israel. He is tiresomely preachy in his talks with non-Israeli leaders, repeating to the point of boredom his odd fact-and-fiction litany of Jewish biblical and legal rights, his self-justification for Irgun atrocities, and his blend of self-righteous arrogance . . . "

□   □   □   □   □

The outrageous attack on Begin, part of a campaign of journalistic indecency, itself beyond the pale, led to charges that *Time* was, at best, biased. The Hadassah Women's Organization, one of the most moderate and comparatively apolitical Jewish groups in the country, basically a fundraising body for Israeli medical efforts, nonetheless declared, *"Time* is no longer a source of news, but of bias."

Clearly, something was going on behind closed doors

at *Time.* Strange reports, personal attacks, and outright cheap shots began showing up regularly. In a September 24, 1979 insert, "Fears for Begin's Health," *Time* went to great length to suggest that Menachem Begin was falling apart in the thick of his first term in office. Wistfully, *Time* wrote, "His health is also a matter of increasing concern to Israelis, who wonder how long the ailing Premier can remain in office." Continuing with the article, *Time* then dropped a bombshell from out of the sky:

> Shortly before the Haifa summit, *Time* correspondent David Halevy learned last week, Begin took a day off from his governmental duties. He was driven to a secluded laboratory, where three non-Israeli neurological experts examined him. One of the specialists was Dr. Jack Fein, a prominent brain surgeon at the Albert Einstein College of Medicine in New York City.

> After the examination, the doctors recommended that Begin restrict himself to a three-hour workday and try to rest as much as possible.... "I am concerned about Mr. Begin's health," said Dr. Fein, "but I admire his courage...."

> Begin seems less and less in control of his fractious ministers.... Even one of Begin's protective aides admits deep concern: "It seems that his physical condition is deteriorating quickly. I do not know when, but he will have to quit the premiership. It might happen tomorrow, next week—or next year."

The article was received in Israel as just short of a hoax. A mischievous hoax. Dan Pattir, Begin's aide, wrote *Time,* deploring its obvious mistake. He listed the errors: Begin did not take a day off shortly before the Haifa summit. He was not driven to a "secluded laboratory" or to any other location for a physical check-up. He never met with a team of "three non-Israeli neurological experts." "In particular," Pattir added, "the Prime Minister never met with a Dr. Jack Fein. Hence, no such team could have given any medical advice to the Prime Minister."

Pattir went on to assert that Begin puts in his regular hours, and any claim to the contrary is incorrect. In conclusion, he wrote, "Given the totally unfounded nature of your report, it is proper that your readers be informed of the above facts."

Heavy stuff.

In the face of this outraged denial by Prime Minister Begin's aide, even *Time* had to moderate its institutionalized bias against Israel to soberly investigate the facts: was the story right, or was the story wrong? Jerusalem bureau chief Dean Fischer looked into the matter.

Because of the story's heavy reliance on anonymous, unnamed sources, it would be necessary to go back to the correspondent who had gathered this big "scoop" for *Time:* David Halevy.

□   □   □   □   □

Born in Israel in March, 1941, David Halevy had joined *Time*'s Israel operation in 1968. Having begun as a part-time stringer attached to *Time*'s Jerusalem bureau, he rose to full-time stringer in 1972 and became a correspondent in 1976. He came with a claim that he had developed a reservoir of top-quality sources, which gave him access to breaking stories faster than other journalists in the area. Like all Israelis, he had done his army service, and he had grown up with people who had risen to positions of importance.

There was another interesting facet of this special "access"enjoyed by Halevy. Contrary to American journalistic standards, he was highly partisan and had joined the Labor Party of Israel during the mid-1960's when he was a student at Tel Aviv University. An outspoken opponent of the Herut-Likud political coalition, deeply antagonistic towards Menachem Begin, David Halevy had secured his "contacts" and "sources" through his partisan politics.

After joining the student organization of the Mapai Labor Party in 1964, Halevy went on to become editor-in-chief of the group's monthly publication. Serving in this role for four years, he soon rose to a new level: Yigal Allon, the powerful Labor Party official, took him on as his press officer from 1968-9.

These were politically exciting years for Halevy. His political leanings crystallized, his rising influence real, David Halevy nonetheless continued writing for *Time* magazine, posturing as an objective, dispassionate observer—posturing, that is, for his American audience. At home, among his Hebrew-speaking associates, there was no need for posturing. David Halevy, after all, was "one of us"—and "us" meant that he was virulently opposed to Begin and his Party.

It was this David Halevy—symbolic of all that was peculiar in *Time*'s Jerusalem bureau—who had filed the story "revealing" Menachem Begin's mysterious physical check-up in a secret, isolated laboratory.

□　□　□　□　□

Dean Fischer, *Time*'s Jerusalem bureau chief, began his investigation with an obvious hope to prove the story accurate, corroborated by as many sources as possible. For Halevy, such exoneration would prove especially valuable, especailly in light of a previous blunder which had already marred his professional reputation.

In the mid-1970's, Yitzhak Rabin, Israel's Prime Minister at the time, took a secret trip up the Mediterranean coastline to Lebanon, where he met privately with the Lebanese president in an effort to begin the process which saw an increasingly close link develop between Israel and the Lebanese Christian community. David Halevy, in reporting on the secret mission, wrote at the time that Rabin had been accompanied on the trip by Shimon Peres, his Defense Minister.

It was a good story.

Only Peres wasn't there.

It became clear that Peres had received a free plug from *Time* magazine, which had put him in one of the most strategically important and politically sensitive meetings in Israel's history. Someone was painting Peres with prime ministerial colors. Eyes turned to Halevy, an ardent Peres supporter.

Had Halevy deliberately inserted a lie into his story in order to promote Peres? He denied it. He wouldn't twist a story for his own political ends. He was a professional.

□   □   □   □   □

Now, Halevy was on the dock over the Begin piece. It was his word against Dan Pattir's word. Pattir was a politician; his objectivity was therefore suspect. Halevy, on the other hand, was a dispassionate reporter. Besides, he had sources.

Dean Fischer contacted Halevy's four anonymous sources, one at a time. One denied knowing anything about the matter. A second source said the same. There were two more good, solid anonymous sources to go.

One called the story a fantasy. The other told Fischer that Halevy had spoken with his wife, never with him.

Fischer did not quit easily. He had Halevy go back to the ubiquitous Dr. Jack Fein in New York City. Halevy called him. Fein fulminated against the absurdity of Halevy's story. Distraught, Halevy would later explain that Dr. Fein had had a bad telephone connection and misunderstood him.

Five strikes, and you're out.

◻   ◻   ◻   ◻   ◻

For Dean Fischer, there was the delicate and embarrassing task of informing *Time's* international headquarters in New York that the story was a boner. For Richard L. Duncan, *Time's* chief of correspondents, there was a real mess on his hands.

Duncan, who had joined *Time* in 1962 and had risen steadily within the corporate ranks over the years, and was responsible for every David Halevy in the world. His official job description obligates him to monitor *Time's* 90 correspondents throughout the world, to evaluate their work, to keep *Time's* reporting flawless.

Now, one of his boys had flubbed — and badly. Duncan had to do something about it. He had already talked with Halevy in 1976 when he learned of his active involvement in the Shimon Peres group. He had explained to Halevy that *Time* reporters cannot be politically identified with one party or the other. Whatever the reality, a *Time* correspondent must at least maintain a veneer—albeit apocryphal—of dispassionate, detached objectivity. Now, Halevy had been caught with his journalistic pants down. And all of *Time* was tainted by the scandal.

After assessing the Fischer investigation, Duncan immediately prepared a "personal and confidential" memorandum, which he distributed to *Time*'s top brass, including managing editor Ray Cave and Henry Anatole Grunwald, *Time*'s editor-in-chief. Duncan praised bureau chief Fischer: "Dean Fischer had reacted well in this situation. He methodically went back to the sources and spotted the problem." Indeed, Fischer's only error, in Duncan's opinion, was in hastily recommending that *Time* issue an apology to Begin.

(As a matter of policy, *Time* does not "appologize." It occasionally expresses a "regret" over an error. But it never, never issues an "apology." According to Grunwald, explaining *Time*'s six-decade-long policy, "the use of the word 'regret' is almost a habit at *Time* . . . I think [Dean Fischer] overspoke if he, in fact, offered an apology, because it is not in his discretion to do so. . . .To the best of my knowledge, *Time* has followed its tradition, its custom of using the word 'regret . . .' It is our custom to use the word 'regret . . .' For consistency we use the word 'regret' [and not 'apologize'] . . . As far as I can recall, we have not used the word 'apology'.")

As for his assessment of Halevy's reporting, Duncan

explained in his memorandum that he had spoken to him about the controversy. Having analyzed all the possible explanations, Duncan was left with the following inference: "At this moment, on the basis of the information given to me by Fischer and of my talks with Halevy, I believe our story is wrong. Inescapably, that conclusion then requires a further decision as to whether Halevy was either (a) inexcusably shoddy in his reporting, or (b) intentionally misled us, or (c) was the victim of an incredibly well orchestrated disinformation plot . . . In my judgment, the balance of the evidence is that our story is wrong . . . ."

A formal retraction of the story appeared in *Time*'s October 22, 1979 issue — a month after the initial publication of the report — in the light of Duncan's decision: *"Time* has rechecked all aspects of its story, which was based on what it believed was firsthand knowledge of a meeting between Prime Minister Begin and three consulting neurologists. *Time* was apparently misled as to the meeting and regrets the error . . . ."

Time did not apologize to Begin, and its use of the word "apparently" in the retraction's second sentence weakened what "regrets" it finally did agree to offer.

□   □   □   □   □

For Richard Duncan, the case was not closed. He met with Halevy in Athens and explained to the correspondent that, he would be compelled to place him on "probation." The one-year probationary status placed on Halevy included the following conditions: (1) he would be expected to do the "fullest possible sourcing" on all

stories, better detailing the anonymous sources he so frequently cited, (2) more than one source would be
necessary in future stories, (3) Halevy would be expected
to do more "meat and potatoes" reporting, rather than
focusing his attention merely on specials and exclusives,
and (4) it was essential that there be "a more obvious effort on your part to insure that what you report to *Time*
. . . is printable, reliable information, reflecting not just
informed speculation, but the *most likely true situation.*
As part of this, I would like to see on your part more effort to evaluate the reliability of various sources, and the
likelihood that they, in fact, *know* what they are saying
. . ."

□   □   □   □   □

It was Duncan's expectation that the incident would be
the last in which Halevy's reporting would bring embar-
rassment to *Time* magazine. In retrospect, one almost
wonders why the magazine stuck with Halevy altogether.
To understand that,it is important to recognize that Halevy
had, in fact, also done some credible reporting, in between the botch-ups. And his anti-Begin politics certainly
did not hurt his job security.

Indeed, *Time's* continued calumny of Israel —
especially targeted against the Begin government and its
ministers — continued uninterrupted throughout this
period. An April 1978 story filed by Halevy, alleging
Israeli abuses against Arab rock-throwers in Judea and
Samaria, included such vitriolic quotations and mean-
spirited reporting that Israeli Defense Minister Ezer Weizman called Halevy at his home to complain bitterly

against the biased account. Halevy passed along a summary of Weizman's complaint in the form of a telegram to New York: "Yesterday, Weizman called me at home and told me the following: "...What a terrible, lying, libelous story on Beit Jala. I do not want to see you again. Your magazine stinks,' and shut the phone." Halevy included in his message to New York the text of an official Israeli statement issued against the *Time* piece.

In the official Israeli response, the Israeli Defense Forces spokesman denied charges of Israeli brutality against Arab civilians and pointed to *Time's* omission of the cause of Israel's arrest of individuals in Judea and Samaria: they had been throwing heavy rocks at Israeli officers. In addition to denouncing as inaccurate much of the Halevy article, the spokesman went on to complain that, while Halevy had launched a vicious story against the Israeli forces who handled the disturbance in Judea and Samaria, he did not bother to include in the published account the text of the Israeli response to the charges leveled.

Six years later, in a New York courtroom, attorney Milton Gould would elicit from Halevy a confession of yet another of his biases: on a personal basis—completely unrelated to his professional role as a reporter—he deeply opposes the Israeli role in Judea and Samaria.

It was this kind of consistently antagonistic coverage of the State of Israel which led Rael Jean Isaac to write in a 1980 cover story in *The New Republic* that *"Time* has engaged in vigorous adversary journalism against

Israel. In doing so, *Time* has practiced subversion—literally, 'the turning of a thing upside down or uprooting it from its position.' *Time* is not simply inaccurate: it stands facts, words, and moral principles on their heads to achieve its portrait of the Arab-Israeli conflict."

Isaac contrasted *Time*'s journalistic mauling of Israel with its kid-gloves treatment of Arab dictatorships and terrorist groups. She provided a systematic look at how *Time* kept publishing reports that Yasser Arafat would be issuing new, moderate policy statements—although such statements never came. While *Time* was busy attacking the Middle East's only democracy, Israel, it was describing surrounding Arab lands as "democratic." In a May 22, 1978 story, *Time* went so far as to call Saudi Arabia a "desert democracy"—even though Saudi Arabia has no parliament, no political parties, not a single elected official, and no press freedom.

Time's appalling prejudice against Israel came into a clearer light when Ze'ev Chafets, a former director of the Israeli Government Press Office, interviewed Bill Marmon, a former *Time* reporter who retired from journalism shortly after encountering the P.L.O.—firsthand. From 1973-1975 Marmom was *Time*'s bureau chief in Israel, and he became well known throughout the country for his sharply critical positions taken against the policies of Jerusalem. When the New York office transferred him to Beirut in 1975, Marmon anticipated a fine welcome, indeed.

But he had committed a grave crime. He had set foot in Israel.

While on assignment for a story in Egypt that summer, Marmon left behind in Beirut his local assistant, Abu Said. One day Lebanese security officers visited Said to tell him that they had received intelligence reports that the P.L.O. had learned of Marmon's stint in Israel—and had, accordingly, targeted him for assassination. Said used his contacts to confirm that the Popular Front for the Liberation of Palestine did, in fact, have Marmon on their death list.

A few months later, with Marmon working in Beirut despite the threat looming over his head, Said came to see him. He had word that P.L.O. gunmen had been looking for Marmon the night before—but they had gone to the wrong apartment.

Marmon got the message. He drove to Beirut airport and caught the first flight out of Lebanon, arriving in Jordan. Marmon contacted Richard L. Duncan, then the deputy chief of correspondents. In a February 1983 interview with Chafets, Marmon remembered the period: "When I got to Amman, Jordan, I immediately contacted Dick Duncan...I reported that I had been essentially expelled from Beirut by the P.L.O. and that my life would be in danger if I tried to return. At the time Duncan was non-commital, but as time went on I realized that New York was upset with *me,* not with them. There was a sense there that the P.L.O. had to be cultivated, not alienated, and that somehow I was responsible for spoiling relations with them."

Marmon was especially surprised that *Time* chose to keep his expulsion secret from its readers—and that, in this unique case, *Time did not defend its reporter with so much as an official protest.*

Marmon continues: "I felt at the time, well, this is all wrong; this isn't the way expulsions are supposed to be dealt with. The special status of the P.L.O. was underscored by *Time's* approach. If this had happened in Russia, say, it sure would have been a story. In this case I felt that I had to justify having offended the Palestinians. It was backwards."

In a shocking revelation to Chafets, Marmon revealed, for the first time, that *Time's* growing anti-Israel prejudice was not merely coincidental, nor was it just a figment of imagination sensed by Israel's staunchest supporters. Said Marmon to Chafets, recalling the 1975 atmosphere when he was assigned to *Time's* Beirut desk: "There was a feeling in New York that Israel was getting too good a deal in the Western press, and that this needed correction." The explicit message from New York was clear. "It was part of my charter to enable the Arab story to emerge in a convincing way."

No, David Halevy's anti-Begin politics certainly did not hurt his job security at *Time* magazine—even if Richard Duncan recognized that his reporting may just have been "inexcusably shoddy."

When war broke out once again in June 1982, during Israel's Operation Peace for Galilee, *Time* was there. Describing the "Israeli onslaught—in effect a blitz," *Time* described the incursion as an act of Israeli defiance.

Ignoring the steps which had led to the fateful decision, *Time* focused its accounts on Ariel Sharon—as though the entire war, backed by a 94 to 3 vote in Israel's democratically elected Knesset parliament, had been the result of one individual's caprice. "Sharon would have his war," wrote *Time,* as though one militarist were running the country. As though all of Israel had not finally had enough of P.L.O terrorism and of the instability and inhuman bombardment to which all of Israel's nothern Galilee region had been subjected to.

In an insert, titled "Subtle Like a Bulldozer," *Time* continued advocating its theory of a one-man war: "Whatever the outcome, it will surely be remembered as his war: no other Middle East conflict has so unmistakably borne the stamp of one man. He had been spoiling for the fight . . . He had intensively lobbied Prime Minister Menachem Begin and his Cabinet to approve it. . ." *Time* went on to question Sharon's reputation, saying that he "does not have a great store of credibility among Israeli politicians or, for that matter, among his military colleagues"– a remarkable innuendo in light of his actual influence and credibility. *Time* spoke of Sharon having been accused in the past of "insubordination." *Time* did not mention that the last time such a charge had been leveled against Sharon – after the Yom Kippur War – the official Agranat Commission named to investigate that and other charges stemming from the difficult 1973 conflict emerged with a clear endorsement of Sharon. The commission vindicated him, and strongly rejected the charges against him.

Time was not finished with the Defense Minister. After admitting that many regard Sharon as a brave military leader, the article continued: "To his critics, among them many of his generals and Cabinet colleagues, he is an arrogant and dangerously ambitious megalomaniac with little or no respect for opposing points of view, much less democratic process." In addition to discussing his supposed "reputation for brutality," the *Time* report got so petty as to describe Sharon's fingers as "stubby."

□   □   □   □   □

Criticize though it did, even *Time* had to admit, as the war was winding down in late August, that "many Israeli observers were ready last week to declare the P.L.O. dead and buried even before the guerrillas evacuated Beirut." It cited a PORI Institute opinion poll taken in Israel which showed that Sharon's popularity in Israel had soared.

If not won over, it appeared at least that *Time* would have to eat a serving of humble pie, recognizing that the war in Lebanon had achieved the fundamental purpose of breaking up the P.L.O. terrorist infrastructure.

V
Shatilla and Sabra

With the August 23 election of Bashir Gemayel, the Maronite Christian leader and head of the Phalangist Party, as Lebanon's next president, things appeared to be moving very much along Israel's path. Gemayel, a strong friend of Israel, had long enjoyed Israel's support for his Phalangist group, and he was an articulate spokesman for the Lebanese drive to rid itself of the P.L.O. menace.

But Lebanon has its own unique chemistry, and two weeks later the dreams for a reconstructed, centralized government—and a restored Lebanon—went up in the ashes of a furious bomb which rocked the East Beirut headquarters of the Phalangists. Bashir Gemayel had been blown to pieces—and, with his assassination, the hopes for a peaceful interlude in Lebanon went the same way. Within a week's time, Israel would be dragged into

Lebanon's muck and mire, unexpectedly—and with grave results.

S   S   S   S   S

When word reached Israel of Bashir Gemayel's murder on September 17, 1982, the country's leadership reacted swiftly to the tragic news. A new air of uncertainty pervaded the political equation, and Israel knew all too well from her experience that a vacuum of leadership would be perilous and might well endanger all that had been achieved by Operation Peace for Galilee.

One of the most dramatic accomplishments of the Lebanon incursion had been the eradication of the P.L.O. from the country. Holed up in West Beirut, having fled to one last civilian center after being routed throughout Lebanon, Arafat and his terrorists waited for days, as Israel made clear that they must leave. Arafat bullied. He threatened. He kissed babies and complained of Israeli persecution. He refused to leave, effectively daring the Israelis to enter West Beirut and throw him out. The Israelis were, of course, deeply frustrated by Arafat's tactics—"How do you fight an army which hides behind women's skirts?" became a popular refrain—but they would not invade West Beirut. They kept the pressure on Arafat until his P.L.O. finally gave in and agreed to evacuate Lebanon.

Under the terms of the agreement, the P.L.O. were to depart by sea; the complete evacuation would be completed by September 1. While the terrorists would be obliged to turn over all weapons to the official Lebanese Army the Israelis did accede to a request that the P.L.O.

retain possession of their sidearms.

As was to be expected, the P.L.O. evacuated by September 1—and they didn't. While they did leave, amidst much ado, some 2,000 terrorists managed to remain behind. Western peacekeeping forces sent to supervise the P.L.O. evacuation attributed the subterfuge to a time-honored P.L.O. trick: dressing men as women and women as men. Accordingly, while careful counts were made to assure that the correct number of Palestinian terrorists had left, no effort was made to ascertain that each and every one of the people leaving were the people who were expected to leave.

In addition to leaving behind their 2,000 fighters, the P.L.O. reneged on its pledge to turn over its heavy weapons and munitions to the duly constituted Lebanese authorities. Instead, they hid much of the arms, and they turned some over to radical Moslem militias which operated in West Beirut and supported the P.L.O. Estimates put the strength of such militias at 7,000 armed men. Together with P.L.O. terrorists who had remained behind, the Israelis estimated that a force of 10,000 fighters were still very much alive and well in the western sector of Lebanon's capital city.

Because of the stickiness of the situation caused by Gemayel's death—the uncertainty, the vacuum of power—Defense Minister Sharon and Chief-of-Staff Eitan decided to send Israeli troops into West Beirut in a desperate attempt to preserve order and to prevent a radicalization process from igniting. When an Israeli attempt to enter the neighborhoods of Shatilla and Sabra in West Beirut was repulsed by heavy Palestinian firepower, leaving three Israeli soldiers dead and nearly 100 wounded, Sharon and Eitan resolved that they simply could not send Israeli Defense Force troops into the two armed nieghborhoods.

Their decision was rooted in their knowledge, by now confirmed and no longer speculation, that both Shatilla and Sabra served as major terrorist nests. Indeed, Shatilla was especially heinous because it had served as the central base for the training of terrorists from all over Europe. Its infamous reputation, its underground tunnel system — stocked with loads of heavy weapons and linking the community to strategic areas in West Beirut proper — made Shatilla a formidable base against which to launch a military operation.

□   □   □   □   □

The Israelis were unwilling to launch an attack on Shatilla or Sabra because they knew that they would be forced to choose between fighting terrorists and injuring civilian bystanders — or standing in paralysis, in the face of the civilian concentration, endangering their own lives and, giving their assailants more time to strike at them.

Besides, the Israelis were not Lebanese. How could they really tell who in Sabra and Shatilla was a native resident — and who was a foreigner?

Fortunately, the Israelis had their Christian Phalangist allies. These soldiers knew the language of Lebanon — and its various dialects. Like an American who can individuate between a Brooklyn accent, a southern twang, and the Kennedy pronunciation of Boston, so could the Phalangists tell locals from outsiders. They would be far more suitable for the operation to maintain order in Sabra and Shatilla.

Compounding this consideration was the growing political unrest back home in Israel, occasioned by a perception that the Israeli Defense Forces had entered Lebanon, driven out the P.L.O. and restored to the country a new hope for peaceful existence—while the Christian Phalangist armies sat back and watched. "Why weren't they doing some of the fighting?" many Israelis asked, as the casualty count from the front steadily rose—over four hundred Israeli soldiers had died in the fighting. The popular feeling was that Israel had sacrificed quite a bit of blood—admittedly, in support of direct Israeli needs and interests—and that the time was long overdue for the Phalangists to join in the effort, to share some of the mortal risks of warfare.

On the other hand, mitigating against too active a role for the Phalangists was Israel's uneasiness over the questionable fighting ethics prevalent throughout Lebanon.

□   □   □   □   □

For a decade, competing armies, militias, and terrorists had exchanged massacres. After a savage, vicious massacre of the Christian community in Damur by Palestinian murderers in early 1976—they butchered 6,000 Christians—a retaliation was inevitable. In the months of June and July of that year, the Christians reciprocated by slaughtering 4,000 civilians in Tel el-Za'atar.

That kind of behavior deeply concerned the Israelis and, in fact, was one of the key reasons that the Phalangists and their army had been asked to play so minor a role in Israel's initial fighting.

By September 1976, however, many Israeli military leaders, and the upper echelons of the highly regarded Mossad intelligence network, felt that the Phalangists had turned the corner, that they were moving towards substantially greater discipline and maturity as a fighting force. There were clear and noticeable improvements in their methods and attitudes. Under close Israeli scrutiny, it was felt, they could be counted on to do a professional military job. Indeed, they had done a splendid job in an operation aimed at clearing out the College of Sciences in Reychan.

Others in the Israeli military establishment sharply disagreed with this assessment of the Phalangist forces. They argued that they would regress, given the opportunity.

In the aftermath of Bashir Gemayel's assassination and the subsequent decision to move into West Beirut to maintain order, Sharon and Eitan decided to send the Phalangist units into the heavily armed Shatilla and Sabra neighborhoods; their objective was to eliminate residual terrorist forces from the area.

□   □   □   □   □

On September 15, Defense Minister Ariel Sharon traveled to Lebanon to pay two important calls. He first met with leaders of the Phalangist forces at their headquarters in Karantin. He than traveled the eight-mile trip to Bikfaya, home of 76-year-old Pierre Gemayel, founding father of the Lebanese Phalangist movement—and grieving father of Bashir. Sharon went to express his condolences and those of the Prime Minister of Israel. He assured the elderly patrician of the Phalangist movement that Israel's support for the Maronite Christian community would continue. Close as the Israelis felt with Bashir, Minister Sharon explained, they recognized a mutuality of interests which transcended the personalities of individuals. Israel would continue to stand by the Lebanese Christian community. He also told Gemayel that the Israeli army would be going into West Beirut to maintain calm. Gemayel thanked Sharon for his visit. Sharon left the stately Gemayel fortress and returned to Israel. Their meeting had lasted fifteen minutes.

By the next day, September 16, the Israeli Defense Forces had already entered West Beirut, according to plan. At 6:00 pm that evening the Phalangists entered the neighborhoods of Sabra and Shatilla. They were to mop up the terrorist enclaves still functioning in the neighborhoods and to search for remaining P.L.O. arms caches. They would have much to find. By war's end there would be reports that over 500 tons of weapons had been stored in those neighborhoods.

But this phase of Israel's Lebanese campaign did not go according to plan. In the hands of the Phalangists, it descended into calamity.

By late evening rumors began to spread among certain Israelis near the Sabra-Shatilla areas that something was not going right. The word was that the Christians were not being as discerning between terrorists and civilians as they were instructed to be. By the next day, word began to spread, as far away as Israel. Something seemed to be going wrong.

By Saturday, September 17, the first confirmations began trickling out. There had been some sort of massacre in Sabra and Shatilla. The Phalangists had killed many civilians. There had been a massacre.

In time, the Red Cross would report 460 people killed; and 35 of them were women and children. That means that *over 90% of the victims were men, mostly of fighting age.* And the victims included not only Palestinians and Lebanese—*but also Pakistanis, Syrians, Iranians, Algerians, and others.* The highly respected *Wall Street Journal,* in an editorial published on October 25, 1983—a year after the killings, when passion had cooled down and reason prevailed—wrote: "It was a further mistake to over-react to the Sabra and Chatilla(sic)killings, in which the official report of the dead—425 men compared with 35 women and children—suggests something more nearly resembling combat than an atrocity." Indeed, the P.L.O. policy of inducting into its fighting forces young boys twelve years of age further beclouds the issue: could any of those children have been involved in combat?

S. Fred Singer, a Senior Fellow at the Heritage Foundation, the highly regarded conservative think-tank based in Washington, D.C., wrote the *New York Times* a letter, published in August 1983, which argued along the same lines:

> The official report informs us that 35 victims were women and children and 425 were men. Not only that: nearly one-half of the total were not even Palestinians but included Lebanese, Syrians, Pakistanis, Iranians, Algerians, and unidentified others.

> Perhaps further investigation will reveal just what
> these people were doing in the Palestinian refugee
> camps. Perhaps the Lebanese authorities will tell us
> someday . . .

But the editorial of the *Wall Street Journal* and the letter in the *New York Times* were to come later, long after
the initial shock waves stirred humanitarians throughout
the world—indeed, throughout Israel proper. Civilians
had been killed, whatever the circumstances. And the
Israelis had been on the scene, in a sense.

As the world newsmedia responded to Shatilla and
Sabra by headlining the killings—and imputing to Israel
a far more heinous role than the facts warranted—the
Israeli public itself was thrown into turmoil. Prime
Minister Begin's political opponents organized a huge
demonstration in Tel Aviv's main square demanding a full
judicial inquiry into the deaths, in an effort to impartial-
ly determine just what role—if any—Israel had played in
the killings.

At the same time, many argued vehemently against the
appointing of such a commission. Begin succinctly and
bluntly summarized this feeling when he sighed, "Gentiles kill Gentiles, and the Jews are blamed." But the
pressure continued to build. Finally, the Prime Minister
agreed to name a formal commission of inquiry into the
events which had transpired between September 16 and
18 in the Palestinian neighborhoods of Shatilla and Sabra.

Named to the committee was Supreme Court Justice
Aharon Barak. He had already established himself as a
man of impartiality when, serving as Attorney General

in the Cabinet of Yitzhak Rabin, he nevertheless fulfill-
ed his duty to prosecute Rabin's wife when she was found
to have maintained an illegal bank account in Washington,
D.C. Later, he impressed Prime Minister Begin through
his contributions during the Camp David meetings in
Washington.

The second man on the three-man tribunal was Major General (Res.) Yonah Efrat, an officer with a
distinguished record. He had served on various military
commissions, and his reputation among the upper
echelons of the Israeli Defense Forces was impeccable.

Finally, Menachem Begin named Chief Justice Yitzhak Kahan to head the committee. (Hence, it became
known as the "Kahan Commission.") By virtue of his
preeminent position as the nation's chief justice, the deeply regarded Kahan was considered the best possible individual to chair the investigation.

Meeting in a specially reserved section of Hebrew
University in Jerusalem, the Kahan Commission heard
testimony from 60 persons, and the staff took 180
statements from an additional 163 witnesses. The investigation openly focused on certain individuals, beginning at the top. Prime Minister Menachem Begin, Foreign
Minister Yitzhak Shamir, Defense Minister Ariel Sharon,
and Chief-of-Staff Rafael Eitan were among the main personalities whose roles were considered by the tribunal.
Among the other key targets of the inquiry were
Brigadier-General Amos Yaron and General Amir Drori,
both of whom played central roles in the Israeli Defense
Forces on the scene during that crucial week. General

Yehoshua Saguy, director of Israeli military intelligence, was also a subject of the study.

When the final report of the Kahan Commission was released in February 1983, it captured world attention because of its extensive effort to determine the scope of Israel's responsibility in the Sabra-Shatilla killings. While it found no Israeli, on any level, guilty of causing the deaths—or even of involvement in planning any anti-civilian assualt—it did impute guilt in a few instances. Central to these findings were its determination that both Defense Minister Sharon and Chief-of-Staff Eitan had erred in not adequately assessing the Phalangist forces as an unreliable force whose veneer of maturity and discipline was bound to be discarded in the aftermath of the assassination of their leader, Bashir Gemayel. Thus, while Israel's top defense leaders were themselves shocked at the killings, and never anticipated that such a thing would transpire by innocently dispatching Christian Phalangist forces into Shatilla and Sabra, the Kahan Commission found the very source of their innocence—their inability to fathom the depths of which the Phalangists could sink, given the opportunity—to be a liability. Accordingly, Defense Minister Ariel Sharon—while exonerated from any charges of direct involvement or conspiracy in the killings—was told to step down from his post as a penalty for his innocent presumption that the Phalangists could be trusted to fight cleanly.

▫   ▫   ▫   ▫   ▫

To many, it was a strange verdict—and an excessively harsh one. Indeed, so many people were unable to understand how so substantial a penalty could be assessed for so questionable a failing that rumors circulated that there must have been secret testimony which implicated Sharon more heavily. It could not be that he would be forced to resign his post because Christians had killed Moslems.

Reflective of the public response in Israel to the Kahan Report and its recommendations were opinion polls taken after the commission issued its findings. Despite the harsh findings aimed at Sharon, at Foreign Minister Shamir, and even at Prime Minister Menachem Begin, the electorate made clear that it would return the Likud coalition to power with a solid mandate were elections held at that time. Nevertheless, Ariel Sharon stepped down from his post as Defense Minister, conforming with the Kahan Commission's recommendation. Prime Minister Begin made a point of asking Sharon to remain in the Cabinet, all the same, as a Minister-without-Portfolio.

Sharon's own feelings about the affair were most clearly expressed in a major Knesset speech he delivered just days after the Shatilla and Sabra killings became known:

> This is a dark day for all of us. Innocent people—old men, women, and children—were murdered for no crime in Beirut. In the cruelest possible way.
>
> The human mind cannot accept that such would be the fate of innocent people. I did not come to explain this terrible tragedy because it is part of another world, not ours, but of those who perpetrated this slaughter. I hope they get their just punishment, although this is not under our control...
>
> I can say clearly and immediately that no soldier and no commander in the Israel Defense Forces partici-

pated in this terrible act. The hands of the I.D.F. are clean.

□   □   □   □   □

When we agreed to the entry of the Phalangists to the refugee camps, senior commanders distinctly told them that a military force would be allowed in the Shatilla camp to seek out and destroy terrorists. In the coordinating meetings, it was stressed that the action was to be against terrorists and not to harm the civilian population, and especially women, children, and the elderly . . .

The I.D.F., its soldiers and commanders, have been performing for three months a wonderful operation in Lebanon, which has brought and will bring great security gains. Every movement of our soldiers was known to us and was reported immediately. That is the tragedy of the camps. We did not know exactly what was taking place . . . We did not know. Would that we had known! . . .

We did not imagine in our worst dreams that the Phalangists would act thus, as they entered the battle at this time of the war. They looked like a regular army in all respects. They promised to fight only against the terrorists. We had a good expeience with them in the past when, during the siege of Beirut, they conquered the Faculty of Sciences, the neighborhood of Reyhan, and Jamhour. In addition, they were active in policing the road blocks between the two parts of the city. And they carried out their operations with efficiency. We passed along to them responsibility over various areas which we conquered, . . .

It is possible that you will come and say that this was an error in judgment in estimating the situation. But I do not say that. And I want you to pay attention.

Three weeks after the start of the war, a noted person came to me and said, "Lord in Heaven, what are the Phalangists doing, they who are our allies in this matter? They told us that at some point the Christians would enter Beirut. After all, it is their capital. They, too, have to do something to liberate their homeland. What's their part in this war? Is their part only that they sprinkle rice on our soldiers and hand out flowers, while we give blood? After all, did not we the Labor alignment open up the path for the Christians to power when we were in the Government?"

When I saw this, I said, "Lord in Heaven, is this *someone* from the National Religious Party?" No, this was the respected member of parliament, Mr. Victor Shemtov. He came to me with this claim. Member of Parliament Victor Shemtov [an outspoken leader in the Labor opposition] . . .

Throughout all these months, I was continually asked, "Why don't the Phalangists fight within Beirut? Why do their hands remain clean?"

You cannot have it both ways. You cannot harp on the fact that the Phalangists do not join the fighting, and then the moment a terrible tragedy happens, for which we are not responsible, roll your righteous eyes heavenward . . .

You will surely understand why letting the Phalangists into the camps while the Lebanese Army refused to go in was a natural step in order to prevent loss of life in our forces. The inhuman tragedy which took place was beyond our control, notwithstanding all the pain and the sorrow. We cannot bear the responsibility on our shoulders . . .

Sharon's impassioned plea for world understanding did not fall on deaf ears. And the subsequent findings of the

Kahan Commission, despite the stiff severity of its recommendations, essentially bore out Sharon's position. Ironically, then, the Kahan Commission—despite its role in forcing Sharon to depart from the Defense Ministry—did Sharon a great service at the same time.

If he had failed to foresee the barbaric tendencies of the Phalangist forces, Ariel Sharon was nonetheless innocent of any role in the planning or conspiring which set the Sabra and Shatilla killings into motion.

Though temporarily set back in his political career, Ariel Sharon could breathe a deep sigh of relief after the verdict came in.

Ariel Sharon had been exonerated. Finally, the murder-conspiracy charge would be laid to rest.

VI
Time's **Blood Libel**

For *Time* magazine's Jerusalem bureau, the entire Shatilla-Sabra story opened yet another new path for deprecating Israel.

Here was a juicy story, made to order. Finally, the Israelis could be implicated in an old-fashioned massacre. This time they would not be able to claim their innocence or rationalize the matter. Here was a gory, juicy page-one massacre.

But, for Jerusalem correspondent David Halevy, that just was not enough. He sought something more, something extra-special.

In the two months which followed the September 16-18 killings, Halevy composed a story which, upon publication, would set off tremors throughout the world—and would rock the State of Israel in a way no previous report of his had ever done.

Halevy based his story on Sharon's September 15 visit to Bikfaya, the Gemayel stronghold in Lebanon, where the Israeli Defense Minister had stopped for a brief condolence call to pay his respects to patrician Pierre Gemayel on the occasion of Bashir's death. Halevy argued that there was more to that Bikfaya meeting than anyone else realized. Sharon, he wrote, had not merely gone to express his respect and to convey Prime Minister Begin's regrets. No. Sharon had something else to talk about as well.

Christian revenge.

◻   ◻   ◻   ◻   ◻

In a December 6, 1982 world-wide memorandum, sent by Halevy to *Time* editors and writers all over the globe, the Jerusalem correspondent broke his scoop under the title: "Green Light for Revenge?" It was shocking:

> (Halevy—Jerusalem) The most crucial findings of the state inquiry commission investigating the Sabra and Shatilla massacre may turn out to be the newly discovered notes which were taken during a conversation between Israel's Defense Minister Ariel Sharon and leaders of the Gemayel clan. Sharon came to the Gemayels' home village, Bikfaya, the morning after Bashir Gemayel was assassinated. He came actually to convey his and the Begin government's condolences. When Sharon landed at Bikfaya, he had with him only one senior Israeli intelligence officer, who went with Sharon to the meeting and took notes during the private session.
>
> According to a highly reliable source who told us about that meeting, present were not only Pierre and

Amin Gemayel but also Fadi Frem, the Phalange Chief of Staff who is married to Bashir's sister. Sharon indicated in advance to the Gemayels that the Israeli army was moving into West Beirut and that he expected them, the Force Lebanese, to go into all the Palestinian refugee camps. He also gave them the feeling after the Gemayels' questioning that he understood their need to take revenge for the assassination of Bashir and assured them that the Israeli army would neither hinder them nor try to stop them.

These minutes will not be published at all, in any form whatsoever, as they indicate a direct involvement and advanced planning by the Gemayel family, including Lebanon's President, Amin Gemayel.

World-wide memoranda, such as the Halevy story, are routinely submitted by *Time* correspondents for internal circulation only. Only *Time* editors read these tidbits of information and gossip. Information included in a world-wide memorandum may not be disclosed outside this controlled group unless its author specifically gives clearance. On December 8, two days after Halevy filed his scoop, New York researcher Helen Doyle, based in the main *Time* headquarters, telexed him, requesting clearance for the memorandum. The next day Halevy telexed Doyle with his reply: "World Memo Item: 'Green Light' Cleared."

With Halevy's World-Wide Memorandum cleared, it was available for inclusion at any time. And it was a hot piece of property. Besides directly linking Amin Gemayel with the Sabra-Shatilla killings, at a time that Gemayel was desperately trying to unify his country, the memo clearly leveled a grave accusation against Sharon. In the key sentence of the memorandum, Halevy had written, "He also gave them the feeling after the Gemayels' questioning that he understood their need to take revenge for the assassination of Bashir and assured them that the Israeli army would neither hinder them nor try to stop them."

Sharon, in blunt terms, had been a major conspirator in organizing the killings, Halevy wrote; he had given the Gemayel family a "green light for revenge."

□   □   □   □   □

The story sat in the files, not so much gathering dust as festering. Like a deadly time bomb it ticked away, steadily, steadily, patient in the knowledge that, in time, it would have its chance to fulfill its destiny and explode.

□   □   □   □   □

Harry Kelly was *Time's* new Jerusalem bureau chief. He had assumed his new position in November 1982, two months after the disquieting events of September. Born in Chicago, he had racked up thirty years experience in journalism, including stints at the *Chicago Tribune,* the *Washington Star,* and *Time's* New York bureau. Now, only one month on the job at his hot new assignment, his man Halevy had uncovered a real shocker of a scoop.

Kelly knew of Halevy only the little he had been able to learn on his own. And this was not much. He had not been told by Dick Duncan, the chief of correspondents, that Halevy had been put on probation in the past because of a "hot story" whose sources proved to be not so hot.

All Kelly knew was that he had on his hands a "hot story," rooted in a "highly reliable source."

Reading through Halevy's memorandum, Kelly made some quick inquiries of Halevy: Are you sure?

Halevy, author of the Begin health story which had created the great stir in 1979, affirmed that he was sure.

On Tuesday, February 8, 1983 Kelly received his copy of the final report of the Kahan Commission. It had just been released. No doubt the Kahan Report would be the bureau's lead story for the week, maybe New York's cover story. Kelly wanted to take that Kahan Report and immortalize it. He was especially enticed by the fact that the tribunal, in issuing its findings, had announced that one segment of the report, "Appendix B," would have to remain sealed from public view. It contained material whose release could jeopardize Israel's national security.

Like a child warned to stay away from the cookie jar, Kelly yearned for a glimpse into the secrets, the sweet secrets, of "Secret Appendix B." He turned to his correspondent, Halevy. He asked him what might be in Appendix B. Halevy returned with the answer: his worldwide memorandum. What else?

It was now Thursday, February 10. Kelly was working on a tight schedule, knowing that New York needed his material right away so that his piece could be incorporated with the dispatches being submitted to New York by other *Time* bureau chiefs around the world, all of them reporting on the Kahan Commission findings. If he had the goods on Secret Appendix B, that would be wonderful. But he had to know. And he had to know fast.

Kelly asked Halevy to check out the sources one last time. Make sure it's right. Make sure.

Halevy returned to his office and placed a phone call to a person he would later describe as "Source C." After some time, he finally reached this anonymous informer on whom so much rested, and he asked, "What the hell is in Appendix B?"

"Source C" replied, "Hey, hey, this is a secret appendix, and I am not going to make any reference to that."

Halevy pleaded, "Okay, tell me at least the nature of Appendix B."

The response was: "It's an index. It's a reference book. The names of the officials appearing there and officers appearing there is a direct reference to their testimony, their minutes or documents that they provided to the commission."

Halevy probed. He got a confirmation that the names of people who had taken notes during the September 15 Karantina and Bikfaya meetings were included in the Appendix listing of names. At that point "Source C" terminated the conversation: "This is as far as I can go."

For David Halevy, put on probation only three years earlier for inadequate sourcing, that was enough. He returned to Kelly, who again asked him whether or not Appendix B actually contained the notes and information which would substantiate Halevy's report that Sharon had given the Gemayels, grieving for Bashir, a "green light for revenge?"

Halevy looked Kelly square in the eye, smiled, and gave him a "thumbs-up" sign. Thumbs up.

The story runs.

Now that he had decided to include his insider's scoop, Kelly tried to call Ariel Sharon to inform him of the charges *Time* would be printing and to ask him for a formal response, for publication alongside the allegations. But Kelly never reached Sharon. The Defense Minister was not at his office. So Kelly considered calling Sharon at his home, in light of the matter's extraordinary gravity. But Kelly could not make the call. The *Time* Jerusalem bureau did not have a current English-language telephone directory. And Kelly, the Jerusalem bureau chief, could neither read nor speak a word of Hebrew. So he never called Sharon.

He filed his story on Thursday afternoon, February 10. In *Time* jargon, the piece was labeled as Kelly's "Take 9", and it was telexed instantly to New York City. In the 700-word news summary, Harry Kelly reported:

> Part of the Report, which is called Appendix B, was not published, "since in our opinion," the commission said non-publication of this material is essential in the interest of protecting the nation's security...
>
> ... Some of it, we understand, was published in *Time*'s world-wide memo, an item by Halevy, December 6, for which we gave clearance, dealing with Sharon's visit to the Gemayel family to pay condolences. Certainly in reading the report, there is a feeling that at least part of the Commission's case against Sharon is between the lines, presumably in the secret portion.

Kelly's "Take 9" speeded along the overseas telex lines

and arrived in the world section of *Time's* editorial offices with enough time to make the issue then being prepared in New York. The Kahan Commission findings had, indeed, been selected as the coming week's cover story, and the task of writing the article was assigned to senior writer William E. Smith.

□   □   □   □   □

The way *Time* compiles articles is unique to the format of the news weekly. Unlike daily newspapers, which carry many late-breaking stories, the weekly magazines tend to carry fewer individual stories, often incorporating into one report four or five separate articles. Thus, a daily newspaper would have reported on the Kahan Commission with a number of different articles, each written by a different reporter. One story might have been the Jerusalem report of the raw text issued by Kahan. A second story could cover local reaction in Israel, while a third column could focus on Jewish reaction in America. A fourth story could give the reaction from Washington; a fifth article could relate European responses, and so on.

A newsweekly like *Time,* on the other hand, would publish one single—albeit extensive—article instead.

Such a difference in style requires a different methodology as well. In the case of daily newspapers, each reporter writes the text of the story he has investigated.

□   □   □   □   □

At a magazine like *Time,* however, the process is necessarily different. Correspondents throughout the world investigate and do their journalistic leg-work. The bureau chiefs then send out story segments, which are called "Takes" in corporate jargon, to the international headquarters in New York City. There, the "Takes" are forwarded to a senior writer who is assigned the task of writing up the extensive story which will ultimately appear in the magazine. The senior writer dutifully immerses himself in the subject about which he will be writing for that week's issue, and he goes through every word sent to him from *Time* bureaus throughout the world. Helping him keep up with the mounds of information and hard-to-check facts is a staff "researcher" whose specific job description is to check every single word for acccuracy. The researcher checks dates, spellings, and sundry other matters, significant and minuscule alike—looking over items coming in and, especially, poring over the senior writer's finished product.

Researched, checked, and corroborated, the finished article is now sent to the section's editor for his comments, suggestions, changes, and ultimate approval. When it is all finished, checked, re-checked, and approved, the perfected text goes through one more phase: the "playback." "Playback," another *Time* magazine insider's term, refers to the final proofreading process. The completed article is sent from New York back overseas or across the country, with copies sent to every bureau whose material may have contributed to the finished product. The respective bureaus review the senior writer's prose and facts in this last phase of the magazine's ostensibly impeccable and unimpeachable editorial review process. When the "playback" is cleared and no other questions remain, the piece may finally—and only then—appear in the magazine.

In this system, the senior writer plays a major role in the compilation of every article in the magazine. He decides what to include and what to omit. He conveys the thoughts and reports of a world-wide network of correspondents into one smooth, homogenized form. And, if he follows the basic rules, he gets his way.

□   □   □   □   □

Unfortunately for Israel, William E. Smith was the last person in the world the Jewish State needed to report on the Kahan findings. In one of his most celebrated—and infamous—blunders, he had chopped up a crucial part of modern Israel's history in a scandalous paragraph he had written for the January 17, 1983 issue. As part of an article whose focus was not really on Zionist history, Smith had inserted this extraordinary sentence: "In 1948 the Jews of Palestine seized control of part of the ancient land of their forefathers and established the State of Israel." He made no reference to the historical background, to the legitimacy inherent in their simple execution of a resolution adopted by the United Nations General Assembly. Indeed, rather than "seize" the land, the founders of the modern State of Israel found themselves the targets of seven fully mobilized Arab national armies which attempted to wipe them from the face of the earth in defiance of the U.N. vote to recognize the State of Israel.

Smith would later admit, in his own words, that *Time* came under heavy criticism after that sentence appeared, that many people regarded the sentence as most improper.

He would say, "It was unfortunate that I did not include the important details in terms of the basis of Israel." In response to Smith's grievous flick of his pen, Susan Tribich of *Time*'s letter-answering department drafted a letter on *Time* stationery admitting that *"Time* erred."

This was the senior writer into whose hands Harry Kelly's "Take 9" had been entrusted: William E. Smith.

Smith began preparing for the cover assignment by reading the Kahan Commission report, a variety of news clippings from around the world, and material which had been filed by *Time*'s Beirut bureau. Material came in at a hectic pace from Jerusalem. As Friday night's deadline approached, he had already received eighteen separate "takes" of news reports from his Jerusalem bureau. One of those reports was Kelly's "Take 9."

After reading "Take 9," Smith decided to go into the files and review Halevy's original December 6, 1982 memorandum which, in fact, served as the basis for Kelly's report. He read Halevy's words:

> According to a highly reliable source. . . [Sharon] expected them, the Force Lebanese, to go into all the Palestinian refugee camps. He also gave them the feeling after the Gemayels' questioning, that he understood their need to take revenge for the assassination of Bashir and assured them that the Israeli army would neither hinder them nor try to stop them.

Smith would later explain how he interpreted the Halevy report. "I took this to mean that, on this condolence visit that he was making that day . . . I learned from this that Sharon during his condolence visit, and immediately after...broached the subject of military moves with the Gemayels, and in the course of the conversation discussed the subject of revenge with them...Mr. Sharon was discussing the grief that their family had suffered and assured them that he understood and that the Israelis would not get in their way..."

Starting with the basic text of "Take 9," senior writer Smith began preparing the crucial segment of his cover story. In the key paragraph, he first used Halevy's terminology, writing that Sharon "also reportedly gave the Gemayels the feeling..."

He looked at those words, at that sentence construction, for ten, fifteen seconds. He didn't like it. It was too weak. It was too passive. It needed more punch, more pizzaz. That's what senior writers are for.

So, employing a bit of poetic license, William Smith changed the words "gave them the feeling" to something more forthright and direct: "discussed." Yes, that was better. "Sharon also reportedly discussed with the Gemayels the need for the Phalangists to take revenge..."

That would do the trick.

Smith worked assiduously through the day of Friday, Ferbruary 11, not leaving his desk until 10 p.m. that evening. In crafting his final draft, he had sculpted an historic paragraph out of the clay which had been "Take 9":

> *Time* has learned that it [Appendix B] also contains further details about Sharon's visit to the Gemayel family on the day after Bashir Gemayel's assassination. Sharon reportedly told the Gemayels that the

Israeli army would be moving into West Beirut and
that he expected the Christian forces to go into the
Palestinian refugee camps. Sharon also reportedly
discussed with the Gemayels the need for the Phalangists to take revenge for the assassination of Bashir,
but the details of the conversation are not known.

□   □   □   □   □

The following morning, Smith was back at his desk.
Weekends are miserable the weeks you have to write the
cover story. This Saturday was Smith's turn. He read and
re-read the article he had prepared the day before and saw
it through to its typeset galley form. He had received comments from Henry Muller, his boss, editor of *Time*'s world
section. Helen Doyle, the researcher assigned to back him
up on the story, had made her suggestions as well. Smith
tightened up the text accordingly and was now satisfied
that he was set.

Helen Doyle, the researcher, had joined *Time* a year-
and-a-half earlier. Together with Nellie Gonzales, she had
been put to work on the Smith article. It was a cover
story—and an extraordinary one at that. A piece of that
magnitude deserved a second researcher.

Doyle found that the voluminous task before her was
aggravated by the great foe of all professional journalists:
the ticking deadline. To speed things along in an effec-
tive and efficient manner, she and Gonzales decided to
split the article up between them. Doyle's portion included
the paragraph asserting that Sharon had discussed with
the Phalangists their need to take revenge for Bashir's
assassination. Her job was to check and to verify, to

research and to bolster.

But how could Helen Doyle, sitting in *Time*'s offices at Rockefeller Center, check on the veracity of Halevy's memo? How could she verify the contents of Secret Appendix B six thousand miles away?

She could compare Smith's report with the primary sources in her possession: Halevy's world-wide memorandum and Kelly's "Take 9." And Doyle also had her own copy of the Kahan Commission report. She spent hours poring through Kahan's published findings and recommendations. She studied Smith's article. She did her job.

She found no problems of great import.Smith had done just fine. In changing the words "gave them the feeling" to "discussed," Smith had acted appropriately, she felt.

With Doyle's concurrence, Smith now had one last step to follow up the ladder of *Time*'s meticulous check-for-accuracy system. The "playback."

Smith telexed the Jerusalem bureau with his final draft. Halevy and Kelly, ever mindful of their duties and responsibilities, perused through Smith's cover story on Sunday, February 13 in their Jerusalem office.

They noticed that Smith had added the proud, beaming phrase, "Time has learned" to the text, an acceptable touch. He wrote that the details of Sharon's condolence visit are not known but that he discussed the need for Phalangist revenge with the Gemayels. They read through his text and found it just fine. They sent back a telex to *Time*'s "world" section in New York, giving their approval. "Story reads very good," Kelly and Halevy wrote. "A fine job in our view."

Well, almost a fine job. In fact, their return telex to New York went on to include no less than seventeen corrections, changes, deletions, and comments. Seventeen — and it was only one day before publication. The presses would be running that night. It was a good thing that telex machines existed.

But in their six hundred words of corrections, changes, deletions, and comments they did not make a single suggestion about the wording of Smith's account of the condolence visit. That paragraph survived the "playback" intact. It "read good." It was a fine job.

The Kelly-Halevy "playback" arrived in New York the same day, and the final touches were put on the grand cover story. Ray Cave, the managing editor, came up with the catchy headline: "The Verdict is Guilty."

By Sunday afternoon, the verdict was sealed — the verdict that Secret Appendix B contained documentation supporting a claim that Ariel Sharon had conspired with the Gemayels in a vengeance plot against the Palestinian residents of Shatilla and Sabra. It would be in the mails and on the newsstands the following morning — six million copies of America's most widely read newsweekly.

□   □   □   □   □

Bob Parker arrived on Sunday and sat down to work at his desk in *Time*'s public-relations department. Every Sunday, or so, Parker would arrive for a hectic day's work. He had been with the corporation since 1948 when he wrote for *Life* in Washington, D.C. He had moved over to *Time* as a writer in 1953 and eventually went on to serve in many other posts at the magazine: news editor, deputy chief of correspondents, public relations. After 30 years in the company, Parker retired in 1978. Since then, he would come by frquently as a part-time independent contractor.

His boss, Brian Brown, manager of *Time*'s publicity department since 1976, describes Parker's important role in the office:

"Usually. . .on a Friday. . .myself or Bob Parker will call the senior editors of the various sections of the magazine, that is: nation, world, business, and so on. And I will, or he will, ask them quite simply: 'Do you have anything that is particularly newsworthy this week in the magazine?' And they will indicate what they have. . .and these are stories that we will then watch for on Sunday.

"The magazine, as you know, closes on Saturday. We write press releases on Sunday, and we write the press release from page proofs, that is, the actual pages, copies of the actual pages that will appear in the magazine. And that, basically, is how we operate."

Bob Parker came in on Sunday to do his job. It is a high-pressure job because he must not only decide what to highlight in the weekly press release but must also finish writing it no later than 3:00 in the afternoon. At that point, the finished copy is reproduced, and a team of messengers fan out over the great Manhattan metropolis, quickly distributing the weekly press release to the 140 recipients on their list: information brokers, daily newspapers, wire services, radio stations which feature important news programs, radio and television networks, and some other major agencies and correspondents based in New York.

As Parker would later explain in a deposition, "always, in the preparation of a press release, the purpose is to try to focus on the matter of what we feel will be the greatest interest to the people we are writing it for, the news editors, the newspapers, wire services, radio, TV stations."

Sunday, February 13, was like any other Sunday. Parker came to work, assessed the situation, canvassed the editors and settled on the story of the week: the cover story, written by one of the writers in the "world" section about that Kahan Commission report. There was something special in *Time's* account of the event, Parker learned. *Time* was breaking some spicy information that was going to rock a few boats.

"It was an interesting piece of news," Parker would later recall. "There is a small professional touch involved, that any time a story has in the text *'Time* has learned' that is a kind of signal to everybody that it is a special piece of news, and it is a signal to me as a promotion person to read it with special care, and very likely put out a press release on that part, where *Time* spotlights the information by saying *'Time* has learned.' I would expect that [people] would read it with special interest and that they might deduce—we hope they would—that this is a piece of information which may not be available anywhere else, that it may be new and exclusive in *Time*."

□   □   □   □   □

Parker was especially lucky this Sunday. He had a winner. The Halevy-Kelly-Smith paragraph. It was too good to miss. Parker wrote his release and slapped on it a great headline, the kind that he gets paid for:

"SHARON SAID TO HAVE URGED LEBANESE TO SEND PHALANGISTS INTO CAMPS"

□ □ □ □ □

In his six-paragraph release Parker reprinted the Sharon condolence-call paragraph verbatim from Smith's final version. The press release was distributed on schedule. The news was out.

□ □ □ □ □

On Monday, the newspapers in Israel went wild with screaming headlines, the first fruits of Parker's catchy press release, transmitted world-wide by the wire services. The daily *Al Hamishmar* reported the *Time* scoop under a subheading "They Will Avenge the Murder":

> . . . Sharon spoke with members of the Gemayel family about the necessity for the Phalange to avenge Bashir's murder . . .

And the mass-circulating afternoon daily *Yediot Aharonot* published a banner headline of its own: *"Time:* On the Eve of the Massacre Sharon Called Upon the Gemayel Family to Avenge the Death of Bashir; Ministry of Defense: A Lie." Elaborating on its headline, *Yediot* continued:

> The day after the assassination of president-elect Bashir Gemayel, Ariel Sharon met with members of the Lebanese leader's family and gave his opinion that the Christian Phalange must avenge his blood, writes the American newsweekly *Time* in its latest issue . . .

As the story spread throughout Israel that Sharon had somehow hidden from the public a direct role in colluding with the Gemayels in planning the Shatilla-Sabra killings, a new wave of resentment and hostility against him erupted throughout the country.

It was a lie, Sharon contended. I did not talk with the Gemayels about anything of that nature. I merely paid a condolence call. It is a lie.

Because the Secret Appendix B was just that—secret—it would be impossible to buttress his claim by pointing to the paragraph itself in support of his refutation.

Sharon was one of a select group of Israelis who were given access to the classified appendix material. As Minister of Defense, he was privy to the entire unabridged report, as were all other Cabinet ministers of Israel. Members of select Knesset committees also saw it.

With a tumultuous wave of controversy sweeping the land, in the wake of the *Time* story, Prime Minister Menachem Begin ascended the Knesset rostrum on Monday, February 14, and used the full power and prestige of this office to make the most bitter denunciation of any periodical he would ever deplore:

> Mr. Speaker, gentlemen, members of the Knesset. I read Appendix #2 to the final report of the Commission of Inquiry, which decided it will be privileged and top secret and, of course, I will not reveal its contents. But I am able to say on the basis of this knowledge that what is written in *Time* magazine, as

if the Minister of Defense went after the assassination of Bashir Gemayel to Beirut and talked to the family of the assassined (sic) about revenge upon Palestinians or on those suspected in the murder, this whole story is entirely a lie and false and has no substance...I call [upon] the editorial board [of *Time*] to apologize immediately to the Minister of Defense and to the State of Israel for the distribution of this libel.

     □   □   □   □   □

At first Kelly, the Jerusalem bureau chief, was completely unaware of the stir and commotion all around him. Unable to read or speak a word of Hebrew, he did not realize that the newsstand copies of *Al Hamishmar* and *Yediot Aharonot,* with their screaming red banner headlines, were talking about him. He had no idea.

     □   □   □   □   □

For Halevy as well, this time it was different. This time he was not merely putting Shimon Peres on a boat ride up the Mediterranean or looking into Menachem Begin's cardiovascular system. This time, he had published a charge of collusion and conspiracy to murder. If true, it was one of the most important journalistic scoops of the century and a valuable contribution to the cause of justice in Israel.

If wrong, it was a blood libel.

Kelly would look back later on that frenzied February 14 and confess his complete amazement at what was happening. "I did not know immediately what was going on. It was very confusing to me. I don't read Hebrew. No one came to me and said such-and-such and so-and-so . . .

Halevy [came into the office the next day and] had a Hebrew newspaper in his hand, and he looked puzzled, and said something: Could they have changed the story [in New York] after we saw it?—or words to that effect..."

(While *Time's* press release, as disseminated by the wire services, had reached Israel by Sunday night, February 13, the actual magazine itself would not arrive for several days...)

Continuing, Kelly would recall, "By this time it was obvious that there was some confusion going on...Then Begin's statement. That's what really altered me...I was stunned."

It is one thing to be confused and stunned. It is another thing to have the power to influence international political events. Kelly, at the center of this storm, began to realize the enormous clout he had wielded. Why, he had just about single-handedly knocked Sharon out of the political ring! And he had achieved all this only three months after assuming his position. He couldn't hold it in. He had to share it with someone. Someone important. He telexed Richard Duncan, The chief of correspondents in New York, with the news:

"That must have been one heck of a news release on the inquiry cover [story], specifically on that fairly innocuously worded *'Time* has learned' [paragraph] about Sharon's meeting with the Gemayel family.

"It was on page one in the papers Monday. Somebody at the Defense Ministry was commenting it was all lies. Then the Press Office put out a statement that the Defense

Ministry response was 'not an official denial.' Then later, in the Knesset Monday, Begin called it 'bald lies and slander' and called on *Time's* editors to apologize to Sharon and the State of Israel 'for disseminating this libel.'

"And I don't think anybody's had a chance to read the story yet . . . We must have struck a nerve. Cheers."

Cheers. We must have struck a nerve. We made page one. Kelly had recuperated from the confusion. He was beginning to enjoy the notoriety.

Cheers.

For Dick Duncan, back at the home office at Rockefeller Center, there was no need to react with concern or alarm when Kelly's telex arrived. It was clear that the boys in Jerusalem were having a swell time, and he knew he could rely on their professional skills in support of the story's veracity. After all, it had been based on secret sources described by one of Duncan's most reliable correspondents, David Halevy. Duncan knew that there was nothing to worry about. Besides, Halevy's probation was already passed. He was a pro again.

Given a choice between a Begin denunciation from the Knesset rostrum and a Halevy thumbs-up confirmation, Duncan knew where to put his money. "I did not regard [Begin's remarks] as serious . . . It seemed to me consistent with the political forum and the kind of vocabulary which upon occasion was used in the Knesset, so that it had somewhat less import than it might have had in another country at another time."

Yes, Mr. Duncan, but how many times, to your

recollection, has the Head-of-State of a country denounced a *Time* article, or a portion of it, as containing bald lies and slander?

That very question would be posed to Duncan two years later. He would answer, "Not very many."

And, if the Head of State in *another* country had made a remark like that on the floor of a "less emotional" parliamentary body would you have taken that more seriously, Mr. Duncan?

"I might have."

So Duncan did not launch an investigation. And, unlike the responsible Jerusalem bureau chief who had pursued the erroneous 1979 Halevy story on Begin's supposed health problem, Harry Kelly did not look into the matter any further.

□   □   □   □   □

Two weeks later, Kelly was attending a social event at one of Jerusalem's better spots, a dinner honoring visiting New York City Mayor Ed Koch. As the appetizers were being served, the man sitting on Kelly's immediate right tapped him on the shoulder. "Hi, my name is Olmert. Ehud Olmert. I'm a Likud Knesset member. Nice to meet you."

Kelly had never before heard of him. He acknowledged the greeting.

Olmert continued. "You know, I serve on the Knesset Foreign Affairs and Security Committee—"

Kelly responded "that's nice."

"—and I had an opportunity to read through the entire Kahan Commission Report, including the secret Appendix B."

Kelly put down his fork.

"And I have to tell you," Olmert said, "that I don't recall seeing in Section B, in Appendix B, anything remotely related to what you wrote about General Sharon."

Kelly was dumbstruck. He paused, considered the words, the surprising, unexpected words suddenly tossed at him in the middle of salad. He composed himself and looked at Olmert, saw that the young Israeli parliamentarian was quite serious, and asked him if he wouldn't be so kind as to review the material one more time. Just to make sure.

Olmert agreed, and he called Kelly at the *Time* office in Jerusalem first thing Monday morning. "I just don't see what you reported in the papers I have," said Olmert. His English is good. Kelly thanked him and politely ended the conversation.

What to do? He had checked the story—or, at least, he had asked Halevy to confirm the facts. And Halevy had given him the thumbs-up. Could something have gone wrong?

Kelly decided to call Duncan in New York and lay the problem on his lap. Since Israel is seven hours ahead of New York time, Kelly would have to wait through the day, until 5:00 p.m., at which time he would be able to reach Duncan starting his work day in Manhattan.

The hours ticked along. It was late afternoon. Just about time to call New York. Duncan would be there any minute.

Suddenly, the phone rang. Jean Max, the office

manager, called Kelly. It was a reporter on the line.

Kelly picked up the phone. "Hello?"

The voice on the other end responded, "Hi, I'm with United Press International here. I'm just calling for a statement from you."

A statement? A statement about what?

"Oh, haven't you heard the news? Ariel Sharon has just filed a multi-million libel suit against *Time* magazine."

Kelly put down the phone.

Cheers.

VII
Sharon's Day in Court

For Ariel Sharon, the Kahan Commission Report had already been a very severe blow. It just wasn't fair, he felt.

For months after his resignation from the Israeli Defense Ministry, he would tell visitors to his farm: "I am the only Defense Minister in the world who was forced to become a farmer because Christians killed Moslems." And he would expand on his small, pained joke by looking back on the events of 1982.

Israel had to silence the P.L.O. guns and destroy the terrorist network and infrastructure in Fatahland and beyond, throughout Lebanon. It was Israel's solemn obligation, a sovereign nation's duty, to protect her citizens and to secure her borders.

So Israel launched Operation Peace for Galilee. A good battle plan was drawn up and almost flawlessly executed. Virtually all the military objectives were attained;

the fundamental goal—Arafat's expulsion from Lebanon
—was achieved. It was really a remarkable victory.

There had been casualties. Nearly 400 soldiers were
killed during the war. It was undeniably tragic. But Israel
has learned that security means sacrifice, and she has had
to sacrifice her sons to protect her borders. The Yom Kippur War of 1973, fought according to a defensive philosophy which stressed the need to absorb the enemy strike
before mobilizing, had resulted in more than 2,500 Israeli
deaths. Even the swift and awesome victory of 1967's Six-
Day War had left behind a statistic of 679 Israeli soldiers
killed. In the face of such numbers, the cries of Sharon's
opponents on the political left did not seem fair.

Had the war been unnecessary? Hardly. The Galilee
was under incessant attack, and the Jewish population had
begun to despair of its future. By early 1982, Jewish
neighborhoods were thinning out, as Jewish residents
decided to move southward to quieter, more secure Israeli
neighborhoods. As a result, the already significant Arab
population in Israel's north was fast becoming a majority. There was a real chance that the situation, if not
dramatically altered, might eventually imperil Israel's very
presence in the region.

Finally, with the shocking discoveries of thousands of
tons of heavy weapons and munitions in P.L.O. storage
facilities (underground tunnels, school yards, hospitals,
and apartment-house basements) throughout Lebanon, it
became apparent that a significant danger existed which
had escaped Israel's own intelligence community: Arafat
may have been planning a full-scale frontal assault on

Israel. Had the Israelis not entered southern Lebanon, waiting instead for Arafat to choose his most propitious moment to invade Israel, the deaths and related casualties could ultimately have been staggeringly higher.

Sharon recognized that some objectives had been snatched from Israel. American pressure strengthened Arafat's hand during the August negotiations while he was holed up in West Beirut. Bashir Gemayel, who could have turned everything around, never lived to give it a try. His assassination was a terrible blow to Israel's long-term hopes as the war wound down.

And, of course, the Shatilla-Sabra killings had ruined the rest of it. An outpouring of anti-Israel invectives and ugly villifications of the Jewish State had set in motion a national reappraisal, which seemed so affected by external condemnations that the Israelis had really lost sight of the great gains charted by the war.

Sharon was bitter. Had the war effort failed, had the strategy been faulty, had its execution been mismanaged, he would have paid a severe price. He knew that, understood that, and accepted that. But the war had been a success. So his opponents had to find a different cross on which to crucify him.

Along came Sabra and Shatilla, and he never had a chance. That was the opening his foes had anticipated eagerly.

The Kahan Commission was yet one more unfathomable step taken by his political enemies to hurt the Begin government—but, in the long run, it would hurt Israel. The idea of a tribunal sitting in judgment of Israelis for their role in the Shatilla-Sabra killings—while no one investigated the actual Lebanese killers—left a sad taste in Sharon's mouth. Perhaps the Kahan Commission represented Israel's superior national moral-ethical conscience, its democratic ideals which regarded no person to be above the law, and the outpouring of a national conscience seeking redemption—but in the long run it would be remembered as a court which handed down convictions against Israelis for crimes they did not perpetrate.

The very title of *Time*'s cover story on the Kahan Report—"The Verdict Is Guilty"—bore out Sharon's deepest fears. *Time* was not alone in reporting the "guilty verdicts" handed down by Kahan, Barak, and Efrat—as though Sharon, Eitan, Yaron, and Saguy were among the guilty.

For this reason Sharon initially refused to step down from his ministerial post, despite the commission's recommendation that he do so. Stepping down would be a tacit acceptance of the finding that indirect responsibility, in the form of an innocent naiveté (on the part of those who simply regarded the Christian Phalangists as regular human beings and not as bloodthirsty animals), constituted a crime parallel to actual, direct guilt.

Sharon was forced to step down by the Begin Cabinet which voted to implement the Kahan recommendations, for better or worse. Really, they had no choice. While many opposed the formation of the commission of inquiry from the outset—let the Lebanese investigate the real killers was this school's thought—even those opponents agreed, in the wake of the Kahan Report, that the recommendations would have to be carried out.

If Sharon was hurt by the Kahan Commission, however, he was also exonerated by it. As condemnations first poured into Israel from throughout the world, it was actually a point of cynical humor in some Israeli circles to consider the sources of the criticism: the Soviet bloc nations, African dictatorships, and Arab tyrannies. Yet more and more people began to whisper that Sharon's hands were personally bloody from those killings. If he had not personally entered the neighborhoods where the killings occurred, he had nonetheless been involved in the conspiracy and actively encouraged it, perhaps even instigated it.

It was in this sense that Kahan's report helped restore Sharon's reputation. It made clear that:

> We have no doubt that no conspiracy or plot was entered into between anyone from the Israeli political echelon or from the military echelon in the I.D.F. and the Phalangists, with the aim of perpetrating atrocities in the camps. The decision to have the Phalangists enter the camps was taken with the aid of preventing further losses [of Israeli soldiers' lives] in the war in Lebanon; to accede to the pressure of public opinion in Israel, which was angry that the Phalangists, who were reaping the fruits of the war, were taking no part in it; and to take advantage of the Phalangists' professional service and their skills in identifying terrorists and in discovering arms caches. No intention existed on the part of any Israeli element to harm the non-combatant population in the camps...We assert that, in having the Phanlangists enter the camps, no intention existed on the part of anyone who acted on

behalf of Israel to harm the non-combatant population, and that the events that followed did not have the
concurrence or assent of anyone from the political or
civilian echelon who was active regarding the Phalangists' entry into the camps.

Cleared of any actual wrong-doing, Ariel Sharon was
exonerated in a very significant and important way, even
though he did bear some criticism in the process. Thus,
while he was asked by his colleagues to comply with the
Kahan recommendation that he give up the Defense Ministry, he was still accepted as a full-fledged Cabinet
minister, with all the power and influence implicit in such
a position. Indeed, when the National Unity Government
was established in 1984, the new Prime Minister Shimon
Peres—the leader of the Labor Party—accepted Sharon
into his Cabinet as Minister of Industry and Trade, a
significant Cabinet post.

Sharon could not have remained in the Cabinet—
indeed, he has continued in the Israeli Cabinet uninterrupted for every day since the February 1983 publication
of the Kahan Report—were it not for Kahan's underlying
exoneration.

It was for that reason that the *Time* story, concocted
by Halevy and processed by Kelly and Smith for publication in the magazine's issue of February 21 *(Time* dates
its magazines a week ahead in order to maximize newsstand timeliness . . . and sales), shook Sharon. Although
exonerated by Kahan and relieved of the terrible burden
of alleged conspiracy to massacre civilians, Sharon's name
was now no longer cleared. The *Time* article reopened the

grave charges. And *Time's* six-million circulation (one quarter of which is outside of the United States), combined with its press release's effectiveness in transmitting the story to every point on the globe where a wire service machine is accessible, assured the accusations the widest possible readership.

Sharon termed the charge a "Blood Libel," recalling an image steeped deeply in Jewry's history of persecution. For centuries, both in Europe and in the Moslem orbit, rumors were circulated by anti-Jewish agitators that Jews drink human blood, or wash their bodies with it, or fill their pockets with it, or bake it into their Passover matzoh. The charge, the lie, gained wide acceptance during the Dark Ages when people had neither televisions nor newspapers nor automobiles nor any of the other modern vehicles of communication which make it possible to encounter Jews first-hand. People who had never seen Jews in their entire lives had no reason to believe that Jews did not do such things. And so, stirred to frenzies by agitators at times of great tragedy, such as during the 1348 Black Death (which saw one-third of Eruope die of bubonic plague), fear-intoxicated mobs accepted the Big Lie and attacked Jews. If a child were missing, perhaps the Jews had taken him. That was the blood libel of the Dark Ages.

In raising the Blood Libel metaphor, Ariel Sharon and Menachem Begin gave expression to their very real sense that segments of the world were blaming the Jewish people for the crimes of others. Whatever the guilt one must assume for indirect responsibility at the time of Shatilla and Sabra, it still is not the same as pulling a trigger and snuffing out a civilian life. It still does not equate with a charge of direct complicity and conspiracy to murder.

Time, in effect, charged Sharon with just that— conspiracy to murder. For Sharon, just breathing his first sighs of exoneration in the wake of the Kahan Comission report, *Time's* new charges damaged his name and reputation gravely. Sharon had not merely been defamed. *Time's* accusation amounted to more than that.

Ariel Sharon had been added to Jewish history's long list of victims of the infamous Blood Libel.

□   □   □   □   □

In contemplating steps to take, Sharon felt that he would have to go through a new legal procedure, all over again, to clear his name once more. Because *Time* is based in the United States, where over four million people receive it every week, Sharon determined that it would not suffice to sue *Time* in Israel only. He therefore decided to file papers in the United States, too, asking for $50,- 000,000 in damages resulting from the libel. Sharon would later explain:

"I think that this article caused a terrible damage to my reputation. What can cause more damage to a reputation of somebody [than] when he is accused of urging or discussing the need to kill and murder civilian people?

What can be more than that? And I speak as a Jew, and I speak as a human being, who believes in the values of life, of people, and in the need to take every care of human life . . .

"And here comes the *Time* magazine, with a circulation of millions all around the world, *Time* comes and libels me...I regard that to be a blood libel, trying to accuse me of urging, of discussing a revenge...

"I would like to emphasize that in the Kahan commission, never—not in one word—have I been accused of committing any murder, or instigating a murder, or discussing a murder, or encouraging a murder. That happened only in the *Time* magazine...."

"And I can tell you, I remember being in the spring of 1983, being in Montreal, facing the most terrible demonstration, and I was shown...those signs, saying: 'Sharon Murderer,' 'Sharon Is a Monster.'

"And I can only say what I felt as a human being, facing all those things. Very hard. It was very hard what I felt, that after the *Time* magazine published it, [there] was a new wave, a new wave of hatred that [erupted]...There were many people that, after they read the *Time* magazine which described me as a man who encouraged murder, changed their attitide toward me."

Sharon's lawyers, in setting forth the basis for their libel suit against *Time*, explained: "The charge made against this man is the most heinous of all offenses— encouraging the slaughter of innocent women and children! That and that alone is what led to this suit.... Truly, what worse could be said of a human being than that he actively incited mass murder? It is to remove that stain that this man seeks his day in court...The libel itself was the product of a magazine infected with a vicious bias against the plaintiff [Sharon], his country, and its leaders ..."

Reflective of the last charge—that *Time*'s bias transcends Sharon and is also one which is actually anti-Israel—was an article in the *New York Times* of December 14, 1984, entitled "In Israel, Even Sharon's Worst Enemies Aren't Friends of *Time.*" Jerusalem correspondent Thomas L. Friedman reported that "the magazine has come to embody all the evils and all the perceived shortcomings of Western news coverage of Israel" in the opinion of some Israelis. Ze'ev Chafets, former director of the Israeli Government Press Office, told Friedman that "*Time* is so disliked here that it has the capacity to make people who despise Sharon want [him] to win."

On this issue, the country shared a widespread sympathy for Sharon's right to have his day in court.

VIII
6,000 Miles to Foley Square

In taking his lawsuit six thousand miles away from home, westward across the Atlantic to New York's Southern District court in Foley Square, Ariel Sharon was not merely suing *Time* in its own backyard. He had a second reason for filing in New York, where *Time* is published:

"You know, I thought that [their libel] was so serious that in order to bring it to the attention of the world, in order that things like that will not be done again . . . it should come to a place, what I would have called an international stage, where a lie like that should be tried. A libel like that should be tried in a place where it will attract the attention of the world."

By the luck of the draw, the case of *Ariel Sharon v. Time Inc.* went to Federal District Court Judge Abraham David Sofaer, a Jew of Sephardic heritage. Born in 1938 in Bombay, India to parents who traced their family roots back to Egypt and Iraq, Sofaer grew up in India, attending several Anglo-Scottish academies. His family moved to the United States when he was fourteen years of age. Four years later, after high school, Sofaer enlisted in the United States Air Force. Discharged from the service in 1959, he became a naturalized American citizen.

Sofaer studied law after his college years and rose like a meteor. After finishing New York University Law School, where he was editor-in-chief of the law review, he went on to clerkships with an appeals court Justice in Washington, D.C. and subsequently with a United States Supreme Court Justice, William J. Brennan, Jr. When he returned to New York in 1967, Sofaer became an assistant United States attorney for the Southern District of New York. From 1969-1979, he taught at Columbia University Law School, where he eventually became a full professor. He developed a relationship with Law School Dean Michael I. Sovern, who went on to become the President of Columbia University. Sovern told James Brooke of the *New York Times* that Sofaer "has a high-powered intellect and an attractive and energetic personality." Sovern also confessed that Sofaer beats him regularly when they play tennis.

Ironically, Sofaer came to the case with two well-known "prejudices": an outspoken record on behalf of press freedoms and rights—and a love for Israel. As a lawyer, he had served on committees working to enhance press freedom. In a 1982 judicial statement, Sofaer said, "Our nation's free and vigorous press...will not and must not be restrained in the lawful pursuit of even the most tasteless aims."

To the degree that *Time* discerned an advantage in Judge Sofaer, however, Sharon's lawyers might have sensed that they were fortunate to have this judge whose commitment to a secure Israel was well known and who vacations in Jerusalem every summer.

Married, with four young children—his daughter Helen turned three years of age, and he spent the Sunday at home at her party, towards the end of the trial—Sofaer had been named a Federal District Court judge in 1979, when he was only 41-years-old.

A forceful advocate of the rights of the free press—and of Israel—Sofaer proved to be the right judge for the case. He remained impeccably professional and impartial throughout the trial, proving his contention that "You can't say that because you're Jewish, you can't sit on a case involving Israel. . . . When you get into a case, it's the issues and the evidence that count."

For two full months, he would adjudicate those issues and evidentiary materials with a professionalism and impartiality whose only trace of fault would be an occasional "corny" joke.

But most of his witticisms were on target, too.

Time never wanted Ariel Sharon's libel suit to reach an American courtroom. It was a specious use of the American system of law by a cynical politician looking to salvage a damaged career and reputation. That was how *Time* saw it. Sharon did it. He knows he did it. Kahan said he did it. We just reported the facts. What does he want from us?

That was *Time's* basic argument in papers they filed to have the case thrown out before Day 1.

Sharon did not see it quite the same way. "I brought it to court because I knew that the day must come and steps must be taken [so] that you will never dare again to libel," he told *Time's* lawyers. "Not the Jewish people, not Israel, and not me—not you and not any other newspaper."

Time retorted in their papers that the charges are "an attempt by a foreign politician to justify his conduct of a war by his state and to enhance his political reputation" as well as to "punish criticism of Israel's conduct during the invasion and occupation of Lebanon." Moreover, Sharon was merely attempting "to shed his responsibility for the massacre of civilians by an armed force acting at his orders and under his command."

□   □   □   □   □

Bernard D. Fischman, one of Sharon's attorneys, responded in his "Memorandum of Law on Behalf of Plaintiff Ariel Sharon in Opposition to Time Motion for Dismissal": "The charge made against this man is the most heinous of all offenses—encouraging the slaughter of innocent women and children! That and that alone is what led to this suit.... Truly, what worse could be said of a human being than that he actively incited mass murder? ...It is to remove that stain that this man seeks his day in court."

Fischman retraced the steps *Time* had marched in the course of their depicting Sharon as a co-conspirator in the Shatilla-Sabra killings. First, there had been the world-wide memorandum by correspondent David Halevy. He had claimed a "highly reliable source" in support of his claim that "Sharon indicated in advance to the Gemayels that the Israeli army was moving into West Beirut and that he expected them. . .to go into all the Palestinian refugee camps. *He also gave them the feeling, after the Gemayels' questioning, that he understood their need to take revenge* for the assassination of Bashir and *assured them that the Israeli army would neither hinder them nor try to stop them.*" (Emphasis added).

Fischman recollected how Halevy's memorandum, after being cleared, found its way into the critical "Take 9" which Harry Kelly, the Jerusalem bureau chief, submitted to New York days after the Kahan Commission issued its final report:

> Part of the report, which is called "Appendix B," was not published "since in our opinion," the commission said "non-publication of this material is essential in the interest of protecting the nation's security or foreign relations."
>
> Some of that published report simply gives the names of agents identified only by single letters in the published report and secret testimony. *And some of it, we understand, was published in Time's world-wide memo, an item by Halevy, Dec. 6, for which we gave clearance,* dealing with Sharon's visit to the Gemayel family to pay condolences. Certainly in reading the report, *there is a feeling that at least part of the Commission's case against Sharon is between the lines, presumably in the secret portion* . . . (Emphasis added).

With Kelly's "Take 9" and Halevy's "world-wide

memorandum" sitting on the desk in front of him, Fischman continued, *Time's* senior writer William E. Smith composed the crucial paragraph which ruined Sharon's reputation:

> ***Time*** has learned that it [Appendix B] also contains further details about Sharon's visit to the Gemayel family on the day after Bashir Gemayel's assassination. Sharon reportedly told the Gemayels that the Israeli army would be moving into West Beirut and that he expected the Christian forces to go into Palestinian refugee camps. *Sharon also reportedly discussed with the Gemayels the need for the Phalangists to take revenge* for the assassination of Bashir, but the details of the conversation are not known. (Emphasis added).

In no time, publicist Robert Parker was distributing to the world's most influential news agencies a press release highlighting that paragraph, which he was led to understand comprised the main story of the week. By the following morning, even before the *Time* issue of February 21, 1983 had hit the stands, newspapers in Israel were reporting Sharon's alleged role in conspiring to murder the civilians of Shatilla and Sabra.

Sharon, just exonerated by Kahan, was now branded a conspirator and accessory to murder by *Time*. That's why he was suing *Time* magazine, said Fischman. "Despite Halevy's known history of inexcusably shoddy reporting, of substituting speculation for the truth, of failing to make certain that his sources actually knew what they were talking about, despite Halevy's demonstrable bias and hatred toward Sharon and the political group of which he was a leader, and, finally, despite the gravity of the charge being leveled against Sharon, no one conferred with Halevy, no one inquired of Halevy about the strength of his alleged 'sources,' no one asked as to his (or Kelly's) bases for stating what was in Appendix B . . . "

"One conclusion is thus clear: either *Time*'s 'process', which starts and ends with the reporter and makes no meaningful effort to confirm or corroborate his story — or that procedure — was entirely ignored in this instance. Either way, recklessness abounds," concluded Fischman.

Olmert, the Knesset member who had spoken to Kelly at the Koch dinner, the man who had given Kelly clear information that the material did not appear in Appendix B, was never cited in *Time*. Begin's Knesset speech denouncing *Time* for its "bald lies and slander" was not quoted in *Time*. Even Sharon's denials were not quoted.

Only one side of the story made its way into the magazine: the story written by Halevy. Halevy, the author of the story about the boatride to Lebanon which Shimon Peres had taken in 1976 — only Peres never took it. Halevy, the author of the scoop about Menachem Begin's deteriorating health in 1979 — only Begin's health was fine then, and all of the "sources" denied having anything to do with the "fantasy" which Halevy had printed. Halevy, who was the only correspondent ever put on probation by Richard Duncan. Halevy, whose activity in the Israeli Labor Party and whose outspoken activism against Menachem Begin and Begin's Likud coalition, was well known.

Only Halevy's side ever made it into the magazine. That is why Sharon was suing and expecting to win.

Sharon's legal papers were submitted by one of the most prominent law firms in the United States, Shea & Gould. Located in the heart of Manhattan on Madison Avenue and 42nd Street, Shea & Gould already had a reputation preceding them.

□　　□　　□　　□　　□

How prominent? How many lawyers do you know who have had major-league stadiums named after them?

Milton Gould—he didn't get any stadiums—was Sharon's main attorney in the case. A 75-year-old firebrand, he dug into the case with a ferocious appetite. This was a really great case. One of the classics in American history. Perhaps it would help define new concepts in American libel law.

Gould understood that this case could run into costs exceeding one million dollars. And he knew that Sharon would never be able to assume such a heavy financial burden alone. So, the firm decided to do this one practically "on the house." It would be Sharon's only chance.

Even with the legal services substantially donated, huge expenses were still inevitable. Thousands of documents would accumulate in a case like this. The final court transcript alone ran over four thousand pages. Someone has to pay for the court costs, the stenographers, the typists, the bailiffs, and everything else in such a case. There would be depositions, trips to Israel, and so many other costs in a case like this.

This was a new lesson for Sharon. The American legal system may be the finest in the world. But justice costs money—even if the lawyers are willing to go free.

Sharon turned to his friends and supporters in the American Jewish community for their help in absorbing some of the expenses. He turned to supporters of Israel, to individuals he knew to be sympathetic to him, and to community leaders who shared his sense that, whether Sharon is a good man or a bad man, in this case he had been wronged by *Time*.

And the Jewish people had been wronged.

Sharon made this point in speeches to Jewish bodies throughout the United States. "*Time* has not only libeled me. They have libeled the Jewish people. They have cast a Blood Libel on all of us, contending that a minister of the Jewish State was a party to the murder of innocents. It is a blood libel."

What surprised many outsiders was the degree to which Sharon's argument touched a nerve in the American Jewish community. At one evening's gathering, at the Hebrew Institute of Riverdale, located in a prosperous section of the Bronx, Rabbi Avraham Weiss introduced Sharon as a person fighting "our fight." Rabbi Weiss recounted *Time's* litany of anti-Israel articles. He urged his congregation to give Minister Sharon a sympathetic hearing. And the congregation did, responding not only with applause but with money.

This was Sharon's case, but in many ways it really did take on a much wider dimension, as American Jews began sending in contributions to Sharon. Maybe *Time* really had stepped on Israel once too much. Maybe Americans were beginning to feel that it was time that Begin rhymed with something else, for a change.

Time did not come into the federal court any less prepared. They had behind them the powerful law firm of Cravath, Swaine, and Moore. Thomas D. Barr, their principal counsel, had already made his reputation by successfully defending the I.B.M. corporation in its fight against a Federal antitrust action. If he could beat the United States of America, Barr could take on Sharon.

Time's, legal fees were also enormous. The case had not even been gaveled to order, and already the magazine had been compelled to send Sharon's attorneys 6,500 pages of documents, while *Time* writers and editors had already spoken 4,000 pages of pre-trial testimony. That's a lot of stenographers. They had run up a bill of over one million dollars . . . and the case had not yet even started.

□   □   □   □   □

Even before the case had begun, the sparring had gotten hot. In a deposition, Sharon accused Barr of "defending a lie." Barr came back at the Israeli leader and told him that, if he said that outside the courtroom, then Barr would sue Sharon for libel!

Nor were *Time's* lawyers more circumspect in choosing their adjectives in describing Sharon. They called him a "bloodthirsty, insubordinate militarist" whose reputation was so bad—even before the 1982 war in Lebanon—that Sharon could not possibly have suffered any damage to his reputation from the *Time* article. How can a reputation be damaged if it doesn't exist?

Shea & Gould let it be known, for their part, that they were quite prepared with a stable of prominent Americans who would be appearing during the case to substantiate how good Sharon's name and reputation had been—before the *Time* story. Gould would be calling United States Senator Al D'amato, New York District Attorney Robert Morgenthau, civil rights leader Bayard Rustin, and author Leon Uris, among others, to speak of Sharon. Indeed, it would be *Time* and its reputation which this trial would demolish. That was Gould's plan.

□   □   □   □   □

Shea & Gould beat Cravath, Swaine, & Moore in their first skirmish, the pre-trial maneuvering. Despite *Time*'s efforts to can the case and ship it back to Jerusalem, Judge Sofaer accepted Gould's arguments and ruled that, whether or not *Time* had actually libeled Sharon, there was enough of a case presented to warrant a full court trial. Indeed, Sharon might even win.

To win, he would have to gain the votes of the six jurors chosen to hear the conflicting arguments, a jury of four women, two men. None was Jewish, but one juror was dating an Israeli. Their job would be to hear the evidence, to read the challenged paragraph, and to interpret to the best of their abilities what the average reader would understand from reading those sentences.

Judge Sofaer elaborated on their responsibilities when the case opened on Tuesday, November 13, at the Foley Square courthouse in lower Manhattan, a few blocks from City Hall. As the jurors filed in for the first time, they saw a packed court room, filled with spectators of every kind and stripe: law students, journalists, media representatives—and housewives and retired senior citizens. The courtroom filled up, day in and day out, through the trial's conclusion. One woman told the *New York Times* that she had come to view the proceedings because a friend told her it was "the best show in town."

And it was. For two months, some of the most powerful people in American journalism, the editors and writers of *Time* magazine, appeared on the stand to tell their story. One of Israel's most famous leaders, the plaintiff, was there every day, too. The proceedings, live and in color, were so exciting that the only thing missing were the curtain calls.

As the case proceeded, it soon became clear that there was a value in relocating to a bigger courtroom, and the trial moved around a few times, from courtroom to courtroom, depending on the day, depending on the availability. Outside, there were always the guards accompanied by their trusted metal detectors. Every spectator seeking entry to view the proceedings was required to first pass through the security device. The first few times, there was great excitement when the machine ran crazy: Metal! Metal! METAL! it screamed.

But the excitement never lasted very long. It was only a set of keys or a couple of coins.

As everyone settled in for the opening statement by the judge, there was a sense of moment in the air. There really was something very special about this trial. Downstairs, in the very same court building, United States General William Westmoreland was suing the CBS television network over its protrayal of his role during the 1960's war in Vietnam. That trial also had its full complement of reporters and spectators, but this one was different. Vietnam was twenty years ago; Lebanon, the P.L.O., Israel— these issues were very much current, very much right now. And, while Westmoreland's place in American history had basically been written, Sharon's was still very much an open book. At the time of the trial his title was Minister of Industry and Trade.

Tomorrow it might be Prime Minister.

Photographs
and
Courtroom Sketches

Sketches by Ida Libby Dengrove
Photographs by *The New York Post*

iii. Lily Sharon and her husband during a court recess.

iv. General Sharon addresses reporter's questions after his first day of testimony.

v. **Ariel Sharon (left) and wife Lily, addressing a press conference after the jury found *Time* guilty of publishing a false story, defaming the Israeli war hero.**

vi. Ariel Sharon (left) and wife Lily, leaving the Federal Court House after the jury found *Time* guilty of publishing a defamation against the Israeli Minister.

vii. The young Ariel Sharon at the start of his military career.

viii. *Time* senior writer William Smith (right) and correspondent David Halevy (center) look on as General Sharon (left) testifies in court.

ix. General Sharon testifying before the court.

x. A dramatic scene in the courtroom: Ariel Sharon (left) on the witness stand being questioned by his attorney, Milton Gould, as Judge Abraham Sofaer (right) looks on.

xi. The six person jury pays heed as Judge Sofaer makes his opening
remarks at the start of trial. Man on right is jury foreman
Richard Zug.

**xii. General Sharon illustrates a point by tracing his steps along a map
of West Beirut.**

xiii. Lily Sharon (left), Ariel Sharon, Judge Sofaer, Milton Gould (Sharon's attorney), Thomas Bar (*Time's* attorney), the jury.

xiv. *Time* managing editor Ray Cave (beard, center) speaks to his lawyers.

IX
The Trial Begins

Judge Sofaer addresses his jury. The case of *Ariel Sharon v. Time Inc.* will ultimately boil down to America's famous libel laws, defined in the 1964 United States Supreme Court decision in the case of *New York Times Co. v. Sullivan.* In that dispute, the nation's highest court laid down the rule that famous people must meet a higher standard than private citizens in proving that they have been libeled. A private citizen need only convince his jurors that he has been the victim of a published article which is false and defamatory. A public figure must establish something additional: the article which wronged him was written with "actual malice," which is to say that the author of the libel knew it was false and showed a reckless disregard as to whether or not it really had any substance.

Speaking to the jury, Judge Sofaer says, "To state that a Minister of Defense, charged with conducting a war, condoned a massacre of innocent civilians or that he lied to a public commission about his role in such a massacre is to defame him."

If Sharon convinces the jury that the article in *Time* did make such an implication, defaming him, Sharon will next have to prove the falsity of the claim. He will have to prove "that he did not engage in such a discussion and that details of such a discussion are not contained in Appendix B. Furthermore, he must satisfy you that nothing occurred at the meeting and that nothing is present in Appendix B or any other secret portion of the Commission report that would make *Time*'s statement substantially true."

And finally, having won the first two rounds, he will have to prove *Time*'s malice. To the jury Sofaer says, "You must inquire into *Time*'s state of mind at the time of publication as evidenced by what *Time*'s employees knew and intended, and determine whether *Time* published the statements with knowledge that they were false or with a reckless disregard as to whether they were false."

□   □   □   □   □

The opening instructions complete, Sofaer asks Milton Gould to rise to present his opening statement to the jury. Outlining his case, Gould *tells* them that Sharon—"a minister, a general, a soldier, a farmer, and a hero in his own country"—was taking on one of the world's most powerful corporate empires, Time Inc., whose weekly *Time* magazine goes to millions of readers at home and abroad. Time has billions of dollars in assets, billions in revenue, thousands of employees. . . .

None of this is relevant. But Gould has the floor. And he knows that his jury is made up of people, simple people, the kind who don't own corporations but work for them, And, after all, they are the ultimate judges in this case.

Gould, whose opening remarks will last some two hours, pounds away at the key issue in its bluntest terms. He talks about the articles, about the memorandum and the "Take 9." And then he just lays it on the line: "That was a lie." It was "contrived" by *Time*.

He speaks of Israel's incursion into Lebanon, aimed at driving the P.L.O. out of its terror nests. He speaks of the Phalangists. And he speaks of Shatilla and Sabra.

"The so-called 'camps' of Shatilla and Sabra were really built-up sections of the city, neighborhoods of West Beirut. They contained thousands of buildings and miles of streets and tunnels . . . and they had a lot of narrow alleys and roadways in them."

The Israelies had tried to enter Shatilla and Sabra on the morning of September 15. But they were repulsed. "It was clear that there were well armed fighting men in the camps and that seemingly they were prepared to resist, and indeed they did inflict a number of casualties on the Israeli troops moving into West Beirut. In other words, fire came from the camps, and Israeli soldiers were killed and wounded by the fire coming. . . . There was indeed an obvious, demonstrated military necessity to clear out of the so-called 'camps' whoever it was in there, the terrorists, whoever were fighting. . . ."

Gould reviews the events of the fateful week between

Bashir Gemayel's assassination and the killings. He recalls that Sharon, as Minister of Defense, had come to Lebanon the day after Bashir's murder—the day before the Phalangists entered Shatilla and Sabra—to meet with Chief of Staff Eitan. The two men discussed the role the Christians would play the following evening in their operation inside the two neighborhoods. The Phalangists would be expected to do a "mopping up," to locate and drive out the terrorists, and to search for and identify P.L.O. arms caches. From his meeting with Eitan, Sharon traveled to Karantina to meet with the Phalangist leaders and then on to Bikfaya, where he payed his condolence call at the home of Pierre Gemayel.

Yes, the next night the Phalangists went beyond their assignment. They broke discipline. On the other hand, they found over 500 tons of military arms, guns, mortars, machine guns, and other weapons.

What was 500 *tons* of weapons doing in a peaceful neighborhood? Gould wants an answer to that one.

Admittedly, the Christians went too far. No two ways about it. That's why there was a Kahan Commission. That's why there was an investigation. But that wasn't enough for *Time*.

"We will prove to you," says Gould, "That Mr. Halevy did not have a highly reliable source on which he based that information, that the information was contrived by him, invented by him, spun by him out of certain ingredients in his mind...."

"This lie festers in the mind of Halevy for two months before it becomes twisted into what is the ultimate lie, the lie contained in the article which is the basis of this action. . . . We will prove to you that, in plain English, this is a charge of mass murder against Ariel Sharon."

Gould is only warming up.

He describes the picture of senior writer William Smith at his desk in New York, piecing together the cover story he has been assigned to write. Smith is incorporating the material written by Halevy, that Sharon "gave them the feeling" that he understood the need for the Christians to seek revenge.

"But Smith makes a fantastic contribution to it. It is the hand of Mr. Smith. . . which makes the contribution, the important introduction into the article, that 'Time has learned'–which is a lot of bull. . . they hadn't learned anything – that Sharon gave them the feeling after the Gemayels' questioning – he changes that. He makes it read: 'Sharon also reportedly discussed.'

"Because it ain't much of a story if you just say 'he gave somebody the feeling,' but it's a scoop if you're the only one in the world that knows that the Minister of Defense actually discussed, conspired, urged, promoted, instigated these people to perpetrate a mass murder."

Gould is still only warming up.

Gould tells the jury that he had interrogated correspondent Halevy during a deposition hearing before the trial. He had asked Halevy what Sharon had said, what were Sharon's words to Gemayel, how exactly had Sharon "given the Gemayels the feeling. . . ."

And Halevy had responded that maybe Sharon hadn't said anything. When Halevy had written in his world-wide memorandum that Sharon had "given them the feeling" that he understood their need for revenge, Sharon had merely given an indication. In Halevy's words: " . . . a body movement, could be silence, could be a non-outspoken rejection of their raising the issue, and could also be indifference to the fact . . . ."

Wow! So Gould now reveals, for the first time in open court, that Halevy himself has testified that he is not sure that Sharon actually *said* he understands the Gemayels' need for revenge. Maybe it was only a shrug. Maybe it was silence.

But Smith doesn't write that. Smith writes that Sharon actively *discussed* revenge.

"Here is this fellow in New York putting in his paper that Sharon *discussed* the matter with the Gemayels, and the only evidence he has got before him is the evidence communicated to him by Halevy, the evidence that he cooked up in December . . . and then Halevy, the author of this infamous thing, says [Sharon] really didn't discuss it, he did it with body language . . . ."

Gould is still warming up. He reminds the jury that *Time* has a self-correction system, the "playback," which requires Smith to send the finished article back to Jerusalem for Kelly's and Halevy's final approval. The article is telexed to Israel, and Kelly and Halevy see the change. And they telex back that everything is fine. "Story reads very good. A fine job, in our view."

Gould is finishing his opening statement now. The *Time* article was "reckless, malicious, and false." He will prove it right in this courtroom. Better, he will get the writers of *Time* magazine to admit it out of their own mouths. You wait and sit back. This is going to be fun.

Gould has hit his stride. The bell rings. End round one.

□   □   □   □   □

If Milton Gould is a feisty, country lawyer, who peppers his impeccable English with a few "aint's" along the way, Thomas Barr is a perfect study in contrasts. He is cool, meticulous, calm, underspoken. He does not say "ain't." Probably not even at home.

□   □   □   □   □

The jury watches Thomas D. Barr, and they understand why he is hired by I.B.M. and by Time. This is a corporate lawyer straight out of the *Wall Street Journal.*

"This is an important case," he tells the jury. The plaintiff will not succeed in bearing the burdens of proof. *Time's* work in this article was highly polished and professional, reflecting the kind of excellence you would expect of the magazine." Barr speaks of the principals in the case: the Kellys, the Smiths, the Caves—each with his own long solid, established journalistic career behind him. These are no amateurs; they are the best in American journalism.

"All these people have extensive experience in reporting and editing." Harry Kelly has been in the business for three decades. He wrote for the Associated Press, covered the Nixon Watergate scandal for the *Chicago Tribune*, and served as associate editor at the *Washington Star*. William Smith has thirty years in the business, too. He was a bureau chief himself, once in Anchorage, then in Nairobi,

Kenya; later, he headed Time's bureau in New Delhi, India. He has been a senior writer in the "world" section since 1976.

And correspondent David Halevy. Barr tells the jury just who David Halevy is. Born in Jerusalem. A soldier and journalist. A patriot of Israel who has been in the Israeli army since age 17, has fought in three wars, and been wounded four times. He "broke" the story of the Yom Kippur War. He was the first journalist on the scene at the 1974 P.L.O. massacre at Maalot. He "broke" the Entebbe rescue. And each time he achieved his break-throughs with the help of his personal network of confidential sources.

Barr, having established the professionals on his side, now turns to the plaintiff, Ariel Sharon. Sharon is not such a nice guy.

Barr tells the jury of Sharon's years in the army, of deadly commando raids Sharon led. A massacre here. Insubordination there.

□   □   □   □   □

"By the time we are done," Barr says, "we will show that there is a lot of tough press about the plaintiff."

Later in the case, Judge Sofaer will tell the jury: "This is not a nice-guy case. People are trying to prove nasty things about each other here. It's not my job to try to get people to be nice to each other in a lawsuit. I try, but sometimes, ladies and gentlemen, I can't succeed...."

Barr continues, arguing the merits of the disputed *Time* article. It is true. He tells the jury that he and *Time* have been trying, so far without any success, to get the

Israeli government to turn over to the court the text of Appendix B. But Israel has refused to do so.

Nevertheless, the article can be shown to have substantial accuracy. "The article is, in substance, true," he says, admitting that some of the events may not have taken place "precisely" where and when *Time* said they did. It is his first disclaimer. It will not be his last.

To buttress his four-hour opening, Barr skillfully uses slides and a display screen, helping the jury follow his well constructed opening. He shows them reproductions of news items reporting negatively against Sharon about events which took place long before the 1982 occurrences at dispute in the trial. He talks about Shatilla and Sabra, pointing a narrow flashlight beam onto a mounted color map of Lebanon to help his jury follow along. "This was not a battle," he says. "It was, pure and simple, a massacre."

Barr may be a low-key corporate lawyer. But he is ready to go tit-for-tat with Gould. It may not be a "nice-guy case," but it will be interesting.

X
Sharon Takes the Stand

It is Wednesday morning, and Barr has finished his opening remarks. The plaintiff calls his first witness to the stand, Ariel Sharon. It is the Israeli general, back on the battlefields of the Middle East, telling his soldiers, "Step aside. I go in first. *Acharai*. Follow me." Sharon takes the stand.

He will be on the stand for the next seven days.

Sharon, sworn in, tells of his childhood. He recalls the long trek of his parents from Eastern Europe to the moshav at Kfar Malal where they eventually established their family in 1922. They had arrived as the Scheinermans of Russia. But they wanted a new name, a name taken from the land. Kfar Malal was located in the Sharon region.

Wearing a dark blue suit, a pale blue shirt, and a striped tie, Sharon exudes an aura of confidence as he speaks. But the silver-haired 56-year-old Israeli leader has not had it easy. There was the poverty, the material deprivation, though he remembers his early years as having been "spiritually, very rich. Very, very rich."

He continues sharing his biography with the jury, as it gets its first chance to size up the man who has flown 6,000 miles across the Atlantic to "fight for the truth," as he puts it.

Continuing with a discussion of his rise in the Israeli Defense Forces, Sharon expresses views which he says are held by all of Israel. "It goes along [with] our religion, it goes with our culture, it comes as our education [to value human life].... That is the important, highly important, the most important thing was always human life.... I would like you to know that for these moral values that brought us to take all the measures in order to avoid casualties among civilian populations, we paid with blood — our blood — a very precious price and a very high price.... I speak about measures and steps taken in order to avoid casualties among [the] Arab civilian population.... We speak about very specific, very high moral values."

Sharon, recounting the wars in which he has fought, disappoints his audience. This general is not interested in delighting the room with old war stories. He paints a different image:

"Wars are terrible things. I participated in all the wars of Israel, and believe me, I know the horrors of war. I saw it myself."

He turns to the difficulties of the 1973 Yom Kippur

War, and then he responds to his lawyer's question, explaining his role: "We managed to contain, to stop, the movement of the Egyptian forces. My division, in one of the hardest battles that ever took place in the history of the Israeli army, managed to cross the canal, the Suez Canal . . . . That was the beginning of turning the tide of the war."

The battle was not pretty. Sharon's face tightens. It was "maybe the most terrible battle that I have ever seen . . . hundreds of our soldiers were lying dead, together with hundreds of Egyptian soldiers. I will say that this was the war of the soldiers, the war of the soldiers. They were facing, I will say, the most horrible things there in the battlefield.

"But we did it."

□   □   □   □   □

After the Yom Kippur War, Sharon returned to civilian life and continued organizing the Likud coalition which would sweep Labor from power in 1977. When the first government of Menachem Begin was formed, he was named Minister of Agriculture.

At this point, there is a pause. The court will recess. Trial to resume on Monday.

Fresh from the weekend, Sharon resumes his testimony, wearing a conservative gray-blue suit. Today he will discuss the events of 1982, the war and the fateful days between Bashir's assassination and the Shatilla-Sabra killings.

Sharon first goes back to 1965 and recounts seventeen years of P.L.O. terror against Israel, her communities, and her civilian population. In less than two decades, he says, they murdered 1,392 people – not all of them Israeli, not all of them Jewish either – and they wounded more than 6,000 people.

After their expulsion from Jordan in 1970, the P.L.O. took root in southern Lebanon, where they established "Fatahland," a state-within-a-state. Slowly, they extended their control, reaching into the suburbs of West Beirut, into the neighborhoods of Sabra and Shatilla.

"For years these neighborhoods were the center of world terrorism. . . . Lebanon became the center – the place of training, of shelter, of getting equipment – of almost every known terrorist organization in the world. All that was headed by the P.L.O. terrorist organization.

"And they established their headquarters, their centers, in West Beirut, mostly in the Palestinian neighborhoods of Sabra, Shatilla, and Fakahan . . . ."

Sharon reaches into his pocket, and he pulls out a pair of reading glasses. He rolls out a piece of paper he has prepared for today, and he begins to read from a long, long list of P.L.O. atrocities, trying to give the jury an insight into the totality of the P.L.O. terror.

He tells of the time the P.L.O. ambushed a school bus, murdering nine children and wounding nineteen others. It was May 22, 1970.

He reads, incident-by-incident. He comes to the terrible five weeks in 1974 which saw, first, the Kiryat Shmoneh massacre in which the P.L.O. went house to house, murdering eighteen people including eight children. The following month, another P.L.O. squad invaded a school building in Ma'alot where they murdered twenty-two more school children and wounded seventy others.

He stops reading. It does not pay to continue. How much can one listen to without understanding just what the P.L.O. is? He has justified, amply well, the need to enter Lebanon and to drive them out. He now comes to the week of Bashir's death:

He was in his car when he received an urgent message to call his office. It was September 14, 1982. At the first military camp along the way, Sharon stopped and called in. He was told of an explosion which had just taken place in the Phalangist headquarters of East Beirut, where Bashir Gemayel was lecturing at the time. Gemayel had been assassinated.

That evening Sharon spoke with Chief of Staff Eitan and with important figures in the Israeli intelligence network, including the head of military intelligence, the head of the Mossad, and the head of the internal security services.

One of the main considerations which had to be faced was the knowledge that, despite a P.L.O. pledge to completely evacuate Beirut by September 1, there were still 2,000 terrorists in the area. Another 7,000 fighters associated with various pro-P.L.O. Moslem militias were also circulating throughout West Beirut. The heavy arms, which the P.L.O. had pledged to turn over to the official army of Lebanon, had been given, instead, to the leftist Moslem militias.

Because of the Lebanese army's inherent weakness as a disorganized, under-trained unit, there was a great danger that the Lebanese capital would be divided again, and that the militias would seize control of West Beirut once more. That had to be prevented. So a decision was made to have the Israeli army enter West Beirut. That decision would be referred to as "Order Number One" and was arrived at just after midnight.

Early on the morning of the fifteenth, Sharon flew to Beirut. "I landed at the Beirut International Airport which was then under the control of our forces. . . . From there I went to the forward command post of the Israeli forces. [At approximately six o'clock in the morning the Israeli Defense Forces began to enter West Beirut.] At the beginning it went very smoothly. . . . Thousands of soldiers were flown in an airlift using big airplanes, flying from Israel to the International Airport of Beirut, where they landed. Others, some thousands, were brought from other parts of Lebanon, and that included big numbers of tanks, armored personnel carriers. Troops were brought from the northern part of Israel and, as I said, from other parts of Lebanon.

"At the beginning it went smoothly. . . . In the morning hours, however, shooting started, and our forces, to the best of my recollection, suffered three people killed and one hundred wounded. . . . The fire came mostly from the area of Shatilla, Sabra, and Fakahan, the centers of terror. . . ."

The fire coming at the Israeli forces intensified, as the morning hours wore on. "I would say, as the hours passed, it became more difficult. I would say, in the beginning, in the morning, it looked altogether simpler. It became more difficult during the day, or during the morning. . . ."

Later in the morning, Sharon met again with Eitan and with other upper-echelon figures, including Major General Drori, who was in charge of the Northern Command. He was the highest ranking officer in the area. Major General Yehoshua Saguy, director of army intelligence, was present as well. The meeting took place on the rooftop of a heavily damaged building overlooking much of West Beirut. This was the Forward Command Post.

At the meeting, they discussed plans to have the Christian Phalangist forces enter Shatilla and Sabra instead of the I.D.F.

"You can see that when we speak of Sabra and Shatilla, we don't speak—you know, the terms which are used are 'camps'; usually, people, when they hear about the 'camps' they envision some tents and some barbed wired fences around it. These were neighborhoods. These were neighborhoods where they had . . . buildings of twelve stories and up. . . . [The population was] about 30,000 in Sabra and 30,000 in Shatilla. . . . They were towns, part of towns."

"There were tunnels that connected over there. There were underground headquarters, underground armed depots. They used to keep underground rocket launchers, artillery, armed vehicles, and tremendous amounts of ammunition. For years, for years those neighborhoods were the center of world terror. . . ."

A decision was agreed on to send the Phalangists into the two neighborhoods "for several reasons. One was to save the lives of our soldiers. We had been fighting already for a long time in Lebanon. We suffered heavy casualties as much as [was] possible."

"Second, that was a center of terror. There were other people living there. There were Lebanese living there. There were civilian populations. There were terrorists. Our soldiers, most of them did not speak Arabic. In order to be able to find the terrorists, the best possible troops could have been Lebanese troops. So I saw the fire, I knew the conditions there; I knew that that is, I would say, an underground town. And I thought that would be a good solution . . . ."

"[I remained at the command post] about an hour. From there I went to the other side of Beirut, to the place called Karantina, to the headquarters of the Lebanese forces, which included, as you know, the Phalangists. . . . The commander-in-chief [of the Phalangists] that day was Fady Frem. . . . He was there. He was, as a matter of fact, the supreme commander after the assassination of Bashir Gemayel. There were others there. . . ."

"I stayed there for, I believe, an hour. . . . The main subject that was discussed was the political developments that occurred after the assassination of the president-elect Bashir Gemayel, the possible development, what might happen according to the Lebanese constitution, what could be done: new elections, or that the President that was then, President Sarkis, would stay—or a third possibility that had already taken place in Lebanon many years earlier, in the beginning of the 1950's, that the Maronite Christian Prime Minister would be appointed until new elections would be taking place."

"I would say that we discussed the various political steps that might be taken in order to continue. . . . I told them that our army was entering into West Beirut and that we expected their army. . .to participate. And I told them that they have to coordinate the details with General Drori, the commanding officer of the Northern Command."

"Of course, we talked. I expressed our sorrow and grief about the assassination of Bashir Gemayel, the President-elect. Both sides expressed their wish to continue relations that were between us and the Christians in Lebanon."

"I will say that those were the issues, more or less, that were discussed."

"I [then] went to the home in Bikfaya which is a few kilometers east of Karantina, in the mountains, the home of the father, the political leader, Sheikh Pierrre Gemayel, the father of the President-elect. I went there. . .I had with me the director of military intelligence, General Saguy. I had the representative of the Mossad, the head of the Secret Services. I had with me Mr. Uri Dan, who was my press counsellor, who also participated with me at the meeting in Karantina. I think we had two representatives of the Mossad there."

"From the Lebanese side there were two people there. One was Amin Gemayel son of Sheikh Pierre. And Sheikh Pierre was the other person present. When I got out of the car, I had to pass through hundreds of Lebanese people waiting outside. I entered the room. It's a very big living room. . . . We entered there. The first man that

I met was Amin Gemayel. I had never met him before. It was the first time that I met him. After a few seconds, Sheikh Pierre, the father of the President-elect, entered."

"He was, as usual, very properly dressed, very calm, with self-restraint. I had the feeling that I am with a man, with a strong man with real self-control. I had met him before. I saw him before in other events that took place."

"I thought about it. I thought about myself. I also had tragedies. I know how you feel when sometimes that happens. So I looked at him. He was properly dressed, talked very slowly, quietly. I saw a man who controls. I felt that the man had control over the situation, that he gained control, and that he controlled himself. We were sitting there. . . ."

"It was a room with pillars inside and arches, oriental, beautiful oriental building, very old building. Maybe Sheikh Pierre himself was born there in this building. I told him that I came to bring the condolences of Prime Minister Begin and the government. Of course, I told him how much we were sorry about what happened. I told him that the Israeli government would proceed with our relations and the support that we were giving them for years. I told him very briefly that our army was entering into West Beirut."

"He then answered. He thanked us for the condolences that I brought on behalf of the Israeli government and Prime Minister Begin. He told me that Israel was the only country in the world that came to the rescue of the Christian community in Lebanon, that they appreciated that, they would like to keep those contacts. He told me that he was aware of talks that I had with Bashir Gemayel. And he said, he emphasized, the last talk that I had with Bashir Gemayel before the assassination — I met with President-elect Bashir Gemayel on the twelfth of September — so he said they were familiar with the conversation that took place there and that he paid very much importance to those talks. And myself, I added that I also had paid very high importance to that talk and that we would proceed at that process that started. That was, more or less, the conversation."

□   □   □   □   □

Ariel Sharon finishes telling the hushed courtroom the facts of the period under dispute, the facts as he remembers them. His attorney, Milton Gould, now asks him a series of questions.

"Did you tell him in any way that you expected the Christian forces to go into the Palestinian refugee camps?"

Sharon answers: "No."

"Was there any mention of that subject in any way?"

"No."

"Did you discuss with him in any way the need for the Phalangists to take revenge for the assassination of Bashir?"

"No."

"Was there anything that happened in that conversation by words or by gestures or by signs which related directly or indirectly to the need to take revenge for the assassination of Bashir?"

"No."

"Not one word?"

Sharon calmly replies: "Not one word."

"Did he say anything to you, he—Sheikh Pierre—or Amin, did they say anything to you about revenge for the assassination of Bashir?"

"No."

"Did they make any signs or give any indications about revenge?"

"No."

Sharon elaborates. "They were sitting calmly, self-restrained. Everything was done quietly, in the calmest possible way. No doubt, one could feel the grief in the air. That was all the atmosphere around. You could see outside the building, where hundreds and hundreds of people were waiting there, but nothing of this kind."

     □   □   □   □   □

Sharon concluded the meeting with Gemayel some fifteen minutes after he had arrived. He departed Bikfaya and returned to Israel via the Beirut International Airport.

The following morning, at 10 a.m., he met with Eitan, Saguy, and some other aides. They finalized a number of arrangements. On that morning, the Israeli Military command issued "Order Number Six": "The refugee camps are not to be entered. Searching and mopping up the camps will be done by the Phalangists. . . ."

That evening the Phalangists entered the Shatilla and Sabra neighborhoods. Sharon got confirmation that the operation had begun.

The following evening, a day after the Christians entered the two Palestinian neighborhoods, Sharon received a phone call at his home from Eitan who was back in

Beirut. Eitan was reporting that the word had arrived that the Phalangists had committed excesses. He reported to Sharon that the following three orders were therefore given: (1) the Phalangists were halted, (2) no Phalangist reinforcements would be permitted into the neighborhoods, and (3) all Phalangists were expected out by 5:00 a.m. the following morning.

That next morning, the Phalangists were all out of the two neighborhoods.

◻   ◻   ◻   ◻   ◻

From there, it was all history. The world outcry. The naming of the Kahan Commission. The four month wait for the findings. The final Kahan Report was released on February 7.

And the *Time* Magazine article was released the following week.

Sharon zeroes in on the *Time* report. He remembers issuing a denial. He remembers Prime Minister Begin denouncing the "bald lies and slander" from the Knesset. He remembers newspapers like Israel's *Yediot Aharonot* publishing the denials. But not *Time*. Not a word of the denials and the denunciations in *Time*.

Sharon is bitter. "I think that this article caused a terrible damage to my reputation. What can cause more damage to a reputation of somebody, when he is accused of urging or discussing the need to kill and murder civilian people? What can be more than that? What can be more than that? And I speak as a Jew, and I speak as a human being, who believes in the value of life, of people, and in the need to take every care of human life, as I tried during all my military service. . . ."

"We, all of us, we looked at that tragic event that took place in the Shatilla and Sabra neighborhoods. They were tragic events. No one of us participated in those terrible deeds and actions and murders that were done there, no one of our soldiers, no one of our commanders, no one of our politicians. And here comes the *Time* magazine, respected, with a circulation of millions around the world. . . comes and libels me, and I will call it a blood libel. . . ."

□   □   □   □   □

On Tuesday, November 20, Thomas Barr begins his cross-examination of the witness. He comes, prepared with slides he will project onto the screen for emphasis, to put forth a major thesis of his counter-case: *Time* magazine did little more than to reflect the severe findings of the Kahan Commission.

He asks Sharon about Eli Hobeika, the Phalangists' chief of intelligence, who is regarded by many to have been the direct instigator of the Shatilla-Sabra killings. He reads *Time* magazine's description of Hobeika: " . . . A man who carries a pistol and knife and hand grenade on his belt, Hobeika was the most feared Phalangist in Lebanon."

Barr asks Sharon, "How well did you know Eli Hobeika?"

Sharon responds that he never knew him until the 1983 war was well underway. And, after that, he got to know him only briefly.

□   □   □   □   □

Barr comes at Sharon from another angle. He wants to know whether or not Sharon is responsible for the decision to allow the Phalangists into the Palestinian neighborhoods. Sharon accepts the responsibility for his role in that decision. "I think it was the right decision [to take at that time], and that is what I did."

But Sharon stresses an additional point. "When it comes to human life, every casualty is a tragedy. But since we [had] entered Lebanon, it never happened, never happened, that there were mass killings of people."

Yes, Sharon was saying, the Phalangists had established a pretty unpretty record. They had committed massacres. But this had changed dramatically from the time Israel entered Lebanon. Israel had undertaken a major effort to straighten them out, to discipline them in the ways of a more Westernized fighting force. The Phalangists were showing signs of improvement, of maturation.

Bar presses. Why the entry into Shatilla and Sabra?

Sharon explains, "We have to understand we were dealing with 2,000 terrorists that found shelter in buildings using [the] civilian population as hostages. They used to do it during all the wars, in Tyre, in Sidon. Before coming to West Beirut they used to keep [the] civilian population, women and children, at the doors, at the windows. The problem was how to search and find those terrorists in order to kill them. . . . They have to be taken prisoners. If not, they have to be killed. For that, you have to look into thousands of buildings. I speak now of about 24,000 buildings in West Beirut itself. And in Shatilla—I mention only the Shatilla neighborhood now—there were more than 2,300 buildings . . . "

Sharon looks at Barr, trying to win him over to his side. "You are an ex-officer," Sharon says to Barr. Surely, you must understand."

Barr smiles. "Only a lieutenant."

Laughter erupts in the courtroom. The judge gavels, "From one enlisted man, I don't like all of this. Let's go ahead with the evidence."

□   □   □   □   □

"It is not a war in trenches," Sharon explains. "It is a different kind of war. It is a search for P.L.O. terrorists that were there finding shelter among the civilian population and using them as hostages. That is the kind of war."

But Barr wants to know about the Phalangists. "General Sharon, didn't you know that the Phalangists had committed many massacres in Lebanon."

Sharon returns to a theme. "We stopped those massive massacres that had taken place there for seven long years. That is what happened."

□   □   □   □   □

The cross-examination continues the next morning. It is Wednesday, and today Barr will focus his attention on the report of the Kahan Commission. It will be a long day and an uncomfortable day for Ariel Sharon. The Kahan Report is not his favorite reading material.

Barr reads the report, saying that it charges Sharon with adopting "the position that no one had imagined the Phalangists would carry out a massacre in the camps and that it was a tragedy that could not be foreseen."

Mr. Barr then reads Kahan's assessment of the Sharon

position: "It is impossible to justify the Minister of Defense's disregard of the danger of a massacre."

Sharon engages Barr, maintaining his position: "If I would have had even the slightest idea that that tragic event could have taken plalce, I would never have allowed the Phalangists to enter the camps—never."

"But the Kahan Commission clearly decided, General Sharon, that you should have felt apprehension about a massacre ensuing if you would send the Phalangists into Shatilla and Sabra. Did you feel apprehension about a massacre in the camps if the Phalange entered?"

Sharon responds, "No."

"But what about the Kahan Report? Don't you accept its findings?"

"Yes", says Sharon, Yes. I accepted its findings of the facts. I accept that events transpired the way the commission says they did. But I never agreed to the conclusions; I never accepted the conclusions."

Barr persists. At Bashir's funeral, his brother Amin was quoted as saying, "Bashir, my brother, we will avenge you." The next day, Eitan told Sharon that the Phalangists were "seething with a feeling of revenge." That night, Eitan spoke again of the enormous sense of vengeance permeating the Phalangists.

Sharon acknowledges hearing about the funeral remarks and the comments by Eitan. "Yes", he heard that there was a real desire for vengeance among the Phalangists. And maybe he overestimated their fundamental humanity and decency. But, "no, never did I believe that they would perpetrate a massacre". The massacres had stopped from June, 1982 when Israel entered Lebanon. There had not been one single mass killing by the Phalangists since the Israelis had entered. Sharon maintains that there was no way to anticipate that, with Israeli troops all around the area, the Phalangists would run wild on September 16. Sharon said it in court yesterday, and he is repeating his position. "I made it very clear, and I can repeat it now, and I will repeat it again and again."

With Thanksgiving eve only hours away, Judge Sofaer adjourns the proceedings to Monday, November 26.

□　□　□　□　□

During the break, Abraham Sofaer and the two teams of attorneys discuss new efforts aimed at getting the Israeli government to release Appendix B—or something related to it—in an effort to help the parties arrive at the ultimate truth of the case.

Now, word comes in from Israel. Attorney General Yitzhak Zamir will agree, in principle, to find some impartial personality, equally acceptable to Sharon's and *Time*'s lawyers, who will review the contested appendix document and attachments. That individual will then be permitted to answer questions posed him in advance by Judge Sofaer. Zamir adds that his position will still require the approval of the Israeli Cabinet.

While nothing concrete has been finalized, an important chapter in this trial is beginning to develop as Zamir pursues his plan to get Israel's reply to the two sides.

With Thanksgiving recess concluded, Sharon returns to the witness stand for his sixth day of interrogation and testimony. He acknowledges right away that Kahan found him guilty, "indirectly responsible for not foreseeing" that the Christians would commit grave excesses in Shatilla and Sabra.

But Sharon has something more to say about the Kahan findings.

"I would like to emphasize that in the Kahan Commission, never—not in one word—have I been accused of committing any murder, or instigating a murder or discussing a murder or encouraging a murder. That happened only in the *Time* magazine."

He cannot say it often enough, compelled to express it again each time the decision he made is impugned:

Two thousand P.L.O. terrorists had remained behind. There were an additional "7,000 armed people belonging to 27 different organizations, mostly communist under Soviet influence or Syrian influence. . . . They were larger than all the forces that the Phalangists had . . . . We speak almost of about 10,000 armed terrorists together that were left . . . having in their hands heavy weapons like tanks, artillery, heavy mortars, medium-range mortars, machine guns, and all kinds of ammunition and weapons, a tremendous depot of arms. . . ."

And the Christians really were maturing. Bashir Gemayel, once described as a "bloodthirsty murderer," had visited Washington, D.C., and had met with Vice President George Bush, Secretary of State Alexander Haig, and the Senate Foreign Affairs Committee. The Phalangists back home were preparing for their ascent to power by cultivating new relationships with the Moslems of Lebanon, aware that they would never enjoy their rise to leadership if the country were to remain hopelessly divided. They wanted a united Lebanon. It would be so contrary, so very contrary, to their own self-interest to perpetrate a severe anti-civilian attack.

Besides, by the latter part of the 1982 war, they were already participating in limited military ventures with Israel. They had secured certain limited targets in coordination with the Israelis. When Israel seized control of the vital Beirut-Damascus highway, the Phalangists were assigned the task of "mopping up" the roadway for a substantial section, eliminating terrorists from the area. They had done an exemplary job.

□   □   □   □   □

In his final day on the stand, Sharon looks back at all that has transpired and deeply regrets the events at Shatilla-Sabra, the events and their results.

"In retrospect, it's clear that we made a mistake, and the civilian population suffered casualties in a tragic event that took place. And I was punished for that—and I paid the price for it. I felt that I was punished without committing any crime. . . ."

"Of course, politically it was very bad for us because that tragic event happened. I said it many times; I can only repeat it. It was a tragic event that happened—to our regret, it happened. We have to admit that it happened. We didn't have anything to do with it, but it happened."

"But that harmed us from the point of view of public relations in the world. It harmed us terribly. It harmed us terribly."

It was in that sense, says Sharon, that the Kahan Commission helped him enormously, even as it was important in Israel.

"Altogether, in the air, there were rumors and there were all kinds of terrible stories that were going on. And during that period, no doubt that many hard things, mostly after the massacre that took place, very hard things that were written. That was the reason for establishing the Kahan Commission. . . ."

"When the Kahan Commission came, the Kahan Commission clarified . . . made it obvious and clear . . . that no one of us, no one of our soldiers, no one of our commanders, no one of our politicians, not the Prime Minister, not anyone, and not myself — not myself — had any direct responsibility. . . ."

"Before the Kahan Commission, [there were] very hard articles. Then the Kahan Commission came and clarified. . . . I felt that it was a relief; it became easier. . . ."

"Then came the *Time* magazine. . . . They came after that. . . . It is very interesting that this small paragraph, that was the paragraph that was released as a press release all around the world. Not the rest, not the compliments to the Kahan Commission [that] it was a high standard of moral showing. What was released by the *Time* magazine as a press release? This small piece. . . ."

"So if I will try to say what were my feelings then, I would say that, after that short relief — it was a short relief — it started again. . . ."

"And I can say only what I felt as a human being. . . . Very hard. It was very hard what I felt, that after the *Time* magazine published it, [there] was a new wave of hatred...."

...On that note, after one of Sharon's more dramatic statements during his seven days of testimony, he completes his turn on the witness stand.

□   □   □   □   □

Two more witnesses of consequence will appear before the day ends. Bayard Rustin, the noted American black leader whose name is synonymous with the long civil-rights movement, takes the stand as a character witness for Sharon. This testimony, though not germane to the central issues of the case, is valuable in the event that Sharon wins the libel case. Testimony like Rustin's paves the way for a future awards argument claiming that Sharon's reputation is, indeed, solid—and, therefore, libel against him is of consequence, notwithstanding *Time's* effort to show that his name is not respected.

The other witness is Ehud Olmert, the Knesset member who had told Harry Kelly at the Jerusalem dinner for Ed Koch that Appendix B contained nothing in any way related to what *Time* claimed. Olmert, an attorney by trade now serving in his fourth Knesset term, tells of the dinner that night at the Jerusalem Sheraton. A really beautiful place. Knesset members get to eat there. So do *Time* bureau chiefs. Olmert tells the jury, "Mr. Kelly asked me whether I had a chance to look at and read Appendix B ...and I said, 'Yes, indeed,' and I told him that I read it and that there is nothing, just nothing in the Appendix B which even resembles the story of *Time* magazine. There was no mention whatsoever of any meeting at Bikfaya and no talk about revenge. . . . I told him this information and I said, 'I think you failed, and the story is entirely baseless.'"

Olmert tells the jury that Kelly asked him to review the secret Appendix B one more time—just to make sure. Olmert did so and then called Kelly that Monday morning. And he told him, "Well, Mr. Kelly, that is what I told you. It's not there. It's just not there. There is nothing about Bikfaya. There is nothing about revenge, reprisals, retaliation, anything of this nature. It's not there."

XI

"... I Was Once Part of It and Them"

There is time for one more witness today. He will be on the stand for a long time.

David Halevy takes the witness seat. In an unusual move, he is called to testify by Milton Gould as a witness for Sharon. Whatever comes out of Halevy's mouth, reasons Gould, can only accrue to Sharon's benefit.

Halevy reviews the basics of his background and biography. He tells of his years in the Mapai—the Israeli Labor Party. He uses the word "Mapai"—a Hebrew acronym of three letters which means "Israeli Labor Party." But Gould, although Jewish, knows little Hebrew. And the jury knows less. So Gould, interested in moving on to another point, simply asks Halevy a brief, simple question.

"Is Mapai part of the Labor Party?"

A simple question. A simple yes will lead on to the next subject. But Halevy is not in a cooperative mood.

He's going to play games. "No," he says, "It is not part of the Labor Party . . . "

The answer surprises Gould. He knows Halevy is a die-hard, card-carrying Labor Party member who is committed to seeing Begin, Sharon, and the rest of the Likud driven out of office. He wants to show the jury that Halevy is not your objective Walter Lippman-type reporter. This is not Edward R. Murrow reporting the news. This is a glorified party hack.

Now, Halevy sees the strategy. He is not going to help out. The party in which he was active, whose young people's journal he edited, was called "Mapai," not "Labor"— they speak Hebrew in Israel.

> Gould probes: "Is Mapai part of the Labor Party?"
> Halevy: "No, it is not part of the Labor Party . . . "
> Cat and mouse.
> Gould: "You were not a member of the Labor Party?"
> Halevy: "No, I was not. I am sorry."
> Gould: "At no time were you a member of the Labor Party?"
> Halevy: "At no time at all."

Gould is going nuts. He can't believe that this guy has come 6,000 miles from Israel to defend his reputation as an honest, objective, unbiased, straightforward journalist—and now he is playing games. Gould knows that Halevy has worked for Yigal Allon, has supported Shimon Peres, both of "Mapai," both of the Labor Party. But it is one thing to know it. It is another thing to drag it out of Halevy's uncooperative mouth.

But Gould is 75-years-old. He's had his Halevys before. He comes ready. Just in case.

Gould pulls out a dusty, old document. Maybe it is the Gettysburg Address. Maybe it is the Dead Sea scrolls. Maybe it is Gould's birth certificate.

"Now, sir," asks Gould, "I would like to direct your attention to a deposition that you gave on May 28, 1982, and I am referring to page ten . . . You remember a lawsuit called *Charoni v. Media International Enterprises?*"

□　　□　　□　　□　　□

Halevy is slightly startled. "Yes, sure. I testified . . . I gave a deposition."

Gould picks this one up on the rebound. "And you testified under oath in your deposition, did you not, in that lawsuit?"

"Yes, sure."

"And you said, did you not, at page ten, that you studied at Tel Aviv University on political science and Middle Eastern affairs, and then you said: 'I joined the Labor Party and served as editor-in-chief of the Labor Party.' Did you not say that?"

Halevy is stone silent for a moment. If Gould keeps this up, they're liable to name a baseball stadium after him, too. Halevy replies: "Yes, sir, I did."

□　　□　　□　　□　　□

Now that the sparring is finished, Gould and Halevy are ready to face off.

Gould wants to establish for the jury not only that the disputed story defamed Sharon and was false. He must also establish actual malice. He has to get Halevy to project a malice so strong that it will shake the jury. But this will be easier for Gould.

◻ ◻ ◻ ◻ ◻

Gould asks, How do you evaluate Sharon now?

Halevy starts carefully. He is trying to be careful, no slip-ups. Mustn't show malice. "I think Minister Sharon is an excellent field commander. He did not become a statesman. He is a politician who is incapable of becoming a statesman –".

He started so well, but Halevy's slipping.

"– He is a ruthless leader. His ambition for power is naked, and I am afraid that he is causing tremendous damage to the State of Israel and to his own environment ... Ruthless, naked ambition for power, a field commander who did not emerge to the level of a statesman, a politician with no principles, with no ideology ... "

◻ ◻ ◻ ◻ ◻

Malice? What malice?

Milton Gould moves away from Sharon-related questions. There will be time for more of that later. This guy, Halevy, is not going to change his tune on this one.

Gould turns to the 1979 *Time* story on Menachem Begin's health. The scoop by Halevy which ended up being retracted after four "reliable sources" denied knowing anything about it, one-by-one.

What happened? Gould asks.

Halevy replies, "Some of the sources for that story bailed out ... "

"But you reported, did you not, that you had a conversation with a man who told you he gave you information about the health of Prime Minister Begin."

Halevy interjects, "Sir, I would prefer if you didn't quote that story because I quoted there a doctor at the Albert Einstein Institute, and I called him from Jerusalem to New York, and I asked him specific questions, and he responded the way he responded. He later said that the line was bad, okay?"

Gould, astonished, "He said what???"

Halevy: "The telephone line was bad."
Gould: "Didn't he say that you had misquoted him, that you had—"
Halevy: "Maybe. It could be. You might be right. I don't remember what he said . . ."

Gould recalls that *Time* retracted that story after Dr. Fein said he was stunned by what was attributed to him, while the other sources ran for the hills. "So we had 'Source A' who said it wasn't true, 'Source B' who said it wasn't true . . . 'Source C' who said the story was a fantasy . . . and 'Source D' who denied any knowledge of the meeting and said that you never even spoke to him, you spoke to his wife, correct?"

Halevy acknowledges that Gould's summary is correct.

Gould: "And then we have a fifth source, Dr. Fein, who said . . . what you said wasn't true."
Halevy: "Probably you are right."
Gould: "So you named five different sources, and each one of them said that what you attributed to them wasn't true."
Halevy: "Yes."

Shortly thereafter, Gould notes for the jury's education, Halevy was put on probation.

The following morning Halevy returns to the stand. He recounts events of the fateful September 15 day when Sharon held the meeting with Pierre Gemayel in Bikfaya. And then he tells Gould and the jury that he had four different, independent sources who filled him in on the details of Sharon's meeting with Pierre Gemayel.

"I had four significant conversations – talks – with four people, all relating to the matter of the meetings that Minister Sharon had with the Phalange leadership – military, political – on September 15 in Beirut . . . "

One of these sources, whom Halevy describes as an Israeli general, told him that Sharon had characterized Bashir's murder as "a Syrian-Palestinian conspiracy" during talks in the Gemayel estate. The source "also gave me a clear indication that General Sharon said or stated that this Syrian-Palestinian conspiracy should not be left without retaliation, reprisal, reaction – some kind of answer."

Another source, whom Halevy called "an Intelligence person," supposedly told him that when Sharon arrived for the Gemayel condolence call, the Israeli Defense Minister told Sheikh Pierre that he had come not merely to pay his respects but also to "talk business."

This same source averred that Sharon told the Phalangists that they should go into the refugee camps. Later, when Pierre made a comment to Sharon along the lines that his son's blood must be avenged, Sharon did not respond.

This silence on Sharon's part, Halevy tells the courtroom, constitutes an acquiescence. Thus, Sharon "gave them the feeling"—by not demurring when Pierre spoke of vengeance.

By law, Halevy need not reveal the names and identities of his sources—assuming that they even exist. He cites this legal privilege to which he is entitled and refuses to tell Gould the identities of his informants.

□   □   □   □   □

Gould comes back to the world-wide memorandum Halevy authored on December 6, 1982, the document which set in motion the entire libel affair. He has established that "gave them the feeling" may be something as indirect as complete silence. And what about the "questioning" Halevy referred to, when he wrote that Sharon "gave them the feeling after the Gemayels' questioning that he understood their need to take revenge . . ."?

Halevy answers, "My understanding then was, and my understanding now is, that when Pierre Gemayel said the blood of Bashir Gemayel should be avenged, Minister Sharon did not respond immediately—it's a form of writing when I said 'questioning,' but this is a statement, and he did not respond to that statement. So this is what I said."

Judge Sofaer interjects a question. "You treated their statement about Bashir as a question?"

Halevy: "I don't know if they expected an answer from him."
Sofaer: "Is that what your source told you, that it was in the form of a question?"
Halevy: "No, he did not."
Sofaer: "And there was no other questioning that you

**have information about when you wrote this? That was
the questioning that you had in mind?"
Halevy: "Yes, yes, sir."**

□   □   □   □   □

The day is winding down, but the dissection of David
Halevy's journalistic credibility is slowly reaching awesome dimensions. He writes "gave them the feeling,"
which gets translated into "discussed"–but which, by his
own testimony, involves silence or a body motion. He
writes of Sharon being "questioned," but then admits that
no questions were actually asked of the Defense Minister.
And, as for his membership in the Israeli Labor Party. . . .

□   □   □   □   □

It is time to close the session. But first Judge Sofaer
wants to keep his promise to the jurors that he would
answer any questions about the case which may be puz-
zling them. Three questions have been submitted to him
on paper slips. He answers the first two with dispatch. But
he confesses to difficulty with the third one.

"The third and certainly most fascinating question that
you raise here is, 'What do the three knocks sounded as
a judge enters the courtroom symbolize?' This question
is as intriguing to all my staff and to the lawyers in this
case as it apparently was to one of you, and we are going
to research this matter very thoroughly. . . ."

□   □   □   □   □

Halevy is back on the stand the following day. He
wants to use a Gould question to reiterate a position he
has begun expressing strongly during the trial: he does
not believe that Sharon encouraged or instigated the kill-

ings at Sabra and Shatilla. Rather, Sharon turned his back on the incident; Sharon "condoned" it.

Halevy expands, "I think he knew that there were some atrocities, that some atrocities might take place in the camps. He knew that there will be some kind of ugly incidents that will take place in the camps. He turned his back on it...But he knew that there will be some atrocities. Any operation of the Phalangists during the operation in Lebanon caused and brought atrocities. It was not one that did not cause it..."

□   □   □   □   □

Gould wants to know why Sharon was not given a chance to respond to Halevy's allegations. "Did you make any effort to communicate with General Sharon about the information that you had received from your sources?"

Halevy, self-righteously indignant, responds, "I am not an informer, sir. I don't tell the ministers of the Cabinet about information that I received....The answer is no."

Gould comes back, "Sir, one of the things you were required to do as a condition of your employment by *Time* was to check into information that you had received... Wasn't it part of your job to check information that you got?"

Halevy acknowledges, "Yes, sir."

"Did you make any effort to check with General Sharon whether the information you had obtained was accurate?"

"No, sir."

□   □   □   □   □

There is something else bothering Gould. Even if

Halevy really had some of those four sources, even if those sources were telling the truth—and Gould does not accept either premise, in light of the journalistic history Halevy brings with him—the question remains as to how Halevy is so sure that that secret Appendix B has these revelations within it?

Halevy surprises the courtroom with this one. For this incredible piece of inside information, he has relied not so much on sources as on his own intuition. "The Kahan Commission report is saying very clearly that they held 60 meetings hearing 58 witnesses; that they got 180 statements from 168 witnesses...I knew that all the participants of the meeting, the advance command post at the Karantina and Bikfaya testified [before the Kahan Commission]. I knew that the note-takers testified. Where are their notes? Where are their testimonies? [That is, the final Kahan Report left it out. It must be somewhere.] In some kind of secret appendix, correct?"

Gould bounces back, "Nobody said that to you, did they?"

Halevy concedes, "That is the way I read it. It's my evaluation, my analysis based on my knowledge of 43 years living in Israel and going through a lot of coverage of government official matters . . . " Halevy's top-secret revelation, his "highly reliable sources," never told him that the material was in secret Appendix B!

There was Jerusalem bureau chief Harry Kelly, so much in pursuit of a great scoop, so much wanting to know what was in Appendix B—just ask Halevy's sources.

And now Halevy tells the jury that his knowledge of Appendix B was merely the result of his "analysis," his deduction after 43 years in the business! A scandal!

□   □   □   □   □

Just as the Appendix B scandal starts heating up in New York, an announcement comes from Jerusalem on Friday, November 30, that the Israeli Cabinet has decided to allow retired Supreme Court Chief Yitzhak Kahan, the man who chaired the Kahan Commission, to review Appendix B and related documents and attachments in an effort to help clarify some of the issues at stake in the *Sharon v. Time Inc.* case. He will review the material, and he will then submit his answers to three questions:

> (1) Does the document contain any evidence or imply that Minister Sharon held a conversation with the Gemayel family or any other Phalangist at Bikfaya or anywhere else in which Minister Sharon discussed the need to avenge the death of Bashir Gemayel?
> (2) Does the document contain any evidence or imply that Minister Sharon held a conversation with any Phalangists in which one of them mentioned the need for revenge?
> (3) Does the document contain any evidence or imply that Minister Sharon knew in advance that the Phalangists would massacre citizens were they to enter the camps not in the company of Israeli Defense Force soldiers?

With weekend recess over, the trial resumes on Monday, December 3. Milton Gould has a surprise for the audience and jury who have not been privy to the depositions. Today he will lay bare, for all to see, what sort of man is this David Halevy, what objectivity and dispassionate detachment he brings with him to his job.

And what his bosses think about it—or don't.

Milton Gould takes a sheet of paper. To the naked eye, it is merely "Plaintiff's Exhibit 38." To the connoisseur of quality investigative research and hard-nosed homework, it is a gem. It is the kind of document which will surely get Gould that baseball stadium. At least in Israel. If Sharon becomes Minister of Sports.

And if they ever bring baseball to Israel.

But, for now, Gould has his ace-in-the-hole. It is a letter, headed "Personal and Confidential"—the best kind—and dated May 17, 1984. It is written by David Halevy and addressed to Richard L. Duncan, chief of correspondents.

Halevy writes Duncan that things are depressing, what with the libel suit and everything. It is May 1984 when this letter is being written—the case has been hanging over Halevy's head for a year, and it will be another six months before it ever gets to court. Halevy is depressed over developments in Israel.

"... There are *some developments*—to which Jewish terrorism should be attached—that seem to me to be *very worrying. These are the actual vindication of Arik Sharon* ... and other signs of mysticism, fascism and radicalism. I don't want to draw historical *analogies* but it seems to me that the difficulty in recording these trends is as complicated as it was in the *twenties and thirties* in Europe and *mainly Germany*. . . ."

"Strange as it may sound, the result of all this is boredom. There is nothing here to cause enthusiasm, nothing rates as a challenge anymore. The political developments are running in a pattern that is easy to predict. The military-defense establishment is taking a route that at best will lead nowhere. And the intelligentsia is taking such a non-ideological approach that no sparks are lighting up the darkness that is engulfing us all.

"If these statements lead you to believe that I have lost my senses, am pessimistic, or have lost the ability to analyze, you will be wrong. I know this country and its people. *I was once part of it and them. This tunnel is going nowhere, and there is no light at the end . . . .*"

"I can no longer become enthusiastic over here and I will not regret what I have written, nor have I said it all because I am in a bad mood. I will not change my decision when the weather improves or when Shimon Peres will (if at all) become Prime Minister. . . ." (Emphasis added).

□   □   □   □   □

There is more to this one. Dick Duncan writes a response to Halevy. Since he is the chief of correspondents, it is useful to mull over his words of encouragement in an effort to assess what kind of person it is whom *Time* has employed over all other correspondents:

> "Dear Dudu [Halevy's nickname],
> Thanks for your letter . . . Even when the facts now tend to vindicate you, the politics are the same. Perhaps not quite the same in the Begin case, but the politico-cultural atmosphere which makes an outcast —or worse—of those who dare to criticize the *Central Myths of Israel* (some of them the finest myths in the west, *some pretty damn debased* and self-serving recently); that atmosphere is unchanged and seems

to be stifling you. As it must stifle many.

Your German analogies frighten me. I know what you mean, I think, but I hope you are not proved right. . . .
Perhaps you could come to the States and rub elbows with all the nice liberal, intelligent, devout Jews here and pick up a little much-needed rosy nostalgia for Israel. You know, singing songs together down on the kibbutz, that sort of thing . . .

Also, please do not do any books on terrorism, especially Israeli. And lie low on Sharon. *You will be rewarded . . . .* (Emphasis added)

> Dick"

□   □   □   □   □

Malice? What malice?

Gould asks Halevy about his letter to Duncan. He learns from Halevy that he was depressed at the time. "Were you depressed about the actual vindication of Arik Sharon?"

Halevy nods, "Definitely so . . . Here we are . . . fifteen months after the Kahan Commission report is out, and Minister Sharon is riding very high . . . It worried me that he got a vindication . . . It took him only fifteen months to be completely vindicated, to achieve a total vindication of the Kahan Commission finding . . ."

"The vindication of Minister Sharon was another sign that, actually, the practice of justice in my country is not working too well . . . It was a worrying sign, an alarming sign, that something is going wrong, something is rotten in the State of Israel . . ."

"I thought then, and I still believe, that the occupation of the West Bank (Judea and Samaria) is corrupting my country, is corrupting my society . . ."

It is not Halevy's proudest day on the stand. Thomas Barr has his work cut out for him.

Barr begins his cross-examination. He has two difficult obstacles before him. He must first convince the jury that Halevy is a fundamentally objective fellow. Then he must show that he really is not a self-hating Israeli; juries don't like that sort of person.

It is one thing to defeat the United States of America on behalf of I.B.M., knows Barr. It is quite another matter to convince six level-headed, average people that Halevy has self-respect, in light of his reference to having "once" been a part of his people and a part of his country.

And objectivity? This is the reporter whose anti-Judea-and-Samaria article so antagonized Ezer Weizman that he called Halevy in 1978, to personally complain. This is the correspondent who, while covering issues of importance in Judea and Samaria, bears a personal prejudice against a continued effort along the lines charted by the Begin-Sharon Likud. He opposes Sharon; he wants him out. Sharon's vindication eats at him, daily. He can't stand it that, fifteen months after the Kahan Report, the people of Israel want him back in active service.

And it is this correspondent's job to give to six million worldwide readers of *Time* an objective insight into Israel.

Barr has a real job on his hands.

He elicits from Halevy the fact that he has four kids. His wife works at Tel Aviv University, and he has been in the Israeli Defense Forces for over ten years, now standing at the rank of Lieutenant Colonel. He has fought in Israel's wars and sustained his share of injuries in battle.

He has broken some major news stories, using his sources to uncover details about: the Yom Kippur War, the 1974 Maalot massacre, the 1976 Entebbe rescue.

And the 1979 Begin health story.

Barr helps Halevy advance a novel argument: the story was right. His sources "bailed out" on him. Dr. Fein had difficulty with the hook-up on the overseas phone call. No matter. It is a legitimate argument to make—especially when there are none others.

Barr now comes to the disputed article. If he can help Halevy make the anonymous sources believable he will be taking a giant step home. They have to be real, breathing, live anonymous sources. They have to be anonymous sources with anonymous flesh, anonymous blood—maybe even an anonymous wife and kids. Maybe even an anonymous pet. But, in their anonymity, they have to sound real. Barr asks the correspondent, tell us about those sources.

Halevy has a description ready in his mind. The first source is a general, an Israeli general. Halevy knows him thirteen, maybe fourteen years. The second source, also a general, has known Halevy for eight years. He has known his third source, a member of Israeli intelligence, for four years; no, make that five. And the fourth source, why, he's an old friend—sixteen years.

Halevy almost apologizes to the courtroom's spectators that he can't bring them out, introduce them. But they are anonymous sources, and the law protects that anonymity he has promised them. Indeed, his refusal to name them reflects his own commitment to honesty and sincerity. He gave them his word that he would not blow their covers; he is prepared to honor that word, even if it hurts him in this case.

And he describes, one last time, his role as a *Time* correspondent. He is not there to contribute magnificent prose; the senior writers are hired for that. His job is to be on the scene, to dig out the small details, to provide readers with the smell, with the color.

When he is good, he does that very well. The only question anyone is wondering is: what happens when you give the wrong smell, the wrong color? Can it destroy a man's reputation?

On Thursday, December 6, both teams of attorneys can agree: No further questions of the witness, your honor.

Judge Sofaer looks at the 43-year-old Israeli who has been at stage center for nearly two weeks. "You can step down, Mr. Halevy," Judge Sofaer says.

Halevy is incredulous. "I can step down?"

XII
"Cheers"

The next witness called to the stand is one Harry John Kelly, Jerusalem bureau chief of *Time* magazine. "Who's minding the store?" asks one wag in the benches. "Never mind," comes the reply, "with all these guys in New York, there's probably no one there to hurt Israel this week."

The courtroom is gaveled to order.

Kelly begins by telling the court something about himself—he has been with *Time* since 1981, was a correspondent in the New York bureau before taking over the Jerusalem office in November, 1982. He is now being transferred to run the Central American bureau. The Contras can hardly wait.

He concedes that he speaks no Hebrew, reads no Hebrew, knows no Hebrew.

Now to business. Milton Gould wants to know about Halevy's world-wide memorandum of December 6, 1982.

Kelly explains that, when he read it, he inferred that it meant "an indirect conversation in which the Gemayels may have raised the issue of revenge, and Mr. Sharon may have responded with a shrug. . . ."

What a coincidence. That's just the way Halevy interpreted it.

□ □ □ □ □

Kelly defends the accuracy of that memo. "It doesn't say revenge in the camp. This meeting took place before the massacre in the camp."

Kelly's strategy becomes apparent: he is arguing that, even if the story proves to be false, it should not be adjudged to be defamatory. Nothing in the article says anything about Sharon planning revenge in the camps. Even if the article says out-and-out that he talked revenge with Gemayel, it should not be read to mean that he talked about revenge in the camps. No, they were just talking about revenge, in general. You know, that kind of stuff.

Judge Sofaer asks a question of Kelly: "You don't think [the reference to a discussion about revenge, as written in the memorandum] relates to that earlier sentence, the sentence before it, the one we are talking about, 'Sharon indicated in advance to the Gemayels that the Israeli army was moving into West Beirut and that he expected them to go into the Palestinian refugee camps'?"

Kelly: "No, I am sorry, your honor."

Sofaer: "The two sentences—you don't read them together?"

Kelly: "No, I don't read that General Sharon knew they were going to take revenge in the camp. . . ."

Kelly reviews events as they transpired: how the Kahan Commission released its report on February 8, 1983; how he turned to Halevy two days later, asking for information on what might be in Appendix B; how Halevy came back and told him that, if there is one thing we can be sure of, it is that the substance of the world-wide memorandum—Sharon's discussion of revenge . . . or shrug . . . or silence—is in Appendix B; how Halevy went out to confirm his story and returned with a thumb pointing upward. . . .

When Kelly saw Halevy's thumbs-up sign, he went full speed ahead.

Judge Sofaer has a question. "Did it ever cross your mind that the information you had originally obtained [through Halevy] might be incorrect in light of the inconsistencies, possible inconsistencies, in the report?"

Kelly replies, "No, sir, it did not."

He elaborates how he inferred that it must be in Appendix B. It was clear from the report that there was a secret appendix, filled with sensitive information. Now, in the part of the report which the Kahan Commission released to the public, there is virtually no mention whatsoever of the disputed condolence meeting in Bikfaya. The whole meeting is mentioned only one single time and then only in the most cursory way with no evident importance attached to it. Kelly read through the Kahan Report and was baffled: Why do they not elaborate on Sharon's condolence call? What happened to it? Where did it go?

Kelly figured that it had to be in Appendix B. That's

what happened to it. It didn't get lost. It was saved and recorded for posterity. In Appendix B.

There could have been a second inference, the one to which Judge Sofaer alluded in his question: the possibility that the meeting in Bikfaya really was the fifteen-minute condolence call Sharon said it was. It was completely irrelevant to the chain of events in which Kahan was interested. It merited no more attention than Sharon's breakfast that morning.

□   □   □   □   □

The judge wants to get the jury clear on Kelly's testimony. "You were inferring from the absence of that information in the public report a keeping, a holding back, by the Commission?–"

Kelly: "Correct, sir."

Sofaer: "–rather than the possibility that you may have incorrect information, isn't that correct?"

Kelly: "I say that would be correct, yes, sir."

□   □   □   □   □

Now, Gould wanted to shift the subject to the change in wording from "gave them the feeling" to "discussed." Halevy had accused Sharon of "giving the Phalangists the feeling" that he understood their need for revenge – a charge that Sharon may have shrugged his shoulders, may have blinked, may have done nothing.

But, by the time that senior writer William Smith had finished with it, the new accusation was that Sharon actively, overtly *discussed* revenge.

Gould will not let Kelly toss the blame only onto Smith. After all, *Time* has a "playback" process, in which

Halevy and Kelly get to read Smith's article before it is published, as a way of assuring accuracy in the final version. In order for Smith's word —"discussed"— to have made it into the magazine instead of Halevy's choice —"gave them the feeling"— there had to be an approval from Jerusalem.

Gould asks, "You saw that change in the playback?"

Kelly confirms that he spotted the change in language — but he didn't complain about it because he was satisfied that it meant the same thing.

Judge Sofaer wants to get to the bottom of it. "If you had thought of it. . . . Is this the way you would normally report as a *Time* reporter, a *Time* correspondent? Would you pick up your typewriter and write out the words "discuss the need for revenge" from the kind of [description you got from Halevy]?"

Kelly is unrepentent. "Sir, at the time I didn't think it was inaccurate. I thought a discussion —"

Sofaer wants to get this ironed out. "I realize you didn't think it was inaccurate at the time. I am asking you now. What is the standard that you would apply as a reporter if you had the minutes [of the Bikfaya condolence meeting, as reported by Halevy] in your hand? Would you write the words 'discuss the need for revenge'?"

Kelly, realizing he doesn't look very good, is evasive. "Sir, I didn't have the minutes in my mind."

Sofaer was not the type of judge to let Kelly squirm out of this one. "I gather you didn't, but WILL YOU ANSWER MY QUESTION? I am asking you if you *did* today, if you *had* the minutes here and the article here, side-by-side, and the minutes said the *Gemayels* said they wanted to avenge the death of Bashir, and the article said that *Sharon* discusses the need for revenge with the Gemayels, would you write *that* article from *those* minutes?"

Kelly is down for the third time in the round. 'I may not, sir—particularly after this."

□   □   □   □   □

Sofaer isn't finished with Kelly. "...I do think that I would like to have an answer to my question about your standards of reporting as a reporter. You have an important position as a chief correspondent in a bureau there, and you have had many years of experience.... If someone else wrote that story from those minutes, would you consider that an accurate story?"

They're born tough in India.

Kelly, beaten, gives up the ghost. "I would not use the word 'discussed.' "

□   □   □   □   □

Now, here comes Gould. Kelly has barely had a chance to recoup.

Gould looks at the "Take 9" which Kelly sent to New York—and compares it with Smith's final version. Kelly had written:

> ... Some of it [Appendix B], we understand, was published in *Time*'s world wide memo, an item by Halevy, Dec. 6, for which we gave clearance, dealing with Sharon's visit to the Gemayel family to pay condolences. Certainly in reading the report there is a feeling that at least part of the commission's case against Sharon is between the lines, presumably in the secret portion.

Gould says to Kelly that he notes the words "we under-stand" and "presumably" in his original report. Those words tell the average reader that we *think* something is so, but we couldn't swear to it. If you are sure, then you just don't say "presumably." But Smith re-wrote "Take 9" in a way in which he removed the doubt, the qualification:

> ... *Time* has learned that it [Appendix B] also con-tains further details ... Sharon also reportedly dis-cussed with the Gemayels the need for the Phalang-ists to take revenge for the assassination of Bashir, but the details of the conversation are not known.

Gould has a question. "It was changed from a state-ment by you which expressed reservations and qualifica-tions to an affirmative statement: '*Time* has learned.'"

Kelly is in trouble. "'*Time* has learned' to me is a qual-ification. . . . If we are stating that they are there, we would say '*Time* has obtained a document' or '*Time* has seen.' In this case, it was only '*Time* has learned.'"

Gould can't believe the answer. This is back to Halevy playing cat-and-mouse over whether or not the Mapai is the Labor Party.

"Mr. Kelly, all I want to do is understand something. You did have reservations and qualifications, correct?"

Kelly agrees. "I had qualifications."

Gould probes carefully. "Whatever you want to call them: you weren't sure about it?"

Kelly, very carefully, "I wasn't positive, no, sir."

□   □   □   □   □

Gould, moving in for the kill, "You wanted New York to know that you weren't positive. And then you get back [from Smith] the statement '*Time* has learned that it also contains,' and you are telling His Honor and the jury that these words also are expressive of qualifications?"

Kelly, retreating, "qualifications, sir, in the sense that '*Time* has learned' means it's an attribution from a source."

Gould, now in command of the exchange: "Is it your testimony, sir, that a reader reading the words '*Time* has learned that it also contains further details about Sharon's visit to the Gemayel family on the day after Bashir Gemayel's assassination,' that that is a statement from which a reader should understand that you are not sure?"

□   □   □   □   □

Gould has made his point. Something's funny about the Jerusalem Bureau Chief. Maybe that's why they're sending him to Central America.

Gould turns to the next issue. He probes Kelly, focusing on how that paragraph rewritten by Smith made it into the magazine. Kelly admits that the paragraph set off a sensation, that Israel's Prime Minister railed against it in the parliament. And, yet, Kelly just does not see how that paragraph got taken so seriously.

"I thought we had done a very fair job of reporting and writing—and Mr. Begin, to my astonishment, had picked out this twentieth paragraph, what I considered a not-very-important paragraph in all this material, and said it was a slander. . . ."

Gould asks, "And you said, or you characterized, this paragraph, paragraph 20 in the playback, you characterized it in your telex as fairly innocuous, correct?"

Kelly nods, "That is the way I thought it was. . . . We

thought we had done a very good job, a very fair job of reporting the whole thing, the turbulence, the [Kahan] report, and on Monday Mr. Begin had picked out this innocuous paragraph. I was stunned."

Gould is inquisitive. "Do you still think it was an innocuous paragraph?"

Kelly, innocent. 'Yes, sir, I do."

□　　□　　□　　□　　□

But then the country went wild. Banner headlines hit the Israeli Hebrew press. Begin was furious. Sharon was suing.

"I did not know immediately what was going on," says Kelly. "It was very confusing to me. I don't read Hebrew. . . . By this time it was obvious that there was some confusion going on."

Gould moves closer. "You mean that it was obvious that people had construed this 'innocuous and not-so-important' paragraph as something that was important? That's what was going on, wasn't it?"

Kelly is still trying to piece it together. "What I am saying is that somebody had somehow misconstrued the paragraph. . . ."

Sofaer interjects an observation, "It wasn't just this one newspaper; it was newspapers in America and in Israel and in Europe."

Gould puts it into Kelly's lap. One last question for this exchange. "Were you aware at all, in any way, from anybody, that your unimportant, innocuous paragraph, and the playback, had created some kind of journalistic sensation?"

Kelly replies, "No, sir."

        □   □   □   □   □

But soon Kelly was beginning to fathom what "Take 9" had wrought. Page one stories. It was then that he excitedly sent his telex to Duncan. "We must have struck a nerve. Cheers."

And then two weeks later, Knesset member Ehud Olmert ruins dinner by approaching Kelly and telling him that Appendix B, which Olmert has read, contains nothing of the sort.

"Did it disturb you," asks Gould, "to learn that this man who said he had gone through the papers had found no reference to Bikfaya in Appendix B?"

Admits Kelly: "Sure it did."

Gould prods, "It disturbed you very much."

Says he: "I was very surprised. . . ."

        □   □   □   □   □

There is one more matter Gould needs to square away. "Kelly, why didn't you call Sharon and ask him to react to your charges?"

Kelly: "The directory we had was a little out-of-date."

Gould is incredulous. "So you didn't call him at home because you didn't have his telephone number. . . and you couldn't get his telephone number because the only directory you had was in Hebrew, and you couldn't read it?"

XIII
"An Unfair Telescoping"

The next witness is sworn in. William E. Smith, a precise, exact man. Born in Pasadena, raised in Los Angeles, Smith joined *Time* in 1957. After a year reporting in L.A., he was transferred to the Alaska bureau until 1960. He then came to work for *Time* in New York, doing all kinds of general reporting. He covered Governor Nelson Rockefeller's unsuccessful pursuit of the Republican Presidential nomination.

After a stint in Nairobi, Kenya and four years of freelancing, Smith returned in 1969 to begin doing the kind of work he does now. Since 1979, he has been the principal writer in the "world" section when it comes to stories dealing with the Middle East.

He begins his testimony by describing to the court how he functions as a senior writer. He writes the story after being given his assignment by the section editor.

Together with the researchers assigned to him, he prepares the material, incorporating the "takes" being filed by correspondents from throughout the world, each one relating to the central theme from a different perspective. In order to get other "takes" he may need, he sends out a "query letter" to the appropriate correspondents in the field, soliciting their input on specific items which he needs. By late Thursday and early Friday, the "takes" are arriving, and he gets to work on the actual writing. Sometimes, an individual bureau may send as many as fifteen or twenty "takes" as part of their work on just one week's main story.

The writer has to make sense out of all this . . . with the deadline drawing ever closer. As the writer finishes each section, the assigned researcher begins working on the copy, checking for accuracy. It then goes on to the section editor, who is also well-read on all the pertinent material. He may add something of his own; he may send a note back to the writer, asking that he do it.

Then comes the playback, in which the edited story is sent back to the contributing bureaus for one last approval. The managing editor, too, is given another shot at the article.

By late Saturday or early Sunday the final touches are made, and the presses start rolling later that Sunday.

□   □   □   □   □

Having explained so thoroughly how he does his job, having conveyed meticulousness, Smith now faces Gould-the-Hunter. He is hunting for Smith.

Smith explains to him that, for the story being disputed in this courtroom, he received eighteen separate "takes" from Kelly's Jerusalem bureau. Smith, simultaneously, read the full text of the Kahan Commission report, a variety of related news reports, and some "takes" filed on the breaking story from *Time*'s bureau in Beirut.

When Smith received Kelly's "Take 9," with its major citation of the Halevy world-wide memorandum, he decided to pull out that document from his files. He saw Halevy's chosen words—"gave them the feeling"—and he understood that to mean a dialogue had taken place.

"I took this to mean that this was part of a conversation in which Mr. Sharon was discussing the grief that this family had suffered and to assure them that he understood and that the Israelis would not get into their way. . . .

"The revenge need was not Mr. Sharon's need. . . . The people who had the revenge need were the Phalangists. I think the question here and the issue here is whether, at this point, this crucial point, Mr. Sharon consciously sought to exploit the Phalangists' revenge need in order to satisfy his own need, which was to get the Phalangists involved in the war. . . ."

Gould turns to Smith and asks, "And you understand also that, if they had to satisfy this need, they had an assurance from the Minister of Defense that the Israeli army would neither hinder them nor try to stop them."

Smith: "That is what this says."

Gould: "In other words, 'If you [Christians] go out and satisfy the need, we—the Israeli army—will not stand in your way in any way.' Isn't that what it means in plain English?"

Smith: "It could very well mean that."

Gould wants to get it all together. "The average person reading these words –'He understood their need'– would [that average person] not equate that with the statement that 'You go ahead and do it, satisfy your need, and we won't interfere with you'?"

Smith: "Yes, sir. I think that is true."

□   □   □   □   □

Gould next moves on to the reason that Smith changed "gave them the feeling" to the more active and direct "discussed." He asks Smith, "When you changed it to the word 'discussed,' what evidentiary basis, if any, did you have for replacing those words with the word 'discussed'?"

Smith sees it as self-evident. "The same evidence you have in front of you.... The basic sentence from which this is taken is the sentence in the world memo item.... This is clearly a conversation.... In the narrowest construction, taking this sentence alone, we have the Gemayels questioning him. I find it impossible to imagine they are not questionig him in words. He is giving them the feeling–let me come back to that–and then, in the next phrase, he is assuring them that. I read that to mean words, words. And "gave them the feeling"–when I read this the first time, that "gave them the feeling" was in reference to words...."

"Apart from this, this is framed in words. You have the Gemayels asking a question or questions of him, and you have him assuring them. That's words. To my mind, clearly, this is a discussion...."

□   □   □   □   □

Maybe Smith sounds logical. Maybe he makes perfect sense. But, if it means words, words, words—and "questioning" means asking questions—then Halevy has some explaining to do. Smith seems unaware that, as he has propounded his own logic, he has put Halevy deeper into the hole.

□   □   □   □   □

Gould wants to know why Smith never checked his interpretation with Halevy. Smith responds, innocently, that he is a writer, not a researcher. He reads words, interprets them, and writes them. Frankly, if he has erred in any way, the "playback" exists as an institution for just that reason. And there is also a researcher working alongside him as an extra protection for factual accuracy. Why had he never checked with Halevy, then? "It never occurred to me, Mr. Gould, that a year-and-a-half later I would be sitting here in this courtroom, and you would be asking me that question."

□   □   □   □   □

And, while he is on the stand, anyway, Gould has one more score to settle with this senior writer. Gould takes another issue of *Time*. He reads from the copy dated January 17, 1983: "In 1948 the Jews of Palestine seized control of part of the ancient land of their forefathers and established the State of Israel."

Now, now, Mr. Smith. "Were you criticized for that language, sir?"

The senior writer responds, "Yes, sir, I was.... Many people felt it was done unfairly. I believe we corrected that... It was certainly an unfair telescoping of an event. . . . It was unfortunate that I did not include the important details in terms of the basis of Israel."

William E. Smith, senior writer, steps down from the stand.

The next few witnesses are supporting actors and bit players in the story. Helen Doyle, the researcher who was responsible for verifying the facts of the disputed article, takes the stand to say that she checked on the accuracy of Smith's article by comparing it with another document she had available — David Halevy's memorandum.

Richard Goldstein, standing in for Milton Gould, wants to know whether or not she spotted Smith's use of the word "discussed" instead of Halevy's expression "gave them the feeling."

Yes, Doyle confirms. She saw the change. It looked appropriate to her. She never went back to it. Besides, if Smith's change were so problematic, the Jerusalem bureau would always be able to straighten it out during the weekend "playback."

And Goldstein wants to know whether Doyle considers it appropriate to put such stock in a memorandum written by a correspondent who was once put on probation.

Doyle's answer: She never was told that Halevy had been on probation.

□   □   □   □   □

After Doyle, the jury hears Goldstein read from a deposition taken of Brian Brown, the manager *Time*'s publicity department. He isn't physically present, but Bob Parker, the author of the press release which shook Israel, is in court. He takes the stand.

After explaining his job, he comes to the reason that his press release publicizing the February 21 issue of *Time* focused in on the "innocuous, not-so-important" twentieth paragraph:

"Well, it was an interesting piece of news," and it was even more attractive to him, as a public-relations professional, because it was introduced by the words *"Time* had learned."

Hold the presses! Parker has just contradicted Kelly, who went to such embarrassing lengths to downplay the meaning of the expression "Time has learned...."

Sharon's attorneys have caught the inconsistency in testimony. "What do you understand readers to have in mind," Parker is asked, "when they see the phrase: *Time* has learned?"

Parker just calls 'em as he sees 'em. "I would expect they would read it with special interest and that they might deduce—we hope they would—that this is a special piece of information which may not be available anywhere else, that it may be new and exclusive in *Time*.

□   □   □   □   □

Meanwhile, behind the scenes, Judge Abraham Sofaer has been quietly wrestling with the State of Israel in his own effort to gain access to information about Appendix B, in one way or another. The Israelis have proposed that retired Justice Yitzhak Kahan review the sought-after documents and submit his answers to three catch-all questions. But *Time* has rejected the offer as unacceptable. With all due respect to Justice Kahan and his sterling reputation, they are saying, we still refuse to accept the arrangement unless we can have a lawyer of our choosing sitting right there in the room, right alongside him, while the papers are being sifted through.

Judge Sofaer sympathizes with *Time.* This is a big case, with big stakes—fifty million dollars, the reputation of a leader in Israel, the reputation of America's largest-circulating weekly—it just won't do to have Kahan review papers without legal counsel representing both parties to the conflict on hand.

In Sofaer's letter to Israel, he explains that both sides have "agreed to accept Justice Kahan's answers as evidence" if the Israelis will allow an attorney for each party to be involved in the process so that they examine the documents, understand the basis for Kahan's answers, and have input into Kahan's decision-making process. "Time Inc. is unwilling, however," Sofaer continued, "to abdicate completely its ability to assess through its own representatives the underlying material on which the evidence to be presented at trial is based."

Judge Sofaer, asking Israel to comply, assures them that "I want to make it clear, however, that I will gladly accept answers to our questions with respect to any or all the documents we have sought to examine, as long as *Time's* representative is offered access to the specific documents involved."

XIV
"To Rub Elbows"

The trial resumes with a new *Time* biggie on the stand. The ubiquitous Richard L. Duncan, chief of correspondents. The man who put Halevy on probation. The man who urged Halevy to come to the States to rub elbows with all the nice, intelligent, liberal Jews of Rockefeller Center and its environs. Dick Duncan, in the flesh.

He explains that he reports directly to *Time's* managing editor, Ray Cave, and he describes his responsibility in supervising *Time's* 90 correspondents throughout the world. One of them is David Halevy in Jerusalem.

It was Duncan to whom Harry Kelly sent the February 1983 "Cheers" telex after the uproar had erupted in Israel over the disputed article about Sharon. How did Duncan react? Was he concerned?

"I did not regard it as serious."

Richard Goldstein, still standing in for his partner, Milton Gould, asks, "How many times, to your recollection, has the head of state of a country denounced a *Time* article, or a portion of it, as containing bald lies and slander?"

Duncan is nonchalant. "Not very many, sir. . . ."

But Duncan elaborates that the condemning was coming from Israel, so he did not regard it as seriously as he might have were the condemnation coming from a "less emotional" country. Accordingly, Duncan did not even launch an internal investigation of Halevy's report. Indeed, when the *New York Times* asked him on March 1, 1983 whether or not he stood behind the story as reported, he replied with an emphatic "Yes."

Goldstein brings Duncan back to the September, 1979 Halevy report about Begin's health. He reviews the botched account, Jerusalem bureau chief Dean Fischer's investigation, Duncan's conclusion that Halevy's story was wrong, and Duncan's decision to put Halevy on probation. Goldstein reads to Duncan the memorandum which he had sent, as chief of correspondents, to Cave and to editor-in-chief Grunwald, informing them that Halevy's story had fallen through and that "I believe our story is wrong. . . ."

Goldstein asks, "Mr. Duncan, how many correspondents have you ever put on probation?"

Duncan answers in a word. "One."

Goldstein, on the rebound. "One. And is that one correspondent the fellow named David Halevy?"

Duncan confesses, "Yes, sir."

Goldstein explores this man Duncan. You told Halevy to get out of organized politics in Israel, but he did not completely follow the orders immediately. He made an important mistake in 1976, helping his man Shimon Peres gain some needed credibility as a world-class statesman, when he incorrectly placed him at a meeting in Lebanon aimed at creating new ties with the local Christians. He brought *Time* to an embarrassing, shameful spot in 1979 when he cooked up a story that three non-Israeli neurologists had inspected Menachem Begin's health in an isolated, secret laboratory. All the sources denied any knowledge of the incident. One called it a "fantasy." One said that Halevy had never even spoken with him; Halevy had only questioned the source's wife.

Goldstein knows that Duncan has put Halevy on probation once already. Why does *Time* continue to back him, to stick with him? Is it a strategy for the trial? What's going on?

Duncan plays down Halevy's probation. It is not as though he were fired. Really, says Duncan, *Time* does not have a formal probationary status. It was just an expression.

□   □   □   □   □

Duncan says Halevy really does good work. He is not reckless. When he was put on probation, it was not even so much due to the inaccurate article as to administrative considerations. In fact, Duncan adds, the Begin Health Story may really have been true, after all. Maybe Halevy's sources really did exist, and they just "bailed out on him" at a bad time.

As Duncan presents his case, he builds new steam in support of the novel contention that Halevy is one darn good correspondent. Waxing poetic, Duncan even suggests that Halevy is one of *Time*'s five best in the world when it comes to digging out sources.

This is too much for Goldstein. Maybe Duncan is an honest fellow, not a liar, but here and now there seems to be a cover-up in progress. Goldstein begins to come on strong, impeaching Duncan's credibility, implying that he does not play with a full deck. It gets mean.

At this point, Judge Sofaer explains to the jury that this case is not a "nice-guy case. People are trying to prove nasty things about each other here."

Remember, this is the Dick Duncan who has a chip on his shoulder against Israel. If Begin condemns *Time,* we don't get excited. If a "less emotional" country complains, then it's a different story.

This is the Dick Duncan who talks about the "Central Myths of Israel . . . some pretty damn debased and self-serving recently." In America, the Jews are better, the "nice, liberal, intelligent" sort.

Duncan has his own set of Israeli dragons, and Begin and the Likud seem to be at the top. Goldstein probes this aspect of Duncan's psyche. He submits as evidence an article written by David Halevy and published on August 7, 1980 in the *Washington Star,* in which Halevy apparently set off Duncan's psyche. He submits as evidence an article written by David Halevy and published on August 7, 1980 in the *Washington Star,* in which Halevy apparently set off yet another storm by violating Israeli protocol and publishing the name of an individual who is supposed to have the same anonymity Halevy wants for his "sources." In the aftermath of that brouhaha, Duncan advised Halevy to come to the U.S. for a while until the controversy died down.

Goldstein wants to explore why Duncan recommended that Halevy leave Israel for a while. "Did you feel that Mr. Halevy had been made a political target?"

"Yes, I did."

"Who did you think was targeting him?"

Duncan spits it back without batting an eyelash. "The Begin People."

□   □   □   □   □

On cross-examination, Duncan continues to build a case for Halevy the professional. Maybe Dean Fischer did not handle the investigation right in 1979, when the question of Begin's health was being studied.

This is too much for Goldstein, who returns to question Duncan. How can you say that Fischer did not do well in his investigation, when the reality is that you, yourself, in a memorandum you never dreamed would end up in this courtroom, praised Fischer, saying, "I also think that Dean Fischer has reacted well in this situation. He methodically went back to the sources and spotted the problem."

How can you say that Halevy's report may really have been accurate when he wrote of Begin's supposed health problems? Didn't you write, "I believe our story is wrong. . . . In my judgment, the balance of the evidence is that our story is wrong."

How can you praise Halevy to the hills and deny that his probation was the result of shoddy journalism, when you wrote him that "the gist of our agreement, as I understand it, was that I felt your work recently to be unsatisfactory. . . ." And then you gave him four points to follow in future reporting, one of which was: "a more obvious effort on your part to insure that what you report to *Time* (and to the *Star*) is printable, reliable information, reflecting not just informed speculation, but the *most likely true situation*. As part of this, I would like to see on your part more effort to evaluate the reliablility of various sources, and the likelihood that they in fact *know* what they are saying." (Emphasis Added)

If Duncan's sincerity has been impeached in this trial, he has done it to himself, a sad spectacle for a courtroom full of observers, contemplating that this is the man who has such influence in determining who covers Israel — and how.

□　　□　　□　　□　　□

The scene shifts, backstage, to the judge's chambers. The trial is beginning to wind down, and Judge Sofaer is beginning to prepare his formal charge to the jury. In the room with him are Milton Gould and Paul Saunders, the latter of Thomas Barr's law firm.

"You will have an opportunity to see every word of my charge in writing," Sofaer tells the two attorneys. "I will edit it, return it to you once again. We will go through the stages just like *Time* magazine does, with a 'playback' and everything."

Milton Gould. Is he going to let that line pass?

"Your Honor, I hope the quality of our editing will be somewhat superior to what I have observed."

Sofaer tells him that "I don't think the quality of editing is at issue in this case."

Gould, humbly, "I just didn't want my failure to respond to be construed as total acquiescence."

XV
"The Buck Stops Here"

It is Wednesday, December 19. Ray Charles Cave, managing editor of *Time* magazine, is sworn in. We learn quickly of his background, his years as executive editor of *Sports Illustrated,* his thirty-five years in journalism, his role as managing editor since 1977.

"I am totally responsible for the editorial material that appears in the magazine . . . for anything in the magazine except its advertising. I hire the most talented people that I feel are available. I oversee their work and trust that they do it well."

    □   □   □   □   □

Cave goes on to explain that he supervises over 500 employees on a budget which exceeds five million dollars a year. He even makes the final decision on which story makes the week's cover.

The buck stops here.

"We probably have as good, or better, a staff, a method, and spend more money on checking the facts we put into print than any major publication in the world. I hire 60 people whose primary role is the accuracy of the magazine. And in addition to that, which I assume has been testified to here, we have a system whereby, when a story is finished, it is sent back out to the field, out to the people who sent the information in, so that they can confirm that the writer's version of the story fits with the information that they sent in. It is a two-tiered process. It is very careful, and it is immensely expensive."

Here, in Ray Cave, the jury is presented with a man who sits atop a smoothly functioning empire, supervising one of mankind's most flawless systems. It costs money but it works, and Ray Cave is the managing editor. The buck stops here.

Milton Gould examines the witness. And suddenly a strange picture begins to emerge. Cave has "no recollection" that the *New York Times* sought *Time*'s reaction to the Sharon lawsuit. He does not remember when he first learned that Sharon had denied all the magazine's charges against him.

What did you think when the Israeli Defense Ministry called the story "lies"?

Cave has "no recollection of somebody saying anything to me in that language...Somebody certainly would have told me that immediately, yes, sir.... I don't have any recollection of being told, sir."

And what about Menachem Begin's heated denial in the Knesset?

"It must have come to my attention, sir."

Gould asks, "But you don't remember that it did?"

"That is correct, sir."

" Do you have any recollection of any action that was taken with respect to either the statement by the Defense Ministry or by Prime Minister Begin?"

Cave, trying to remember, "Do I have a recollection of the action that was taken?. . . . A great deal of action, sir, would have been taken."

Gould, pressing, "What was it? What was done about it?"

Cave, trying so hard to remember, "I can't answer your question, sir, because I wasn't the officer who would have done it. . . . I don't know . . . Duncan was handling it and telling me, I am sure—I have no recollection, but I am sure, keeping me informed about what was taking place."

". . . Do you remember what you were told about the substance of the press reaction?"

"No, sir—about the substance of the press reaction, I certainly would have been told that the press reaction in Israel—I think it may even be characterized in this wire here—was that the story was creating a great controversy in Israel even before the magazine had reached Israel. Yes, I was aware of it."

"Do you remember what it was about the story that created the great controversy?"

"I think it was the offending paragraph, this paragraph was causing—there may have been other things. I simply don't recall."

□   □   □   □   □

"And were you told what it was about that paragraph that was creating the reaction?"

The courtroom is hushed. Silent.

Ray Cave answers, "I don't recall."

□   □   □   □   □

Now the real boss comes in. Henry Anatole Grunwald, editor-in-chief of Time Inc. since 1979. Cave reports to him—when he recalls. Grunwald, in turn, reports to the Board of Directors.

Gould has one sticky point he wants to work out with Grunwald: What's the problem? Why don't you guys ever apologize?

Grunwald explains that *Time* has a proud tradition going back 60 years. *Time* does not apologize. It may "regret" an error. It may retract a statement. It does not use the term "apologize."

How come?

I guess they just don't. It must be a tradition or a custom over there.

The exchange between Gould and Grunwald continues along those lines. Gould finally gives up. If he wins this libel suit, he may win regrets from *Time*. But an apology? Never.

□   □   □   □   □

As Grunwald steps down from the witness stand, Sharon's attorneys inform the judge and jury that the plaintiff rests his case.

Time will present its defense as of tomorrow morning.

□   □   □   □   □

It is Thursday, December 20, and the packed courtroom awaits the fiery counter-case which *Time* will present. Paul Saunders will begin *Time's* offensive in the afternoon session, the morning reserved for Milton Gould to submit remaining documentary evidence and exhibits. It is now Saunders' turn.

He arises, as the jury enters. It is 2:15 p.m.

"Your honor, we rest."

It is an astonishing announcement. How can they rest? Do they have no witnesses of their own?

Saunders explains that, essentially, *Time* has presented its case through its cross-examination of the plaintiff's witnesses, the majority of whom were *Time* employees. They have made their arguments. And by resting, they deny Shea & Gould the chance to bring Sharon back onto the stand to rebut the defense. If the defense presents no case, then the plaintiff has nothing to rebut.

Earlier in the day, Stuart Gould (the *Time* lawyer) had moved once again to have the case summarily thrown out. And, once again, Judge Sofaer rejected the motion. "I think the jury could well conclude that the plaintiff, on the basis of all the evidence on the record, has established clear and convincing evidence that the statements in the paragraph that he had a discussion about the need for revenge and that that discussion is contained in Appendix B were false."

"I think the jury has ample evidence in addition to Mr. Halevy's own testimony upon which to make a finding of actual malice, intentional falsity."

In a nice way, Sofaer is making a statement about *Time's* remarkable arrogance, in the face of a trial which has devastated its public image already, as reporters from all over the world have begun filing stories for their newspapers about the problems in *Time*'s accuracy system. There is a real sense outside the courtroom that *Time* will be lucky if it gets off the hook, by a technicality, over the actual malice issue. All agree that *Time* has done very poorly so far.

XVI
"For Out of Zion
Shall Go Forth the Law..."

A critical new piece of evidence now appears on the scene as the trial takes a two-week recess for the end-of-season holidays. The law firms of Cravath, Swaine, & Moore and of Shea & Gould will hardly be vacationing. Each must prepare final summations, and those are expected to run some six hours apiece. The judge will be working assiduously on the final drafting of his charge to the jury.

And everyone will be trying to assess the implications of new rumblings from Israel that a deal may be worked out to gain access, in one form or another, to secret Appendix B.

    □   □   □   □   □

On the evening of December 31, the word comes from Israel. An Israeli ministerial committee led by Prime Minister Shimon Peres has agreed to a formula proposed by Judge Sofaer and approved by Attorney-General Yitzhak Zamir. A lawyer for *Time* and a lawyer for Sharon will be permitted to review secret Appendix B together with the retired chief of the Israeli Supreme Court, Yitzhak Kahan. Justice Kahan will then answer the three questions agreed upon:

> (1) Does the document say that Sharon held a conversation with the Gemayel family or any other Phalangist in which he discussed the need to avenge the death of Bashir Gemayel?
>
> (2) Does it say any Phalangist mentioned the need for revenge to Mr. Sharon?
>
> (3) Does it say whether Mr. Sharon knew in advance that Phalangists would massacre civilians if they entered the refugee camps unaccompanied by Israeli troops?

Ariel Sharon designates his attorney for the Kahan session, Dov Weissglas, an Israeli lawyer who has been at this side during the entire trial. *Time* picks Haim Zadok, a former Labor party Knesset leader who served as Minister of Justice of Israel when Labor was in power.

On January 2, 1985, as the case resumes, Judge Sofaer informs the jury that there will be a slight delay in nailing the case closed. There is some important evidentiary material which may be arriving from Israel shortly. We will wait a few more days to see what transpires.

The plan is for Kahan, Zadok, and Weissglas to review the materials on Sunday, January 6. The answers and related documents will be rushed to America on the first plane departing from Israel on Monday. In the meantime, Sofaer, Gould, and Barr will get together around noontime in New York City. Since Israeli time is seven hours later, the assumption is that, by then, they will be able to get the news from Israel together, all at once. But Sofaer won't be available *all* day, if he can help it. He has promised his three-year-old daughter that he wll be at her birthday party on Sunday. And a judge must tell the truth.

It is Monday morning, January 7, and the world knows the answer from Israel. Justice Yitzhak Kahan has determined that *Time* blew it. "In none of the documents or testimony is there any evidence or suggestion that Minister Sharon had any discussion with a Phalangist in which either person mentioned the need for revenge. There is no mention in the said documents or testimony of the possibility of the massacre of civilians if the Phalangists were to enter the camps unaccompanied by I.D.F. troops."

Time is devastated. All over the world newspapers are putting on their front pages headlines like the subdued title which appears on the front of today's *New York Times:* "Report by Israeli Supports Sharon; Israeli Report on Secret File Contradicts *Time* on Sharon." Euphorically, Ariel Sharon is holding press conferences today, accepting the congratulations from well wishers who have declared him the victor. The jury has not yet begun its deliberations, but Sharon is clear on the significance of Kahan's new findings: *"Time* published a lie."

Haim Zadok is still upset. He believes that he has been denied access to certain documents which could still prove *Time's* case. Yes, Appendix B contradicts *Time*. Yes, testimony before the Commission contradicts *Time*. But Zadok claims that in the mounds of secret written testimony, statements, and depositions which were also submitted to the Commission, there may be proof to corroborate the Halevy account.

Kahan won't hear of it. We have gone through all the documents you had asked us to inspect. We had a very clear agreement among all the parties. We cannot change the ground rules now."

Zadok feels that *Time* has been short-changed, that the truth — *Time*'s version of the truth — is out there in the written testimony. He wants it. He writes a letter of reservation which he will personally fly from Israel, challenging Kahan's decision. Milton Gould is calling him "Last Ditch Zadok."

There is irony abundant here. Sharon, who once gave up his Cabinet post under the pressure of Kahan, is praising Kahan today. And *Time* magazine, which saw Justice Kahan as the last best hope of Israel only two short years ago, now wants his scalp.

In *Time*'s official letter of protest, it says: "Time Inc. objects strongly to the limitations imposed in yesterday's examination of documents at the Prime Minister's residence in Jerusalem."

"According to Justice Kahan's letter . . . Time Inc.'s lawyer, former Minister of Justice Haim Zadok, believed that the examination should include 'not only the testimony of the witnesses who appeared before the Kahan Commission, but also the material gathered by the staff investigators for the commission, including the statements taken from persons who did not give testimony before the commission.'"

" . . . We at Time Inc. believe we have been denied potentially crucial information concerning the meetings on September 15, 1982 at Bikfaya and Karantina. This information could include the testimony of the most objective parties present at the meeting . . . "

□   □   □   □   □

As for Milton Gould, he is singing a somewhat happier tune. Kahan's determination, says Gould, "confirms everything that we have said in the case." He expresses to newsmen his interest and curiosity in seeing whether or not *Time* will publish a retraction of the disputed story, now that Kahan has zapped them.

□   □   □   □   □

Indeed, *Time* does publish a "retraction"—but is it a retraction? Or is this the best one can expect from the magazine which never "apologizes"?

A STATEMENT BY TIME:

In its February 21, 1983 cover story, "The Verdict is Guilty," *Time* reported that Israel's official commission of inquiry found that Ariel Sharon, then Defense Minister . . . shared an "indirect" responsibility for the massacre by Lebanese Phalangist soldiers of hundreds of civilians in the Palestinian refugee camps of Sabra and Shatilla that began two days after the assassination of Lebanese President-elect Bashir Gemayel. In one paragraph of its article, *Time* reported that a secret appendix to the commission's published report —known as Appendix B—contained "further details about Sharon's visit to the Gemayel family on the day after Bashir Gemayel's assassination."

Almost two years after Minister Sharon began litigation against *Time* over this paragraph, the Israeli

government has permitted an Israeli attorney representing *Time* to examine this secret appendix. Based
upon this examination last week, *Time* now issues a
correction: Appendix B does not contain further details about Sharon's visit to the Gemayel family. *Time*
regrets that error.

Time stands by the substance of the paragraph in
question that "Sharon also reportedly discussed with
the Gemayels the need for the Phalangists to take revenge for the assassination of Bashir, but the details
of the conversation are not known. . . ."

□   □   □   □   □

It is Wednesday, January 9, and the court is back in
session. Behind closed doors, Thomas Barr is asking
Judge Sofaer's permission to put Haim Zadok on the stand
so that the jury can meet this man, can get an insight into
his character, in order to better evaluate what kind of man
it is who is protesting Kahan's findings.

Milton Gould tells Sofaer he does not mind as long
as it is made clear that Zadok "was appearing there as a
lawyer for *Time* magazine and that he was paid for his
services".

Barr agrees to that stipulation.

Gould: "—Just like you and me."

Gould pauses a moment, considering his special arrangement with Sharon. "Well, certainly just like you. I
don't know about me."

□   □   □   □   □

The principals proceed to open court. The jury is
present. Judge Sofaer will now explain what has happened
in the communications with Israel.

"Good morning, ladies and gentlemen. . . We are now prepared to tell you of the results of the long efforts that were made by the parties and myself to obtain evidence, answers to questions about the documents you have been hearing about. . . ."

" . . . The results of [the examination conducted by Kahan] have been admitted into evidence by me. They consist of three letters."

Sofaer then describes the three letters, their chronology, and reads the letters into evidence. It is a blockbuster. The very last item admitted as evidence in the trial may be the most important document in the last two months of pages of exhibits, deposition, and news articles.

Summations will begin this afternoon.

□   □   □   □   □

Late in the afternoon, a minor emergency occurs. One of the jurors has become very ill and was found lying across two chairs in the jury room, vomiting. A nurse tells the judge that the juror seems quite ill; his skin is clammy and he is suffering with cold sweat.

Judge Sofaer has two alternate jurors from whom he can designate a substitute. But there is a sense of compassion here. The juror has patiently and devotedly sat through two months of intense hearings. This is the last week of the case. He is interested, if at all possible, in sitting through the end. The judge wants to give him a chance. The case has run this long; it can be postponed to tomorrow morning. If the juror is all right by then, he can continue. Otherwise, he will have to be replaced.

□   □   □   □   □

The courtroom is even more packed and tense than usual, as final summations begin on the morning of Thursday, January 10. The juror who had taken ill is back and in the usual seat. This jury will go the distance.

Judge Sofaer looks at the six citizens, embodying one of America's greatest principles, that a citizen has the right to be judged not by noblemen and not by specially placed people of influence—but by peers, by secretaries, by salesmen, by engineers, by retired senior citizens... by people.

The jurors settle into their seats for the homestretch. Thomas Barr, back in form, will do *Time's* summation. Tomorrow Gould will get his chance. In their final presentations, they will be trying to win over the jury on three issues. Defamation. Falsity. Actual Malice.

In behind-the-scenes negotiations both parties have arrived at certain agreements to help process the jury's decision most equitably. To win the verdict of defamation, Sharon must convince the jury that the *Time* article in question conveyed either, or both, of two accusations: (1) Sharon *consciously intended* to permit the Phalangists to take acts of revenge extending to the deliberate killing of the civilians in Shatilla and Sabra, and/or (2) Sharon *actively encouraged* the Phalangists to take such acts of revenge. Any other interpretation will not be enough for Sharon to win the judgment.

He must next prove falsity. *Time* will be conceding that the material attributed to Appendix B, indeed, does not appear there. Sharon will have to prove that such a meeting and such a discussion as described in the disputed paragraph did not happen anywhere else either. That the account is totally false.

Finally, he will have to convince the jury that *Time* published the defamatory and false material with "actual malice," with a reckless disregard for the truth.

Sharon has a heavy burden. But his chances look a lot better today than they did when he filed suit two years ago, a man tried and convicted of conspiracy to murder in the pages of *Time*.

◻   ◻   ◻   ◻   ◻

Thomas Barr begins his summation.

XVII
"Times' Summation"

Thomas Barr faces the four women and two men of the jury. He begins:

May it please the court, ladies and gentlemen of the jury. I have to begin by thanking all of you for your attention and for all the time this has taken. You have been very attentive, unusually so, and we all appreciate that. . . .

You must decide what the facts are, and you must decide, therefore, who is telling the truth. . . . The reporting of the story was difficult, not just for *Time*. . . . The war in Lebanon is not easy to understand. . . . The whole story of what happened on those critical days in September 1982 is not known and probably never will be fully known. It is probably not even really knowable. . . .

I think you recall how the press broke the story and pushed the story out in the open. . . . The press was the first to report the massacre. . . . How the press does that in a situation like this is . . . largely through confidential sources. Nobody is going to issue a press release in a situation like this saying, "I was responsible for the massacre." . . . You are all familiar with the story of Watergate and with the story about how "Deep Throat" wrote gradually in pieces the story to the *Washington Post's* reporters. . . .

You heard also here about examples of earlier stories that David Halevy had gotten through confidential sources, how *Time* changed the cover just before the 1973 war in Israel because Halevy, on his way to that war, knew from his confidential sources and got the word to *Time* . . . . And you remember him reporting on the Entebbe raid (and on Maalot). . . . All of those things came from confidential sources. . . .

The Kahan Commission report, of course, is very central to this case. . . . You remember that Kelly, Halevy, Smith, Ms. Doyle, they all studied the Kahan Commission report. . . . Digging out what is behind things like the Kahan Commission report and the massacre is . . . a very important part of the reason why the press, why words themselves have to be free. . . .

I am sure you all remember that I told you in my opening that none of us had ever seen Appendix B. Since we last saw you, we have learned new information. . . . I do, indeed, concede that the plaintiff has carried his burden of proving that the information we said was in Appendix B in the article is not there. . . . But that does not mean that *Time* did not believe in February of 1983 when it wrote this article that that information was in Appendix B. . . .

The plaintiff has the burden of proof on three issues. . . . The plaintiff now says that the words mean two things. . . first, that in permitting the Phalangists to enter Sabra and Shatilla, Minister Sharon *consciously intended* to permit the Phalangists to take acts of revenge extending to the deliberate killing of noncombatants in the camps. Then the plaintiff says those words also may mean, in context, that Minister Sharon *actively encouraged* the Phalangists in their intention to commit acts of revenge . . . extending to the deliberate killing of noncombatants. . . .

The next question is: Were those meanings false? Again, the plaintiff has the burden of proving, this time by a standard of proof that is higher, by clear and convincing evidence, that those statements were false. . . that he did not engage in any discussion with Phalangists, prior to the massacre, of the need to take revenge for the death of Bashir Gemayel. . . .

The third issue is the issue that lawyers call actual malice. . . whether the *Time* writers and reporters knew or had a high degree of awareness that what were printing was false. . . .

Let's turn to [the disputed *Time*] article. . . . You have all had an opportunity to study it. . . . Surely, the average reader, if he had gone through this article, would have seen a number of things. The average reader might have found adverse findings of the Kahan Commission, worldwide reaction, an impressive discharge of responsibility by the Israeli democracy, the reaction of General Sharon to the Kahan Commission. . . . Would the average reader have paused over a particular paragraph on page 4 which is the subject of this lawsuit?. . . . Would the average reader indeed have even paused over the paragraph, have spent much attention to it?. . . . It's not a question of what some other newspaper would have written, but the critical first step in your analysis is . . . the average reader. . . .

Now, the plaintiff says it has two [defamatory] meanings. . . . Now, look at that paragraph. . . . Does it say that? Does it mean that to you? If it doesn't mean that, if it doesn't man one of these two things, then this case is over. . . . Now, of course, you look at the words. The words don't say that, and they don't mean either of those two things. . . .

Now, revenge is a word that appears in the paragraph. . . . What does revenge mean? Does it mean a massacre? Does it mean punishing whoever did the killing of Bashir Gemayel in this case? . . . What does it mean? . . .

Now, in trying to make that determination you will be thinking, "What did the Kahan Commission say?". . . That is what everybody was reading and thinking about, and I am going to turn to that now. . . .

By the middle of the early morning of the 15th [of September] the whole deal was done. By that time the Phalange had been ordered to go into the camps. . . . The deal was already done. . . . The Gemayels' private army, the Phalange, was committed to enter the camps without the I.D.F. . . . The Kahan Commission report says: "From the forward command post the Minister of Defense went to the Phalangist headquarters." This is at Karantina. It is about 9:00 in the morning. . . .

Minister Sharon testified that the only subjects that were discussed were political developments, condolences, and that the I.D.F. was moving into West Beirut. That's all. Was the entry of the Phalange into the camps of so little interest that nobody talked about it at the meeting? What else was more important? . . . Minister Sharon tells you they didn't even talk about it. . . .

The next event. The next event is the meeting at Bikfaya. . . . Note, this is a meeting of the highest government. The Gemayels are Israel's most important ally on the northern border. . . . The meeting took place between 11:00 and 12:00 in the morning. It is either a critical meeting in the chain of events that I am discussing, or it is totally irrelevant. It is irrelevant, I submit to you, if the Gemayels have already given their approval to sending their private army, the Phalange, into the camps. . . . But it is a critical meeting if either the Gemayels have not yet approved or if Sharon doesn't know whether they have approved or not. . . . Sharon says there was no conversation with anyone at Bikfaya about revenge or about the Phalange entering the camps. . . . If these subjects were not discussed, I ask you to think: why not? Why were they not discussed? Certainly they were important. They were critically important. . . . I can certainly understand, and I think you can understand, why Kelly and Halevy and Smith and Doyle thought they must have talked about it. . . .

Was the meeting of any importance? Was it critical? Did the parties discuss what was important and on their minds? You have to decide that, and you have to decide whether it was reasonable for Halevy and Kelly and Smith and Doyle to believe that. . . .

I am going to turn now to what is really the last part of the argument. . . the reporting of the story. I now want to talk about what the [*Time*] people did and what they thought, and this really, in a major way, relates to the third part of the plaintiff's burden of proof, the actual malice portion of the case. . . Now, this focuses on what the *Time* people believed at the time they wrote the story. . . . You have got to put yourselves into the hearts and minds of the reporters and the writers because this test, this actual malice, is a subjective test. . . . It does ask you to determine: What did they really think? What did they really feel? What was really on their minds? Were they trying to be honest, forthright, decent reporters and put the truth on the table in the magazine, or were they trying to concoct or fabricate something?. . . .

Let's start with this fellow Halevy. I think that we know that Halevy has had a long and brilliant military and journalistic career. He is a patriot, a rather old-fashioned patriot. . . . He has had a lot of scoops and they have been based on confidential sources. He knows everybody in Israel. He has interviewed all the prime ministers, all the defense ministers, all the generals. More importantly, probably, not only does he know them; they know him. . . .

What sort of typified his career to me was the fact that

on the way to the 1973 war, where he fought as a tank officer, he called *Time* magazine in New York and said,
"There is a war coming in the Middle East," stop the presses. *Time* stopped the cover, held the cover. War broke
out, and *Time* printed a new cover in response to the
Halevy warning. . . .

After the massacre he continued to report the story.
The Phalangists denied everything. . . . But as he and the
other journalists sought to get the story out, to push it out,
they got a big help, as the press often does from people. . . . You heard Halevy testify at very, very great
length about his sources, and your job is to figure out
whether he was telling you the truth. . . . Did he really
believe what he was getting from his sources? . . .

Let me go on quickly to the next actor on the scene,
who was Harry Kelly. . . . On Thursday, as the closing
for the story draws near, Kelly is wrapping it up and says:
"What is in Appendix B. . . . Stop to think about it. . . .
The Commission came down very hard on Sharon, and
I read all that to you, really, much harder, significantly
harder than anybody else. And yet the words of exoneration, they seem to apply equally to everyone, and the
words regarding indirect responsibility. There was really
something about the Commission report that didn't quite
fit, didn't quite make sense. . . . The information that they
thought probably condemned Sharon was in Appendix B,
where it might logically be. . . .

Whatever the truth is, and we now know from our visit to Jerusalem on Sunday what the truth is, the question
is: What did Kelly and Halevy and the rest believe, and

what did they have good reason to believe, and that is for you now to decide. . . .

Smith did change Kelly's "We understand" to "*Time* has learned," which means that *Time* has a source. But that is no particular big deal. . . . The article was checked carefully and *Time*'s checking procedures, I think, are close to the best in the world. . . . I think you need to ask yourself, in evaluating how they testified and what they said, put yourself in their place. . . .

Let me touch on a couple of the problems: Begin's health. . . . He must at least have talked to the people that they went back to check with, and if he was going to fabricate the story, why would he pick Dr. Jack Fein out and put his name in the story? . . . Moreover, even if you were to assume that Halevy got the story wrong from the source at the time—if you folks never made mistakes, I certainly have. That doesn't mean because you make a mistake—and Halevy didn't make one here, but let's assume that he did—that doesn't mean when you get to judging this question of actual malice that, because a mistake was made, that years later, after brilliantly reporting a number of other stories, that doesn't mean that all of a sudden you are an unreliable journalist. If you think that—I suppose it sort of comes down to he who is guiltless can throw the first stone. But if that is making the test for when you decide somebody is suddenly unreliable, then I guess all of us are pretty much in the same boat. I certainly have made more than my share. I suspect others in the room have made their share, too. . . .

What do the people at *Time* think of Halevy? Smith

said he was "dazzled." Duncan said he was one of the top four or five people. . . . Isn't David Halevy, isn't he what you hope reporters will be? Isn't he just the kind of enterprising, straightforward man than you would want to be out there digging for the news that you need to know. . . ?

□　　□　　□　　□　　□

Many jurors have heard Barr with great sympathy. He has presented his case.

The jury will be back tomorrow. The second summation will be heard.

Milton Gould has been waiting for this one for seventy-five years.

XVIII

"...Help Us Stamp Out
This Infamy"

With fire in his eyes, Milton Gould faces the jury.
These are his words:

Ladies and gentlemen of the jury, before I address
myself to the substance of the summation, I want to point
out to you that we were all witnesses to a very momen-
tous event last night, an event in which *Time* came as
close as *Time* ever comes to admitting that it was wrong
about something. . . . Mr. Barr told you last night "I now
concede to you that the plaintiff has carried his burden
on the second part of the falsity issues . . ." That is *Time's*
way of saying: "All of the stuff we wrote about Appendix B is wrong. There is nothing in Appendix B." But that
is the way they say it. *Time* speaks. . . .

Now let's get down to what this case is about . . . I
really don't want you to pass judgment on the career of
Mr. Halevy. He may have done some good things in his

life . . . I don't know anybody that didn't do some good things in his life, but the number of good things in your life hardly relieves you from paying the penalty for some of the bad things. . . And so as you sat here last night and listened to this recital of the vast journalistic achievements of Halevy, this stuff about how, as a wounded soldier, he persisted in going back into action and how in the midst of the war, bleeding I suppose from a dozen wounds, he reached into his blood-stained fatigues for his credit card so he could call his editor at *Time* . . .

What does that have to do with whether he was right or wrong in this case? . . .

Now, ladies and gentlemen. . . your verdict will go a long way to determine whether Ariel Sharon will go down in history . . . as a great man. . . or, on the basis of the lies and the vicious speculation. . . whether he will go down as a kind of monster, another Herod, a man who ordered a massacre of women and children . . .

It's not in Appendix B. . . and now it's out there in the open. And it's not "sustaining a burden." It's a lie, and it's a lie that they are afraid to admit in language that any ordinary human being can understand. . . "Sustain a burden," indeed! Why don't they come out in the open and say, "We told a lie. We are sorry. We shouldn't have done it." . . .

This really is a remarkably simple case. It centers on a single paragraph. . . . I listened last night with patient endurance to my friend, Mr. Barr, tell you, "Well, this teensy-weensy little paragraph buried way down at the bottom of the article, one quarter of one percent of what is in the whole article. . . . Let me tell you, if I wanted to put a bomb in the Empire State building, I could probably do it within the confines of a shoe box . . .

Let me address what I think . . . has to be the most important event in the whole case . . . I refer of course . . . to the [Kahan responses to the three questions] . . . And what is left of *Time*'s story? They have admitted to you after two years of claiming . . . to stand behind their story — *Time* never apologizes — after two years of that kind of stuff, Appendix B contained nothing like what they claim they had learned it contained . . .

The other part of the story is just as fake, just as spurious, just as unsupported by evidence of revenge talk at the condolence call or elsewhere . . . Kahan establishes for you, the jurors, that Halevy knowingly, ruthlessly, recklessly fabricated the story and that his sworn testimony is false . . . And to fabricate a story is malice. . . .

Halevy's information was false . . . It was rooted in a kind of personal bias in the complex personality of this man . . . It has been handled with the same lack of care, that same cavalier imprecision which earlier had gotten him into trouble with his superiors in the Begin story. There isn't a heck of a lot of difference between what that fellow did to Sharon and what he tried to do to Begin, except in the Begin story he didn't get away with it; and in this story *Time* closed the ranks and said, "We are going to die in the last ditch with this guy . . ."

I don't think anyone suggests that Sharon is a maniac, but only a maniac knowing that he had sat [in Bikfaya] and had such a conversation, and that [minutes of] the and had such a conversation, and that [minutes of] the conversation was taken down by somebody connected with the Israeli government, some Mossad fellow, stenographer... You got to be nuts, and Sharon ain't nuts. He may be fat, but he ain't crazy... He is supposed to sit there at Bikfaya with a guy taking this down, and then he says to the Kahan Commission, "Have an investigation. I would love to have an investigation... Don't overlook the notetaker. He put down everything I said. He will tell you I said I understood about revenge, and I said we wouldn't bother them; they could do what they please." What kind of lunacy is this?

But that is the made-up story encapsulated in that paragraph. That is what they have the nerve to come in here and urge on intelligent human beings ... So this brings us to the next thing in this case.

There was a painstaking, careful, thorough investigation of all these events by the Kahan Commission... It was better than a court. It was a tribunal specifically constituted and set up by the Israeli government to get at the heart of a slander, a lie... The claim that Israelis, men with the tradition of humanity and decency, an army inculcated with a respect for the lives and feelings of civilians, had perpetrated an outrage like this. Not just Sharon—the rest of them... It was better than a court because it wasn't subject to any rules at all. They could get anything they wanted, and they did get anything they wanted...

Now, the world-wide memorandum that Halevy wrote ... If you read the world-wide memo, [the

Phalangists] advance-planned it with the Minister of Defence . . . They probably advance-planned it among themselves, and he was sitting there, and his only contribution was, "It's all right, fellows. I heard what you said." This is Halevy's interpretation of the silence. "I heard what you said. And, by the way, don't worry about us. We won't hinder you or deter you in any way. You want your knives sharpened, fellows? Just let us know . . ."

I suggest, ladies and gentlemen, that you are being victimized in this case . . . by witnesses from *Time* magazine who, in one breath, tell you that the [Kahan] report is one of the greatest things ever done . . . and out of the same mouths comes the charge that not only did Sharon do it but that the commissioners . . . somehow contrived to cover it up . . . Make no mistake about it . . . the Kahan Commission . . . very carefully and very clearly found that neither General Sharon nor any other Israeli had any direct involvement in the massacre or knew in any way that it would occur or had any intention to let it happen . . .

Well, if Halevy is right, if *Time* is right, then the Commission are a bunch of liars . . . The Minister of Defense had sat with the Gemayels and had discussed with words, with body language, with silence, with smoke signals . . . their need for revenge and had comforted them with the knowledge that the Israeli Defense Forces wouldn't interfere with them, and he had done it with a stenographer sitting there putting it down, but the Commission concealed it from history. They concealed it from the Israeli authorities.

They concealed it from everybody except that great news hawk, Halevy. He found it out. He knew it. Nobody else, just Halevy . . .

Nodody ever accused [Sharon] of murder until along came *Time* and said, "You sat with the murderers, and you practically sharpened the daggers for them . . . "

I suppose that when you were first handed your copies of the Commission's report . . . you must have expected you were going to find ten or fifteen pages in which the Commission . . . discussed Bikfaya, what happened at Bikfaya . . . So let's look at what they said. This — and this alone — is what they say: "From there (meaning from Karantina) the Minister of Defense went to Bikfaya, to the Gemayel family home, to pay a condolence call . . . " Now, that's all there is about Bikfaya in the Commission's report . . .

Now, why would Halevy do a thing like this? . . . Well, I am not going to waste a lot of time with Mr. Halevy's political history, which was extracted from him, but you know, he has been one of the members of the Labor Party going way back . . . His activities as a member or an adherent or a sympathizer of the Labor Party was sufficiently well known so that in 1978 Mr. Duncan, in his position as chief of correspondents, finds it necessary to warn Halevy to soft-pedal his political activities . . . But we had a little trouble getting this out of Halevy [when] he was asked whether he had ever worked for the Labor Party . . . Now, why does Halevy want to conceal from anybody, from you in this case, what were his ties to the Labor Party? . . . He must have a reason. There is nothing

inherently disgraceful in being a member of the Labor
Party. Some of the greatest people in Israel were members
of the Labor Party . . . So Halevy was well aware that, if
he admitted in your presence, that he had continued to
support Mr. Peres after Duncan's warning, that might be
seen—and properly seen—as a kind of conflict-of-interest,
especially when he is undertaking to write about
Sharon. . . .

Now, if you want to examine the soul of our friend,
Halevy, I suggest that you get hold of Plaintiff's Exhibit
38 in this case . . . It's a letter, a personal and confidential communication, that Halevy writes to Dick Duncan
in 1984 . . . He worries over the political popularity of
Sharon, the fellow against whom he has no bias . . . One
of the things he worries about is the . . . "actual vindication of Arik Sharon." Well, it indicates to you that he has
a very open mind on Arik Sharon. Just the guy you want
running around with his notebook trying to get honest
information and giving objective reporting on Arik
Sharon . . . I think you ought to read that letter, but there
is something else in the letter. Do you remember the
lengths to which this man went to establish his devotion
to the State of Israel, his deep patriotism? . . . And what
does he say to his boss? Get me out of here! Get me out
of Israel! . . .

Ladies and gentlemen, I don't think there is anything
wrong with a man wanting to get out of one place and go
live in another . . . but I think that when a man comes into
a courtroom here, and puts on a parade of national devotion, puts on a show of the depth of his patriotism in the

same year in which he is asking his boss to get him out of a place that he compares with Nazi Germany, it is very, very important in one respect. It demonstrates to you the quality of the man, the nature of his sincerity, and whether you can rely on him in what he says . . .

We spent a lot of time with the Begin story because the Begin story gave us a perfect opportunity really to x-ray this guy, to give a demonstration of how he operates. All the baloney about the secret sources. "Don't interfere with my secret sources. They are very valuable. You mustn't do that. I am a very important guy to *Time* magazine because every general — I know every general. I know them all the way down. They were all in school with me." You heard all that stuff.

Begin, the Begin Story. That strips him bare for what he is . . . I suggest to you that the Begin story, more graphically than anything else, illustrates his technique, Halevy's technique for manufacturing a scoop, for fabricating bits and pieces of fanciful speculations into facts, of synthesizing what he hears, what he thinks, what he believes, half truths, speculations into scoops . . . You attribute it to sources, and he has a talent for putting in the ring of authority . . . lies like the Begin story, lies like that . . . So what happens with the Begin story? *"Time* has learned" again through those ears of Mr. Halevy, through those secret sources, unidentified, *"Time* has learned . . . ."

But what did he learn? . . . What he had learned, according to the confidential memorandum from Mr. Duncan to Grunwald, editor-in-chief, the Grand Panjandrum of all the *Time* publications, the man who can't find it in his heart ever to say "We were wrong," never apologized.

What did he learn? . . . Let's see. What does it say? . . . He called Source C. Source C. What does he say about the story? Fantastic. A fantasy. Crazy. Never happened. He called Begin's two doctors. They denied ever hearing of the meeting.

He called D, another one of these secret sources. You know, it goes back to the good old days when he and Halevy were in kindergarten together in Tel Aviv . . . He called D, who denied any knowledge of the meeting. Then there is a little filler, which tells you a little something about this crack reporter, who said his wife, not he, answered the phone when Dudu called . . . So much for— let's call it anatomic dissection . . .

And even *Time* , even *Time* reacted with what for them — after all, this vast company which never admits it was wrong about anything, never apologizes — even they acted with vigor. They put him on probation . . . Duncan says the only correspondent he ever — *Time* ever — placed on probation . . . He writes him a letter, putting him on probation. And he puts some good stuff in the letter.

What does he want him to do? "Dudu, you star, you comet in the constellation of journalism, what you want to do is to make a more obvious effort to insure that what you report to *Time* is printable, reliable information, not fantasies; information reflecting the most likely true situation."

How would you like to get a letter like that from your boss? "Stop fooling. Stop telling us a lot a baloney, but just give us the most likely true situation . . ." Ah, even in Duncan's mind [there] is beginning to creep a little doubt about the validity of these sources, these guys that he knows from back in the gym in Tel Aviv . . .

Then Duncan goes on. He wants to get him back on the track. "And you are really a good guy, Dudu, but this is what I want you to do." And then there comes a wonderful little phrase. Really, very illuminating. It tells you a lot more than I can tell you. It says, "I realize that these points that I made in the letter are designed to help things work again. I realize that they may cramp your style some."

You bet they would have cramped his style! They would have made him tell the truth, and that would have been fatal to this guy. "Gee Wiz! You mean, I can't put in six million copies a lot of malarkey like that stuff and a lot of lies like that stuff? Oh, that would cramp my style very much."

You bet it would cramp his style. But I didn't write all of this. This comes from Mr. Duncan, his own boss . . .

When the journalist, in his pursuit of sensation, in his pursuit of rumor, in his pursuit of scoops, in his desire to make more money, sell more papers, sell more magazines, when he puts truth in the second place and his own speculations and his own rumors and his own half-truths, and the bits and pieces he picks up in barrooms, when he puts them before truth, the reputation of decent people, the reputations are shattered, destroyed, and good men like Sharon are transformed into men who are supposed to have *consciously intended* the massacre of other human beings, who are supposed to have *encouraged* a bunch of men with a potential for mass murder to go ahead and do it, and that's what they did.

That's what he did here, and that's what he got caught doing to Begin, and that's what he was put on probation for . . .

Imagine the difference if Halevy had been an honest fellow when he walked out of Kelly's office that day, that fateful day when Kelly said, "Go, find out what is in Appendix B." And, instead of coming back and giving him that "thumbs-up . . . " he could have said, "Harry, in my opinion, based on my evaluation and the experience that I have accumulated over all these years, I believe the information is in Appendix B."

And so, Mr. Kelly, instead of writing the lie that he wrote in "Take 9," would have said, "We got a fellow here in our office in Jerusalem who knows more about this subject than anybody that ever lived . . . He thinks the proof of Bikfaya is in Appendix B, and nobody is going to lay a hand on him."

Nobody would have printed it because it's not very interesting to say that Halevy thinks so. It's only interesting to say, "Halevy has learned, *Time* has learned,"–that is interesting . . .

I think it's worthwhile spending a little time [so that] we talk about one of Mr. Halevy's masterpieces, the so-called world-wide memo . . . When the gentleman who is the source of the whole lie wrote his first piece about it, the world-wide memo, he talks about a single conversation at a single place. And he says in that thing that he learned from "a highly reliable source." You know, that troubled us because when you say "a highly reliable source," if you are familiar with the English language, that means one single guy . . .

Now, why is that important to you? Because the process in which we are engaged, a search for the truth, a search for who is a hell of a liar and who is telling the truth, involves an examination of what he said at different times . . . So, we start off with Mr. Halevy very confidently writing for the eyes of all his colleagues in *Time* magazine in the world-wide memo, that he has learned something from "a highly reliable source."

Now, at the trial here, he had abandoned "a highly reliable source," and he had a different story for you. He had *four* sources for that item. He told us during his deposition—he told us there—that he had *three* sources for the item. Well, gee, that is terrible.

Here is this very important thing. And one day, when he writes the memo he has "a" source—which, to unsophisticated human beings like you and me, means a *single* source. And then he is testifying [at the deposition] under oath; he says he had *three* sources. And then he is testifying in this courtroom, and he says he had *four* sources.

And to Mr. Kelly, who spoke to him about the time he wrote the memo, he told yet another version. Oh, this is getting bad! Isn't it?

He told Kelly he had *two* sources.

So we have 1, we have 2, we have 3, we have 4—and, I suggest to you, we really have *none*. I really believe there were none . . . You know, a long time ago, about 2,000 years ago, there was a great writer on the subject of ethics and rhetoric, and his name was Quintillian. He said, "A liar has got to have an awful good memory . . ."

It's a cooked-up, made-up, fabricated story . . . He lied to Kelly as he lied to you, as he lied to everybody else . . .

I say to you that what was done to General Sharon in this case, done recklessly, done without a decent concern for the rights of another human being . . . what was done to him is an infamy, an infamy. And it falls to you six American citizens, who never heard of any of these people and have no interest, to do your duty and eradicate that infamy . . . Help us stamp out this infamy.

Thank you very much.

XIX
"Exoneration and Vindication"

On Monday, January 14, Judge Sofaer delivers his charge of law, a meticulously crafted legal statement aimed at spelling out the issues of the case, defining acceptable forms of evidence to be considered, spelling out in clear terms just what constitutes "defamation, falsity, and actual malice" for the purposes of this case. He places the final verdict in the hands of the jury, having devised a novel formula: the jury is being asked to determine guilt and innocence, issue-by-issue. They are first to determine whether *Time* has defamed Ariel Sharon. If so, then they are to deliberate as to whether the defamation is false. And, finally, if they have found for Sharon on the first two issues, they are to deliberate a third time on the question of actual malice.

The jury retires from the public's view.

They are out of sight for only two days. On January 16, the jury returns to a filled courtroom. The clerk asks, "Mr. Foreman, has the jury agreed upon a verdict?"

Mr. Zug responds, "We have."

The clerk requests, "Please read the verdict."

Mr. Zug reads. "We find the plaintiff has proved by a preponderance of the evidence that the statement or statements in the challenged paragraph in the article "The Verdict is Guilty," read in context, defames the plaintiff in some actionable manner as defined by the instructions on the subject . . . We find that the paragraph in context states that, in permitting the Phalangists to enter Sabra and Shatilla, Minister Sharon consciously intended to permit the Phalangists to take acts of revenge extending to the deliberate killing of non-combatants in the camps. . . .

"We do find that the defamatory effect of the paragraph was aggravated by the *Time* statement that the details of the alleged conversation were contained in Appendix B of the Commission report."

□   □   □   □   □

Outside the courtroom there is pandemonium, as *Time* arrogantly ignores the first finding and its implications. "*Time* continues to believe that the article was substantially true, and we could have proven that had we been given adequate access to secret Israeli documents and testimony . . . The jury completely misread what *Time* said . . ."

Ariel Sharon, speaking to reporters on the courthouse steps, enjoyed the spectacle of *Time* arguing with the jury. "I was sorry that *Time* magazine is shouting that the jury does not understand plain English," Sharon commented.

□   □   □   □   □

It is two days later. Friday, January 18. The jury has reached its second verdict. Richard Zug begins to read the jury's findings at 2:35 p.m. The room is as quiet as a tomb.

"The verdict on falsity. The question is: 'Has plaintiff proved by clear and convincing evidence the falsity of the facts in the paragraph that implied the defamatory statement or statements we found *Time* has made?' We found: yes, the plaintiff has so proved...In rendering our verdict we have kept in mind the defendant has conceded that plaintiff has proved by clear and convincing evidence that Appendix B of the Commission report contains no details of the discussion by Minister Sharon with the Phalangists, prior to the massacre, of the need to take revenge for the death of Bashir Gemayel.... In answer to the following question, 'Has plaintiff proved by clear and convincing evidence that he did not engage in any discussion with the Phalangists, prior to the massacre, of the need to take revenge for the death of Bashir Gemayel?' we find: yes, they have so proved."

□   □   □   □   □

Time's response is predictable. Ray Cave, managing editor, pulls out a prepared statement to read to the media. With cameras rolling, he speaks, "*Time* is gratified that . . ."

He stops abruptly. Glances at the rest of the statement. "Wrong statement," says he.

After a swithcheroo, he reads an equally arrogant affirmation of the false article's essential veracity. "Time Inc. still believes that the article was substantially true..." The evidence showed only "a relatively minor inaccuracy."

Again, Sharon is euphoric. "It is a long way to arrive at the truth, but it is a rewarding one. What has been proved now is that *Time* magazine lied—they lied when they printed what they printed almost two years ago. They lied. They libeled not just a blood libel against me but against the State of Israel and against the Jewish people. We showed clearly that we spoke the truth, and *Time* magazine lied."

Marvin Smilon, the *New York Post*'s correspondent covering the trial, spots Ray Cave. "Ray, do you think the jury made a mistake?"

Says he: "Of course."

Smilon also catches a glimpse of David Halevy outside the court house. He looks dazed.

□   □   □   □   □

And the wait begins once more. This time there is greater tension—a finding for Sharon may mean big bucks. But, on a strangely different level, Sharon is relieved of the greater burden. He has fundamentally won his case, proving that he was indeed the victim of a false and defamatory report. He is so satisfied, in fact, that he tells a press conference that he will return home to Israel after the jury hands in its third verdict—even if they find that *Time* is guilty of actual malice. He tells reporters that, having won his points, he must now return to guide his Ministry of Industry and Trade. He does not intend to remain in New York for the deliberations over monetary damages. And, whatever is awarded him in the case will be used to create a fund to protect Jewish rights throughout the world. He does not want to keep a single penny of it for his personal use.

On Thursday, January 24, the stir begins once more. The jury has decided. Spectators desperately swarm in, vying for whatever seats there are to be had. This is it.

Mr. Zug reads his statement. "Actual malice. To the question, 'Has plaintiff proved by clear and convincing evidence that a person or persons at Time Incorporated responsible for either reporting, writing, editing, or publishing the paragraph at issue did so with actual malice in that he, she, or they knew, at the time of publishing any statement we have found was false and defamatory, that the defamatory statement was false or had serious doubts as to its truth?' To that question, we find: The answer is no, plaintiff has not so proved by clear and convincing evidence . . ."

Mr. Zug has been given permission by Judge Sofaer to read a most extraordingary supplementary statement. "The statement that amplifies what we found: We found that certain *Time* employees, particularly correspondent David Halevy, acted negligently and carelessly in reporting and verifying the information which ultimately found its way into the published paragraph of interest in this case."

An incredible condemnation. Of Halevy. Maybe of Kelly or Smith; that is not clear. And a mighty blow against any further arrogance *Time* may manifest in this case.

What has the jury wrought! It has, in complying with the strict standards of the 1964 *New York Times v. Sullivan* precedent, withheld a technical "libel" judgement because of the awesome consideration that public figures like Ariel Sharon must prove actual malice. Yet, the jury has been moved by this case, by Sharon's pain and victimization, by *Time*'s continuted arrogance, to send a message home to both. That is the "amplification statement."

To *Time* magazine: Don't you dare walk out of this court room claiming victory and vindication. You did a shoddy, negligent, careless job, defaming a public figure with a terrible falsehood. You should be ashamed, deeply ashamed. Your article, your arrogance as an institution is a disgrace.

To Ariel Sharon: You will be traveling six thousand miles back home. You will not be returning with money or with a formal libel verdict you can frame and hang on your wall. But you won, Minister Sharon. You showed us what kind of reporter this Halevy is. Our laws may protect him, but our consciences demand that we speak out. He almost ruined you with careless and negligent reporting. His cohorts did not acquit themselves well. We cannot send you home with money, Minister Sharon. The law won't allow us that. But we have found a trick, between the lines, to give you something to bring home with you. That is why this extraordinary statement was read. We send this small gift from us back to your farm in Israel.

Please accept from us, Arik, the gift of Vindication. The Blood Libel has been cleared.

XX
The Last Word

As the news of the jury's extraordinary statement spreads throughout the world, a soft voice speaks out in Jerusalem. It is a voice heard infrequently in Israel these days. But the voice has been inspired by the case and the results to say a few words:

"Ariel Sharon has won a complete and absolute victory. This case was never one rooted in monetary considerations. There is an absolute moral victory for Minister General Ariel Sharon in this case."

The statement has been issued by Menachem Begin.

Appendices

(Note: All Appendices have been retypeset for easier readability.)

THE COMMISSION OF INQUIRY INTO THE EVENTS AT THE REFUGEE CAMPS IN BEIRUT

1983

FINAL REPORT
(AUTHORIZED TRANSLATION)

YITZHAK KAHAN
President of the Supreme Court
Commission Chairman

AHARON BARAK
Justice of the Supreme Court

YONA EFRAT
Major General (Res.)
Israel Defense Forces

INTRODUCTION

At a meeting of the Cabinet on 28 September 1982, the Government of Israel resolved to establish a commission of inquiry in accordance with the Commissions of Inquiry Law of 1968. The Cabinet charged the commission as follows:

"The matter which will be subjected to inquiry is: all the facts and factors connected with the atrocity carried out by a unit of the Lebanese Forces against the civilian population in the Shatilla and Sabra camps."

In the wake of this resolution, the President of the Supreme Colurt, by virtue of the authority vested in him under Section 4 of the aforementioned law, appointed a commission of inquiry comprised as follows:

Yitzhak Kahan, President of the Supreme Court, commission chairman; **Aharon Barak,** Justice of the Supreme Court; **Yona Efrat,** Major General (Res.).

The commission *held 60 sessions, hearing 58 witnesses.* As per the commission's requests of the Cabinet Secretary, the Office of the Minister of Defense, the General Staff of the Israel Defense Forces (henceforth, the I.D.F.), the Ministry for Foreign Affairs, and other public and governmental institutions, the commission was provided with many documents, some of which were, in the course of the deliberations, submitted to the commission as exhibits. The commission decided, in accordance with Section 13(A) of the law, that there was a need to collect data necessary for its investigation. Appointed as staff investigators were: Ms. Dorit Beinish, Deputy State Attorney, and Ms. Edna Arbel, Senior Assistant to the District Attorney (Central District), who were seconded to the commission by the Attorney General; and Assistant Police Commander Alex Ish-Shalom, who was seconded to the commission by the Inspector General of the Israel Police. Judge David Bartov was appointed commission coordinator. The staff investigators collected, by virtue of the authority vested in them under Sections 13(C), 180 statements from 163 witnesses. Before the commission began its deliberations, it visited Beirut, but it was not allowed to enter the area of the events. The commission also viewed television footage filmed near the time of the events at the camps and their surroundings.

The commission published notices to the public in the press and other media, inviting all who wish to testify or submit a document or bring any information to the commission's attention to submit to the commission in writing details of the material he possessed or wished to bring to the commission's attention. There was not much response to these appeals. The commission made an effort to collect testimony also from people who live outside the juridical boundaries of the State of Israel; and all necessary steps were taken to bring witnesses from outside of Israel, when this was possible. The commission's requests in this matter were not always honored. For example, the "New York Times" correspondent Mr. Thomas Friedman, who published in the aforementioned newspaper a famous article on what transpired during the period under deliberation here, refused to appear before the commission, claiming that this was contrary to his paper's editorial policy. We did not receive a satisfactory answer as the why the paper's publisher prevented its reporter from appearing before the commission and thus helping it uncover all the important facts.

Some of the commission's hearings were held in open session, but most of the sessions were in camera. In this matter we acted in accordance with the instructions of Section 18(A) of the law, according to which a commission of inquiry is required to deliberate in camera if it is convinced that "it is necessary to do so in the interest of protecting the security of the State . . . the foreign relations of the State . . . " and for other reasons stipulated in that section. It became clear to the commission that with regard to certain matters about which witnesses testified before it, open hearings would be liable to affect adversely the nation's security or foreign relations; and therefore it heard most of its testimony in camera. It should be noted that during sessions held in camera, witnesses also said things whose publication would not cause any harm; however, because of the difficulty in separating those things whose publication would be permissible from those whose publication would be forbidden, it was imperative in a substantial number of cases to hear the entire testimony in camera.

In accordance with Section 20(A) of the law, this report is being published together with an appendix that will be called Appendix A. In the event that we will need recourse in this report to testimony whose publication would not be damaging to the nation's security or foreign relations, we shall present it in a section of the report that will be published. On the other hand, in accordance with

Section 20(A) of the law, a *portion of this report, to be called Appendix B, will not be published, since, in our opinion, non-publication of this material is essential in the interest of protecting the nation's security or foreign relations.*

As we have said, the commission's task, as stipulated by the Cabinet's resolution, is "to investigate all the facts and factors connected with the atrocity which was carried out by a unit of the Lebanese Forces against the civilian population of the Shatilla and Sabra camps." *These acts were perpetrated between Thursday, 16 September 1982, and Saturday, 18 September 1982.* The establishment of the facts and the conclusions in this report relate only to the facts and factors connected with the acts perpetrated in the aforementioned time frame, and the commission did not deliberate or investigate matters whose connection with the aforementioned acts is indirect or remote. The commission refrained, therefore, from drawing conclusions with regard to various issues connected with activities during the war that took place in Lebanon from 6 June 1982 onward or with regard to policy decisions taken by the Government before or during the war, unless the activities or decisions were directly related to the events that are the subject of this investigation. Descriptions of facts presented in this report that deviate from the framework of the commission's authority (as defined above) have been cited only as background material, in order to better understand and illustrate the chain of events.

In one area we have found it necessary to deviate

somewhat from the stipulation of the Cabinet's resolution, which represents the commission's terms of reference. The resolution speaks of atrocities carried out by "a unit of the Lebanese Forces." The expression "Lebanese Forces" refers to an armed force known by the name "Phalangists" ot "Keta'ib" (henceforth, Phalangists). It is our opinion that we would not be properly fulfilling our task if we did not look into the question of whether the atrocities spoken of in the Cabinet's resolution were indeed perpetrated by the Phalangists, and this question will indeed be treated in the course of this report.

The commission's deliberations can be divided into two stages. In the first stage, the commission heard witnesses who had been summoned by it, as well as witnesses who had expressed the desire to appear before it. The commission asked questions of these witnesses, and they were given the opportunity of bringing before the commission everything known to them of the matters that constitute the subject of the investigation. When this stage terminated, the commission issued a resolution in accordance with Section 15(A) of the aforementioned law, concerning the harm that might be caused certain people as a result of the investigation or its results; this was done in order to enable these people to study the material, to appear before the commission and to testify (for the text of the resolution, see section 1 of appendix A). In accordance with this resolution, the chairman of the commission sent notices to nine people; the notices detailed how each one of them might be harmed. The material in the commission's possession was placed at the disposal of those receiving the notices and of the attorneys appointed to represent them. During the second stage of the deliberations, we heard witnesses who had been summoned at the request of the lawyers, and thus some of the witnesses who had testified during the first stage were cross-examined.

Afterwards, written summations were submitted, and the opportunity to supplement these summations by presenting oral arguments was given. We should already note that involving the lawyers in the commission's deliberations did not in any way make the commission's work more difficult; it even helped us in fulfilling our task. The lawyers who appeared before us were able to clarify properly, though not at excessive length, the various points that were the subject of the controversy; and thus they rendered valuable assistance to the commission's task, without in any way prejudicing their professional obligation to properly represent and defend their clients.

When we resolved to issue, in accordance with Section 15(A) of the law, notices about harm to the nine people, we were not oblivious to the fact that, during the course of the investigation, facts were uncovered that could be the prima facie basis for results that might cause harm to other persons as well. Our consideration in limiting the notices about possible harm to only nine persons was based on [the conception] that it is our duty, as a public judicial commission dealing with an extremely important issue—one which had raised a furor among the general public in Israel and other nations—to deliberate and reach findings and conclusions with regards to the major and important things connected with the aforementioned events, and to the question of the responsibility of those persons whose decisions and actions could have decisively influenced the course of events. We felt that with regard to the other people who were involved in one way or another in the events we are investigating, but whose role was secondary, it would be better that the clarification or investigation, if deemed necessary, be carried out in another manner, viz., before the military authorities, in accordance with the relevant stipulations of the military legal code and other legislation. We chose this path so that the matters under investigation would not expand and become overly-complicated and so that we could complete our task in not too long a time.

In the course of the investigation, not a few contradictions came out regarding various facts about which we had heard testimony. In those cases where the contradictions referred to facts important for establishing findings and drawing subsequent conclusions, we shall decide between the variant versions in accordance with the usual criteria in judicial and quasi-judicial tribunals. *Our procedures are not those of a criminal court; and therefore the criterion of criminal courts that stipulates that in order to convict someone his guilt must be proven beyond a reasonable doubt, does not apply in this case.* Nevertheless, since we are aware that our findings and conclusions are liable to be of significant influence from a social and ethical standpoint, and to harm also in other ways persons involved in our deliberations, no finding of significant harm was established with regard to any one of those to whom notices were sent, unless convincing evidence on which to base such a finding was found, and we shall not be satisfied with evidence that leaves room for real doubt. We shall not pretend to find a solution to all the contradictions in testimony. In many instances, these contradictions relate to the content of conversations that took place between various people without the presence of witnesses, or when the witnesses' attention was not focused on the content of the conversation, and there are no exact notes on these conversations. In such cases, it is only natural that there exist several versions with regard to what was said, and the differences between them do not necessarily derive from a desire to conceal the truth but rather are sometimes the natural result of a failure of the human memory. We do not see the need to rule about those contradictions which surround unimportant details that do not influence the decision about points in controversy.

We shall conclude this part of the report by expressing appreciation and gratitude to all those who helped us in fulfilling our task. It is only fitting that we note that all the institutions and various functionaries in the Government, the I.D.F., and other authorities whose help we needed rendered us all the necessary assistance and placed at our disposal all the relevant material, without reservation. Our special thanks go to the coordinator of the commission, Judge David Bartov, who showed great capability in handling the administrative aspects of the commission's work and without whose enterprise and devoted and efficient work it is very doubtful whether we would have succeeded in properly carrying out our task.

Our appreciation and gratitude also go to the staff investigators, Dorit Beinish, Edna Arbel and Alex Ish-Shalom, who, by virtue of their expertise, initiative and dedication, succeeded in placing at our disposal much material which served as the basis of the commission's deliberations and findings. Similarly, our thanks go to the entire staff of commission employees, whose loyalty and faithfulness enabled us to carry out and complete our task.

THE ASSASSINATION OF BASHIR JEMAYEL AND THE I.D.F.'S ENTRY INTO WEST BEIRUT

On Tuesday afternoon, 14.9.82, a large bomb exploded in a building in Ashrafiyeh, Beirut, where Bashir Jemayel was [meeting] with a group of commanders and other Phalangists. For the first few hours after the explosion, it was not clear what had happened to Bashir, and there were rumors that he had only been slightly wounded. Word of the attempt on his life reached the Prime Minister, the Defense Minister, the Chief of Staff, the director of Military Intelligence [Major General Yehoshua Saguy] and others in the early hours of the evening. *During the evening, before it became clear what had befallen Bashir, the Defense Minister spoke with the Chief of Staff, the director of Military Intelligence, the head of the Mossad, and the head of the General Security Services about possible developments.* He also spoke a number of times with the Prime Minister. Moreover, there were a number of conversations that evening between the Prime Minister and the Chief of Staff. *Word of Bashir's death reached Israel at about 11.00 P.M., and it was then that*

*the deceision was taken—in conversations between the
Prime Minister and the Minister of Defense and between
the Prime Minister and the Chief of Staff—that the I.D.F.
would enter West Beirut.* In one of the consultations between the Minister of Defense and the Chief of Staff, there
was mention of including the Phalangists in the entry into
West Beirut. The question of including the Phalangists
was not mentioned at that stage in conversations with the
Prime Minister.

Once the decision was made to have the I.D.F. enter
West Beirut, the *appropriate operational orders were
issued. Order Number 1 was issued at 12.20 A.M. on the
night between 14.9.82 and 15.9.82.* Orders Number 2 and
3 were issued on Wednesday, 15.9.82, and Order Number
4 was issued that same day at 2.00 P.M.; Order Number 5 was issued at 3.00 A.M. on 16.9.82; and Order
Number 6 was issued on the morning of 16.9.82. *The first
five orders said nothing about entering the refugee camps,
and only in Order Number 6 were the following* things
stated (clause 2, document no. 6, exhibit 4):

> **"The refugee camps are not to be entered. Searching
> and mopping up the camps will be done by the Pha-
> langist/Lebanese Army."**

Clause 7 of the same order also states that the
Lebanese Army "is entitled to enter any place in Beirut,
according to its request."

Execution of the I.D.F.'s entry into West Beirut began
during the early morning hours of 15.9.82.

On the night between 14.9.82 and 15.9.82, the Chief
of Staff flew to Beirut with a number of people and met

there with the G.O.C. Northern Command [Major General Amir Drori] and with the commander of the division (henceforth the division). Afterwards, the Chief of Staff, together with the people accompanying him, went to the Phalangists' headquarters, where, according to his testimony (p. 210), he ordered the Phalangist commanders to effect a general mobilization of all their forces, impose a general curfew on all the areas under control, and be ready to take part in the fighting. The response of the Phalangist commanders who took part in that meeting was that they needed 24 hours to organize. *The Chief of Staff requested that a Phalangist liaison officer come to the place where the division's forward command post was located* (henceforth forward command post) *under the command of Brigadier-General Amos Yaron.* At that meeting, the Phalangist commanders were told by the Chief of Staff that the I.D.F. would not enter the refugee camps in West Beirut but that the fighting this entails would be undertaken by the Phalangists (Chief of Staff's testimony, p. 211). The Chief of Staff testified that the entry of the Phalangists into the refugee camps was agreed upon between the *Minister of Defense and himself at 8.30 P.M.* on the previous evening. The camps in question were Sabra and Shatilla. After the meeting in the Phalangists' camp, the Chief of Staff went to the forward command post.

The forward command post was located on the roof of a five-story building about 200 meters southwest of the Shatilla camp. The borders of the two camps were not defined exactly. The Sabra camp extended over an area of some 300 x 200 meters and Shatilla over an area of about 500 x 500 meters (testimony of the deputy assistant to the director of Military Intelligence, p. 29). *The two camps were essentially residential neighborhoods* containing, in the area entered by the Phalangists, as will be stated below, *low permanent structures along narrow alleys and streets. From the roof of the forward command post it was possible to see the area of the camps generally* but—as all witnesses who visited the roof of the command post stated, and these were a good number of witnesses whose word we consider reliable—*it was impossible to see what was happening within the alleys in the camp from the roof of the command post,* not even with the *aid of the 20 x 120 binoculars that were on the command post roof.* Appended to this report are an aerial photograph and map of the area of the camps, as well as a general map of Beirut (sections 3, 4, and 5 of Appendix A).

It was not possible to obtain exact details on the *civilian population in the refugee camps in* Beirut. An estimate of the number of refugees in the four refugee camps in West Beirut (Burj el-Barajneh, Fakahani, Sabra, and Shatilla) *is about 85,000* people. The war led to the flight of the population, but when the fighting subsided, a movement back to the camps began. According to an inexact estimate, in mid-September 1982 there were about *56,000 people in the Sabra camp* (protocol, p. 29) but there is no assurance that this number reflects reality.

The Chief of Staff was in the forward command post from the early morning hours of Wednesday, 15.9.82. The I.D.F. began to enter West Beirut shortly after 6:00 A.M.

During the first hours of the I.D.F. entry, there was no armed resistance to the I.D.F. forces, evidently because the armed forces that were in West Beirut were taken by surprise. *Within a few hours, the I.D.F forces encountered fire from armed forces that remained in a number of places in West Beirut, and combat operations began.* The resistance caused delays in the I.D.F.'s taking over a number of points in the city and caused a change in the routine of advance. In the course of this *fighting three I.D.F. soldiers were killed and more than 100 were wounded. Heavy fire coming out of Shatilla was directed at one I.D.F. battalion* (henceforth the battalion) advancing east of Shatilla. *One of the battalion's soldiers was killed, 20 were injured, and the advance of the battalion in this direction was halted.* Throughout Wednesday and to a lesser degree on Thursday and Friday (16-17.9.82). *R.P.G. and light-weapons fire from the Sabra and Shatilla camps was directed at the forward command post and the battalion's forces nearby, and fire was returned by the I.D.F. forces.*

On Wednesday, 15.9.82, the *Minister of Defense arrived at the forward command post between 8:00 and 9:00 A.M.* He met with the chief of Staff there, and the latter reported on what had been agreed upon with the Phalangists, namely, a general mobilization, curfew, and the entry of the Phalangists into the camps. The Minister of Defense approved this agreement. From the roof of the command post, the *Minister of Defense phoned the Prime Minister and informed him that there was no resistance in Beirut* and that all the operations were going well.

During the aforementioned meeting between the Minister of Defense and the Chief of Staff, present on the roof of the forward command post were the Defense Minister's aide, Mr. Avi Duda'i; the director of Military Intelligence, who came to this meeting together with the Minister of Defense; representative A of the Mossad (his full name appears in the list of names, section 1, Appendix B); Major-General Drori; Brigadier-General Yaron; Intelligence officer B; the head of the General Security Services; Deputy Chief of Staff Major-General Moshe Levi; and other I.D.F. officers who were accompanying the Minister of Defense. Duda'i recorded in his notebook what was said and agreed upon at that meeting. According to Dudai's testimony, he later copied these notes into another notebook, pages of which were presented before us (exhibit 103). These notes started, inter alia, that the Phalangists were to be sent into the camps. The *Minister of Defense spoke with the Prime Minister twice from the roof of the command post.* According to the record of these conversations (exhibits 100 and 101), in one of them the wording of the I.D.F. Spokesman's announcement was agreed upon as follows:

"Following the murder of President-elect Bashir Jemayel, I.D.F. forces entered West Beirut tonight to prevent possible grave occurences and to ensure quiet.

"The entry of the I.D.F. forces was executed without resistance."

From the forward command post the Minister of Defense went to the Phalangist headquarters. A record was made of this meeting, which was attended by a number of Phalangists commanders as well as the Minister of Defense, the director of Military Intelligence, the head of the General Security Services and representatives of the Mossad (exhibit 79). At that meeting, the Minister of Defense stated, inter alia, that the I.D.F. would take over focal points and junctions in West Beirut, but that the Phalangist army would also have to enter West Beirut after the I.D.F. and that the Phalangist commanders should maintain contact with Major-General Drori, G.O.C. Northern Command, regarding the modes of operation. A record of this meeting was made by Intelligence officer B (exhibit 28). *From there the Minister of Defense went to Bikfaya, to the Jemayel family home, to pay a condolence call.*

From the meeting with the Jemayel family in Bikfaya, the Minister of Defence went to the airport, and *on the way he met with Major-General Drori at a gas station.* This meeting took place in the presence of a number of people, including the director of Military Intelligence, the head of the General Security Services, Mr. Duda'i, and the bureau chief of the director of Military Intelligence, Lieutenant-Colonel Hevroni. The *situation of the forces was discussed at this meeting, and Major-General Drori reported on the course of events during the I.D.F.'s entry into* West Beirut. From there the *Minister of Defense went on to the airport and met there with the Chief of Staff and the Deputy Chief of Staff at about 2:00 P.M.,* after which the Minister of Defense returned to Israel.

That same day, 15.9.82, while the Minister of Defense was in Beirut, a *meeting took place at 11:30 A.M. in the*

Prime Minister's Office between the Prime Minister and others from the American embassy in Israel. During that meeting (protocol of the meeting, exhibit 120), the Prime Minister informed Mr. Draper that I.D.F. forces had entered West Beirut beginning in the morning hours, that there were no real clashes, that the I.D.F. action was undertaken in order to prevent certain possible events, and that we were concerned that there might be bloodshed even during the night. *The Prime Minister also said that the Phalangists were behaving properly; their commander had not been injured in the assassination and was in control of his forces; he is a good man and we trust him not to cause any clashes,* but there is no assurance regarding other forces. He added that the primary immediate task was to preserve quiet, for as long as quiet is maintained it will be possible to talk; otherwise there might have been pogroms, and the calm was preserved for the time being (exhibit 120).

At 4:00 P.M. on Wednesday, 15.9.82, a briefing took place at the office of the Deputy Chief of Staff with the participation of the I.D.F. branch heads, including the assistant for research to the director of Military Intelligence. The meeting began with a review by the assistant for research to the director of Military Intelligence of possible political developments in Lebanon following the death of Bashir Jemayel. He stated, inter alia (page 4 of the transcript of the discussion, exhibit 130), *that the I.D.F.'s entry into West Beirut was perceived as vital not only by the Christians but also by the Muslims, who regarded the I.D.F. as the only factor that could prevent bloodshed in the area and protect the Sunni Muslims from the Phalangists.* The Intelligence officer also stated that according to what was known to Military Intelligence, the attack on Bashir was carried out by the Mourabitoun, though that was not certain. During the meeting, the head of Operations Department announced that the Phalangists "are encouraging entry into the camps" (p. 7 of exhibit 130). *The Deputy Chief of Staff reported his impressions of the meeting at Phalangist headquarters in Beirut that day and said that the intention was to send the Phalangists into the refugee camps and afterwards perhaps into the city as well.* He added that this "might create an uproar," because the armed forces in West Beirut that were then quiet might stir up a commotion upon learning that Phalangists are coming in behind the I.D.F. (page 11, exhibit 130).

At 6:00 P.M. the Minister of Defense spoke with the Prime Minister from his home and reported (exhibit 99) that by evening the I.D.F. would be in all the places; that he had conveyed the Prime Minister's words to Pierre Jemayel; and that "everything is in order" and the decision made on the previous night to send the I.D.F. into Bierut had been most important and [indeed] should not have been delayed.

The Chief of Staff remained at the forward command post in Beirut and followed the development of the I.D.F. actions from there. On that day the Phalangist officers did not arrive at the forward command post to coordinate operations, but Major-General Drori met with them in the evening and told them generally that their entry into the camps would be from the direction of Shatilla. *Major-General Drori, who was not at ease with the plan to send the Phalangists into the camps, made an effort to persuade the commanders of the Lebanese Army that their forces should enter the camps and that they should prevail upon the Prime Minister of Lebanon to agree to this move. The reply of the Lebanese Army at the time was negative.*

In the early morning hours of Thursday, 16.9.82, the Chief of Staff left the forward command post and returned to Tel Aviv. That same morning, in the wake of political pressure, *an order was issued by the Minister of Defense to half the I.D.F.'s combat operations; but after a short time the Minister of Defense rescinded the order.* At 10:00 A.M. the Minister of Defense held a consultation in his office with the Chief of Staff; the director of Military Intelligence, Brigadier-General Y. Saguy; Lieutenant-Colonel Zecharin, the Chief of Staff's burearu chief; and Mr. Duda'i (exhibit 27 is a record of what was said at that meeting). *The meeting was opened by the Chief of Staff who announced that "the whole city is in our hands, complete quiet prevails now, the camps are closed and surrounded; the Phalangists are to go in at 11:00-12:00.* Yesterday we spoke to them. . . The situation now is that the entire city is in our hands, the camps are all closed." Later on in his statement, while pointing to a map, the Chief of Staff stated that the areas marked on the map were in the hands of the I.D.F. *and that the Fakahani, Sabra, and Shatilla camps were surrounded.* He also said that if the Phalangists came to a coordinating session and wanted to go in, it was agreed with them that they would go in and that the Lebanese Army could also enter the city wherever it chose. At this discussion, *the Minister of Defense spoke of the heavy American pressure to have the I.D.F. leave West Beirut* and of the political pressure from other sources. In the course of the meeting, the Chief of Staff repeated a number of times that at that moment everything was quiet in West Beirut. *As for going into the camps, the Minister of Defense stated that he would send the Phalangists into the refugee camps (p.5, exhibit 27).* At the time of the consultation, the Minister of Defense informed the Prime Minister by phone that "the fighting has ended. The refugee camps are surrounded. The firing has stopped. We have not suffered any more casualties. Everything is calm and quiet. Sitting opposite me is the Chief of Staff, who has just come from there. All the key points are in our hands. Everything's over. I am bringing the Chief of Staff to the Cabinet meeting. That's the situation as of now . . ." After this conversation, the Chief of Staff reported on the contacts during the night 14.9.82 with the members of the Mourabitoun, in which the members of this militia said that they were unable to hide, that they were Lebanese, and that they would undoubtedly all be killed by the Phalangists, whether immediately or some time later. The Chief of Staff added that "there's such a dual kind of situation that they're confused. They're seething with a feeling of revenge, and there might have been rivers of blood there. We won't go into the refugee camps" (p.7, exhibit 27). As stated, participating in this consultation was the director of Military Intelligence, who in the course of the discussion stated a number of things that appear in the aforementioned record.

The commanders of the Phalangists arrived for their first coordinating session regarding the entry of their forces into the camps at about 11:00 A.M. on Thursday, 16.9.82 and met with Major-General Drori at the headquarters of one of the divisions. It was agreed at that meeting that they would *enter the camps and coordinate this action with Brigadier-General Yaron, commander of the division.* This coordination between Brigadier-General Yaron and the Phalangist commanders *would take place on Thursday afternoon at the forward command post.* It was likewise agreed at that meeting that a company of *150 fighters from the Phalangist force would enter the camps and that they would do so from south to north and from west to east. Brigadier-General Yaron spoke with the Phalangists about the places where the terrorists were located in the camps and also warned them not to harm the civilian population.* He had mentioned that, he stated, because he knew that the Phalangists' norms of conduct are not like those of the I.D.F. and he had had arguments with the Phalangists over this issue in the past. Brigadier-General Yaron set up lookout posts on the roof of the forward command post and on a nearby roof even though he knew that it was impossible to see very much of what was going on in the camps from these lookouts. An order was also issued regarding an additional precautionary measure whose purpose was to ascertain the actions of the Phalangist forces during their operation in the camps (this measure is cited in section 5, Appendix B). It was also agreed that a Phalangist liaison officer with a communications set would be present at all times on the roof of the forward command post—in addition to the Mossad liaison officer at the Phalangist headquarters. The *Phalangist unit that was supposed to enter the camps was an intelligence unit headed, as we have said, by Elie Hobeika. Hobeika did not go into the camps with his unit and was on the roof of the forward command post during the night* (testimony of Brigadier-General Yaron, p.726). This unit was assigned the task of entering the camps at that time for two reasons, first—since the . . . Phalangists had difficulty recruiting another appropriate force till then; second— *since the members of this unit were considered specially trained in discovering terrorists who tried to hide among the civilian population.*

On 16.9.82 a document was issued by the Defense Minister's office, signed by the personal aide to the Defense Minister, Mr. Avi Duda'i, which contained *"The Defense Minister's Summary of 15 September 1982." This document is (exhibit 34) a summary of the things which Mr. Duda'i had recorded during his visit with the Defense Minister in Beirut on 15.9.83*, as detailed above. In various paragraphs of the document there is mention of the Defense Minister's instructions regarding the entry into West Beirut. The instruction in paragraph F. is important to the matter at hand; it is stated there:

"F. Only one element, and that is The I.D.F., shall command the forces in the area. *For the operation in the camps the Phalangists should be sent in"*

The document is directed to the Chief of Staff, the Deputy Chief of Staff and the director of Military Intelligence. The Document was received at the office of the director of Military Intelligence, according to the stamp appearing on the copy (exhibit 35), on 17.9.82.

In the testimonies we have heard, different interpretations were given to the instruction that only the I.D.F. command the forces in the area. According to one interpretation, and this is the interpretation given the document by the Chief of Staff (p.257), the meaning if the instruction is that in contacts with external elements, and especially with the Phalangists only the I.D.F., and not another Israeli element, such as the Mossad, will command the forces in the area—but this does not mean that the Phalangist force will be under the command of the I.D.F. On the other hand, according to the interpretation given the document by the director of Military Intelligence (pp. 127, 1523), the meaning is that all forces operating in the area, including the Phalangists, will be under the authority of the I.D.F. and will act according to its instructions.

The entry of the Phalangists into the camps began at about 18:00 on Thursday, 16.9.82. At that time there were armed terrorist forces in the camps. We cannot establish the extent of these forces, but they possessed various types of arms, which they used—even before the entry of the Phalangists—against I.D.F. forces that had approached the area, as well as against the I.D.F. headquarters at the forward command post. It is possible to determine that *this armed terrorist force had not been evacuated during the general evacuation, but had stayed in the camps for two purposes, which were — renewal of underground terrorist activity at a later period,* and to protect the civilian population which had remained in the camps, keeping in mind that given the hostility prevailing between the various sects and organizations, a population without armed protection was in danger of massacre. It should be added here that during the negotiations for evacuation, a guarantee for the safety of the Muslims in West Beirut was given by the representative of the United States who conducted the negotiations, following assurances received from the government of Israel and from Lebanon.

Meanwhile, as we have said, the multi-national force left Lebanon, and all the previous plans regarding the control of West Beirut by the Lebanese government were disrupted due to the assassination of President-elect Bashir Gemayel.

The Begin Health Story
(*Time*, September 24, 1979)

Fears for Begin's Health

At his Haifa summit meeting with Menachem Begin, Anwar Sadat took aside his close friend Israeli Defense Minister Ezer Weizman and asked him to "look after Begin." The Israeli Premier's health is indeed precarious: now 66, he has survived a heart attack, and is still recovering from a mild stroke he suffered last July. Worries over Begin's well-being could be an important factor in Sadat's determination to move forward on the peace agreement with Israel as soon as possible. His health is also a matter of increasing concern to Israelis, who wonder how long the ailing Premier can remain in office.

Shortly before the Haifa summit, *Time* Correspondent David Halevy learned last week, Begin took a day off from his governmental duties. He was driven to a secluded laboratory, where three non-Israeli neurological experts examined him. One of the specialists was Dr. Jack Fein, a prominent brain surgeon at the Albert Einstein College of Medicine in New York City.

After the examination, the doctors recommended that Begin restrict himself to a three-hour workday and try to rest as much as possible. They apparently feared that the medication that Begin takes for his heart condition has affected his body's ability to recover from the stroke. "I am concerned about Mr. Begin's health," said Dr. Fein, "but I admire his courage." Begin is now forced to spend far fewer hours in his office than any previous Israeli Premier. For Golda Meir and Yitzhak Rabin, 18-hour days were normal. By contrast, Begin usually arrives at 8:30 in the morning and leaves between 11:30 and noon. He often returns in late afternoon for another hour or so, but since his stroke he has done this less frequently. Aides say that he works at home, but Begin has seldom seen any Israeli official, politician or even family friends at his Jerusalem house since the stroke.

Begin seems less and less in control of his fractious ministers. At the Cabinet meeting that led to the bitter exchange between Yadin and Sharon, the Premier admitted that he had not read the minutes of the committee report on the settlements, despite the fact that they had been sent to his home. Even one of Begin's protective aides admits deep concern. "It seems that his physical condition is deteriorating quickly. I do not know when, but he will have to quit the premiership. It might happen tomorrow, next week—or next year."

Appendix C
Memo From Duncan To Top Brass
Regarding Halevy's Reporting
(September 26, 1979)

Personal and Confidential

TO: Henry Grunwald
        Ralph Graves
        Ray Cave

FROM: Dick Duncan   September 26, 1979

Here is a review of where we stand as of Wednesday, October 26th on the Begin health story.

Dean Fischer has given me a lengthy memo by packet recounting his experiences in rechecking the story. I have talked with David Halevy, and he will be filing what he promises to be dramatic confirmation of the story late Thursday or early Friday. It will be distributed to you. We will need to evaluate this account in the light of David's personal and professional position. On the other hand, we must recognize the difficulty of getting anyone on the record in Israel on a story which is so obviously to the detriment of this government. David will also be coming back here to talk to me. He will be arriving this weekend.

At this moment, on the basis of the information given to me by Fischer and of my talks with Halevy, I believe our story is wrong. Inescapably, that conclusion then requires a further decision as to whether Halevy was either (a) inexcusably shoddy in his reporting or (b) intentionally misled us, or (c) was the victim of an incredibly well orchestrated disinformation plot.

Dudu has told Fischer that his original source for the story was "A." He also said he had discussed it with "B."

He also says he had confirmed the story with "C." In confirming the story, he says he talked to Dr. Jack Fein in New York and "D."

Both Halevy and Fischer agreed that Fischer supervised Halevy closely during the reporting, questioning Halevy as to his sources and what they said.

Stunned by Begin's early morning phone call denying the story and by reports that Dr. Fein (who was quoted in the story) also denied that the meeting had taken place, Fischer began to make some phone calls.

He called "C" who said the story was "fantastic".

He called Begin's two doctors, who denied any knowledge of the meeting and denied knowing Dr. Fein.

He called "D" who denied any knowledge of the meeting and said that his wife, not he, answered the phone when Dudu called.

He called Dr. Fein, who said "he never asked me specifically if I was in attendance". Fein denied having any knowledge of the examination.

He telephoned "A" who denied any knowledge that the meeting had taken place and that he was Dudu's source. He did not call "B" who figures only as a tipster and a close friend of Halevy's.

Denials from "C" and "A" are, I think, routine given the fact of Begin's vehement denial. Begin's personal protest is not routine, and I consider that it essentially discredits the story. "D" 's denial is very disturbing because he does not appear to be someone who would come under quick pressure from the government. Somewhat the same evaluation applies to Fein.

I have asked Strobe for his sources' evaluation of our report. The best intelligence neither confirms or discredits it at this point.

In my judgment, the balance of the evidence is that our story is wrong. I have sent Ray a suggested admission to this effect which would follow "C" 's letter in the magazine.

I also think that Dean Fischer has reacted well in this situation. He methodically went back to the sources and spotted the problem. In his dealings with "C" he overspoke when he suggested we might make an "apology", but I'm afraid that is the kind of communication error which can happen under pressure.

Halevy's case rests on establishing that there is indeed, as he says, a huge "cover up". It is possible, but I'm afraid that he must prove that case, and prove it with much better evidence than he has for the original story.

RLD

Begin's Health

Your report "Fears for Begin's Health" (Sept. 24) is regrettable for the serious misinformation it contains. On the basis of the most authoritative examination of the real facts, I am able to inform your readers that contrary to your correspondent's assertions, the Prime Minister did not take a day off from his governmental duties shortly before the Haifa summit with President Sadat; he was not driven to a "secluded laboratory" or to any other location for a physical checkup, and he has never met with a team of "three non-Israeli neurological experts." He could, therefore, never have been examined by them. In particular, the Prime Minister never met with a Dr. Jack Fein. Hence, no such team could have given any medical advice to the Prime Minister.

Following the Prime Minister's release from the Hadassah Medical Center, and after a brief rest period at his home, he resumed his regular daily duties, with the full approval of the two physicians who treated him, Professor Marvin Gottesman and Professor Sylvan Lavie. The story in your report, that the Prime Minister has to put in a shorter working day, or is working less hours, is incorrect.

307

Given the totally unfounded nature of your report, it is proper that your readers be informed of the above facts.

Dan Pattir
Counselor to the Prime Minister of Israel
Jerusalem

TIME *has rechecked all aspects of its story, which was based on what it believed was firsthand knowledge of a meeting between Prime Minister Begin and three consulting neurologists.* TIME *was apparently misled as to the meeting and regrets the error.* TIME *stands by its report that for a period of weeks following his stroke on July 19 the Prime Minister's work load was significantly reduced.*

Appendix E
Letter from Duncan to Halevy
(February 13, 1980)

Dear David:

This is the letter I promised you confirming our conversation in Athens. I must tell you that I did not come away from our conversation feeling satisfied that I really knew the full story on a number of the points we discussed. But I did feel that there was sufficient reason to say just that to you, and then drop the subject completely, because we are going ahead on a different footing now. I want to make this work, and I feel you do too.

The gist of our agreement, as I understand it, was that I felt your work recently to be unsatisfactory and, that without necessarily agreeing with me on all points, you accepted conditions necessary to correct that situation.

The conditions, for the period of one year in which you will be on this probationary status, are as follows:

1. The fullest possible sourcing on all reports, which includes the name if possible, but if not, then the closest kind of characterization of the nationality and affiliation of the source. When it is not possible to put this kind of information on the wire, it must at least be available to the bureau chief or to me in some manner.

2. Multiple sourcing when at all possible.

3. A consistent effort on your part to report, and also to suggest, the "meat and potatoes" everyday (or every week) stories from the bureau, not just specials and exclusives.

4.   A more obvious effort on your part to insure that what you report to TIME (and to the Star) is printable, reliable information, reflecting not just informed speculation, but the <u>most likely true situation</u>. As part of this, I would like to see on your part more effort to evaluate the reliability of various sources, and the likelihood that they in fact <u>know</u> what they are saying.

On our part, I realize that we must continue to understand the special nature of some of your source relationships and the information you get from them. You spoke to Dean and me about needing better guidance on the use of attribution and sourcing on your files, and you have a right to expect that Dean will give it to you. And so will I.

Dudu, I want very badly to get you and the magazine back on the highly productive relationship we have enjoyed in the past. For various reasons, that relationship seems to be suffering. The points I have made in this letter are designed to help things work again. I realize they may cramp your style some, and where they are unreasonable you can certainly ask for relief. But what I want to do is get you, and your best reporting, back into print, in sizable and important stories. I hope you agree with me that it will work this way. I believe it will.

Best,

Dick Duncan

cc: Dean Fischer
    Jerusalem Bureau Chief

    Mr. David Halevy
    Jerusalem
    RD/kkm

Appendix F

Halevy's World-Wide Memorandum
(December 6, 1983)

JERU/1/LON   6 DECEMBER 1982
TO: LONDON BUREAU   FOR: WORLD MEMO
FROM: JERUSALEM   BY: HALEVY
SLUG: WORLDWIDE MEMO

(HALEVY—JERUSALEM)   THE MOST CRUCIAL FINDINGS OF THE
STATE INQUIRY COMMISSION INVESTIGATING THE SABRA AND
SHATILA MASSACRE, MIGHT TURN OUT TO BE THE NEWLY
DISCOVERED NOTES WHICH WERE TAKEN DURING A
CONVERSATION BETWEEN ISRAEL'S DEFENSE MINISTER ARIK
SHARON AND LEADERS OF THE GEMAYEL CLAN. SHARON CAME TO
THE GEMAYELS' HOME VILLAGE, BIKFAYA, THE MORNING AFTER
BASHIR GEMAYEL WAS ASSASSINATED. HE CAME ACTUALLY TO
CONVEY HIS AND THE BEGIN GOVERNMENT'S CONDOLENCES. WHEN
SHARON LANDED AT BIKFAYA HE HAD WITH HIM ONLY ONE SENIOR
ISRAELI INTELLIGENCE OFFICER, WHO WENT WITH SHARON TO
THE MEETING AND TOOK NOTES DURING THE PRIVATE SESSION.
    ACCORDING TO A HIGHLY RELIABLE SOURCE WHO TOLD US
ABOUT THAT MEETING, PRESENT WERE NOT ONLY PIERRE AND
AMIN GEMAYEL BUT ALSO FADI FREM, THE PHALANGE CHIEF OF
STAFF WHO IS MARRIED TO BASHIR'S SISTER. SHARON INDICATED
IN ADVANCE TO THE GEMAYELS THAT THE ISRAELI ARMY WAS
MOVING INTO WEST BEIRUT AND THAT HE EXPECTED THEM, THE
FORCE LEBANESE, TO GO INTO ALL THE PALESTINIAN REFUGEE
CAMPS. ALSO GAVE THEM THE FEELING AFTER THE GEMAYELS'
QUESTIONING, THAT HE UNDERSTOOD THEIR NEED TO TAKE
REVENGE FOR THE ASSASSINATION OF BASHIR AND ASSURED
THEM THAT THE ISRAELI ARMY WOULD NEITHER HINDER THEM,
NOR TRY TO STOP THEM.

    THESE MINUTES WILL NOT BE PUBLISHED AT ALL, IN ANY
FORM WHATSOEVER, AS THEY INDICATE A DIRECT INVOLVEMENT
AND ADVANCED PLANNING BY THE GEMAYEL FAMILY, INCLUDING
LEBANON'S PRESIDENT, AMIN GEMAYEL.

Appendix G

Doyle Requests Clearance
(December 8, 1982)


```
           DEC 8 82
TO: JERUSALEM FOR: HALEVY
FROM: TIME WORLD     BY: DOYLE
SLUG: WEEK'S EVENTS    CLOSE: 12/10    ECH:
    REQUESTING CLEARANCE FOR YOUR ITEM GREEN LIGHT IN
THIS WEEK'S WORLD MEMO.
PAT/215P
```

Appendix H

Halevy Clears Memorandum

(December 9, 1982)

9 DEC 82
TO: TIME WORLD   FOR: DOYLE
FROM: JERUSALEM   BY: HALEVY
SLUG: WEEK'S EVENTS   CLOSE: 12/10   ECH:

WORLD MEMO ITEM: "GREEN LIGHT" CLEARED.

Kelly's "Take 9"

(February 10, 1983)

STM: JERU/12/NYK   10 FEB 83   MSG: FIL
TO: TIME WORLD
FROM: JERUSALEM   BY: KELLY
SLUG: MIDEAST EVENTS
        (COMMISSION)   CLOSE: 2/11   TK: 9 EOH:

PART OF THE REPORT, WHICH IS CALLED APPENDIX B, WAS NOT PUBLISHED, "SINCE IN OUR OPINION," THE COMMISSION SAID NON-PUBLICATION OF THIS MATERIAL IS ESSENTIAL IN THE INTEREST OF PROTECTING THE NATION'S SECURITY OR FOREIGN RELATIONS."

SOME OF THAT PUBLISHED REPORT SIMPLY GIVES THE NAMES OF AGENTS IDENTIFIED ONLY BY SINGLE LETTERS IN THE PUBLISHED REPORT AND SECRET TESTIMONY. AND SOME OF IT, WE UNDERSTAND, WAS PUBLISHED IN TIME'S WORLD WIDE MEMO, AN ITEM BY HALEVY, DEC. 6, FOR WHICH WE GAVE CLEARANCE, DEALING WITH SHARON'S VISIT TO THE GEMAYEL FAMILY TO PAY CONDOLENCES. CERTAINLY IN READING THE REPORT, THERE IS A FEELING THAT AT LEAST PART OF THE COMMISSION'S CASE AGAINST SHARON IS BETWEEN THE LINES, PRESUMABLY IN THE SECRET PORTION.

IT IS CLEAR THAT THE COMMISSION MEMBERS BELIEVED THAT THERE WERE SO MANY RED FLAGS FLYING THAT PRACTICALLY ANYONE SHOULD HAVE KNOWN WHAT WOULD HAPPEN IF THE PHALANGISTS WERE ALLOWED IN THE REFUGEE CAMPS. THE REPORT MENTIONS THAT HIDDEN IN APPENDIX B IS TESTIMONY BY AN INTELLIGENCE OFFICER ON "THE LIQUIDATION OF PALESTINIANS CARRIED OUT BY THE INTELLIGENCE UNIT OF ELIE HOBEIKA," WHICH IT TURNS OUT WAS THE SAME UNIT OF THE PHALANGISTS TURNED LOOSE IN SHATILLA AND SABRA CAMPS. HOBEIKA WAS THE PERSON WHO WAS RESPONSIBLE FOR THE ASSASSINATED GEMAYEL'S SECURITY. SO WHY SHOULD ANYONE BE SURPRISED AT WHAT HAPPENED?

THE MOSSAD APPARENTLY WAS: THE REPORT DOES NOTHING TO ENHANCE THE REPUTATION OF ISRAEL'S CIA.

WHEN THE WAR BROKE OUT IN JUNE 1982, THE COMMISSION NOTED, "THE PREVAILING OPINION AMONG MOSSAD AGENTS WHO

HAD MAINTAINED CONTACTS WITH THE PHALANGIST LEADERSHIP WAS THAT THE ATROCITIES AND MASSACRES WERE A THING OF THE PAST, AND THAT THE PHALANGIST FORCES HAD REACHED A STAGE OF POLITICAL AND ORGANIZATIONAL MATURITY THAT WOULD ENSURE THAT SUCH ACTIONS WOULD NOT REPEAT THEMSELVES."

THE COMMISSION NOTED "THERE WERE CERTAIN FACTS THAT WERE NOT COMPATIBLE WITH THIS OUTLOOK." FOR EXAMPLE, AT MEETINGS MOSSAD OFFICIALS HAD WITH BASHIR BEMAYEL, [SIC] THE REPORT SAID, "THEY HEARD THINGS FROM HIM THAT LEFT NO ROOM FOR DOUBT THAT THE INTENTION OF THIS PHALANGIST LEADER WAS TO ELIMINATE THE PALESTINIAN PROBLEM IN LEBANON WHEN HE CAME TO POWER—EVEN IF THAT MEANT RESORTING TO ABERRANT METHODS AGAINST THE PALESTINIANS WHEN HE CAME TO POWER. SIMILAR REMARKS WERE HEARD FROM OTHER PHALANGIST LEADERS."

THE COMMISSION'S INVESTIGATION CONCLUDED THAT NO ISRAELI SOLDIERS WERE INSIDE THE CAMP AT THE TIME OF THE MASSACRES. IT ALSO FOUND THAT MAJ. HADDAD'S FORCES, THE LEBANESE MILITIA LINKED TO THE IDF, WERE NOT INVOLVED DESPITE SUSPICIONS AT THE TIME THAT THEY WERE.

THE COMMISSION ALSO DEALT WITH OBJECTIONS TO ITS INQUIRY, THAT IF IT WERE FOUND THAT ISRAEL HAD NO DIRECT RESPONSIBILITY FOR THE MASSACRE—' THAT THE BLOOD OF THOSE KILLED WAS NOT SHED BY IDF SOLDIERS AND IDF FORCES, OR THAT OTHERS OPERATING AT THE BEHEST OF THE STATE WERE NOT PARTIES TO THE ATROCITIES'—THEN THERE WAS NO REASON TO PROBE THE PROBLEM OF DIRECT RESPONSIBILITY.

THE COMMISSION REFERRED INDIRECTLY TO BEGIN'S SARCASTIC PHRASE "GOYIM KILL GOYIM, AND THEY COME TO HANG THE JEWS"—IN NOTING THAT IT COULDN'T ACCEPT THE ARGUMENT THAT NO RESPONSIBILITY SHOULD BE LAID ON ISRAEL "FOR DEEDS PERPETRATED OUTSIDE OF ITS BORDERS BY MEMBERS OF THE CHRISTIAN COMMUNITY AGAINST PALESTINIANS."

"WHEN WE ARE DEALING WITH THE ISSUE OF INDIRECT RESPONSIBILITY," LECTURED THE COMMISSION, "IT SHOULD ALSO NOT BE FORGOTTEN THAT THE JEWS IN VARIOUS LANDS OF EXILE, AND ALSO IN THE LANDS OF ISRAEL WHEN IT WAS UNDER FOREIGN RULE, SUFFERED GREATLY FROM POGRAMS PERPETRATED BY VARIOUS HOOLIGANS: AND THE DANGER OF

DISTURBANCES AGAINST JEWS IN VARIOUS LANDS, IT SEEMS
EVIDENT, HAS NOT YET PASSED. THE JEWISH PUBLIC'S STAND HAS
ALWAYS BEEN THAT THE RESPONSIBILITY FOR SUCH DEEDS FALLS
NOT ONLY ON THOSE WHO RIOTED AND COMMITTED THE
ATROCITIES, BUT ALSO ON THOSE WHO WERE RESPONSIBLE FOR
SAFETY AND PUBLIC ORDER, WHO COULD HAVE PREVENTED THE
DISTURBANCES AND DID NOT RPT NOT FULFILL THEIR
OBLIGATIONS IN THIS RESPECT."

ONE NOTE. IT WOULD SEEM THAT THE ONLY EXPLANATION FOR
THE REACTION OF OFFICERS LIKE YARON AND CERTAINLY THE
TANK BATTALION COMMANDER WHO APPARENTLY FAILED TO PASS
ON HIS SUBORDINATES' WARNINGS OF CIVILIAN KILLINGS WAS
THEY UNDERSTOOD THE SIGNALS FROM THE TOP WERE TO STAND
CLEAR AND SHUT UP, RATHER THAN AS YARON STATED,
INSENSITIVITY.

Appendix J
The Disputed Paragraph
(*Time,* February 21, 1983)

Time has learned that it [Appendix B] also contains further details about Sharon's visit to the Gemayel family on the day after Bashir Gemayel's assassination. Sharon reportedly told the Gemayels that the Israeli army would be moving into West Beirut and that he expected the Christian forces to go into the Palestinian refugee camps. Sharon also reportedly discussed with the Gemayels the need for the Phalangists to take revenge for the assassination of Bashir, but the details of the conversation are not known.

Appendix K

The Jerusalem "Playback"
(February 12, 1983)

STM: JERU/3/NYK   12 FEB 83   MSG: CAC
TO: TIME WORLD
FROM: JERUSALEM   BY: KELLY/HALEVY/SLATER
SLUG: MIDEAST EVENTS   CLOSE: 2/11   EOH:

STORY READS VERY GOOD. A FINE JOB, IN OUR VIEW. FEW
POINTS ONLY:

PARA 2, LINE 5: CAN WE CHANGE THAT TO "WHEN ISRAELIS
ALLOWED" WE PREFER THIS, BECAUSE IT'S ONLY PARTLY TRUE
THAT COMMANDERS ALLOWED THE PHALANGISTS INTO THE
CAMPS. POLITICIANS WERE INVOLVED TOO.

SAME PARA, LINE 13: "STINGING INDICTMENT": PLEASE
DELETE PHRASE "AND SEVERAL OTHER CIVILIAN". THE STINGING
INDICTMENT SHOULD ONLY REFER TO SHARON AND THE MILITARY.
THE OTHER CIVILIANS NAMED—BEGIN, SHAMIR, AND THE MOSSAD
CHIEF—WERE CRITICIZED BUT NOT THAT HARSHLY (DEFINITELY
NOT "INDICTED IN STINGING TERMS").

SAME PARA, LAST LINE: LET'S MAKE THAT "FOUR TOP
MILITARY COMMANDERS" FULL STOP (DELETE THE WORD "THE"
BEFORE THE PHRASE "FOUR TOP MILITARY COMMANDERS" AND
DELETE THE PHRASE "WHO WERE INVOLVED IN THE INVASION OF
LEBANON.") COMMISSION REPORT SPOKE ONLY OF THEIR
INVOLVEMENT IN WEST BEIRUT. FURTHERMORE, SAGUY WAS NOT
STRICTLY A COMMANDER IN THE SENSE OF BEING A COMBAT
OFFICER.

PARA 6: SORRY, WE MUST NOT HAVE MADE OURSELVES CLEAR.
SECTION BEGINNING "IN A KNESSET DEBATE" TO "BY AN ANGRY
CROWD" HAD BEEN IN REFERENCE TO THE TONE OF ISRAELI
POLITICS IN AN EARLIER WEEK IN THE DISPUTE OVER THE
LEBANESE INVASION. IN THE CONTEXT

PAGE 2   JERU/3/NYK   12 FEB 83
OF THE PARAGRAPH, IT REALLY OUGHT TO BE DELETED. PERHAPS,
IT COULD BE REPLACED WITH PRO-SHARON PROTESTORS YELLING
"PLO AGENTS" AND "TRAITORS" TO THE PEACE NOW ANTI-

GOVERNMENT DEMONSTRATORS WHO IN TURN WERE SHOUTING "MURDERER" AT SHARON.

IF YOU WANT TO HIGHLIGHT THE ISRAELI SHOCK AT THE HAND GRENADE INCIDENT, YOU COULD MENTION THAT THIS WAS THE FIRST TIME THAT AN ISRAELI WAS KILLED IN VIOLENCE IN THE INTERNAL POLITICAL DEBATE.

PARA 7: LET'S MAKE THAT QUOTE CONSISTENT WITH OUR LAST REFERENCE IN THE JANUARY 3RD EDITION: "GOYIM KILL GOYIM, AND THEY COME TO HANG THE JEWS".

PARA 11: HOBEIKA CAN BE DESCRIBED AS "LATE 20S, WHOSE INTELLIGENCE UNIT HAD BEEN BLAMED FOR A PREVIOUS MASSACRE AGAINST PALESTINIANS. (IF YOU WANT MORE ON HIM, SEE TIME EDITION OCTOBER 4, PAGE 9).

SAME PARA: "MURDEROUS HARASSMENT": THIS MAY BE A QUIBBLE ON THE WORD "MURDEROUS" BUT THE PHALANGISTS MENACED BUT DID NOT KILL THE DOCTORS AND NURSES IN THE GAZA HOSPITAL INCIDENT.

SAME PARA: BEGIN TUNED IN THE BBC ON SATURDAY IN LATE AFTERNOON.
(SEPTEMBER 18).
                    ⸺.3 0—4—:
SAME PARA: YARON WAS NOT RPT NOT IN CHARGE OF THE OPERATION. RATHER, HE WAS THE COMMANDER IN CHARGE OF ISRAELI TROOPS IN THE AREA.

PARA 13: SHAMIR GOT THE PHONE CALL FROM ZIPPORI ON FRIDAY, SEPTEMBER 17.

PARA 15: EITAN'S AGE IS FIFTY-FOUR YEARS OLD. HE IS A VETERAN OF ALL ISRAELI WARS, WHO IS KNOWN FOR HIS BATTLEFIELD VALOR AND COOLNESS UNDER FIRE.

NEXT SENTENCE: EITAN HAD PREDICTED TO THE CABINET ETC.

PARA 17: YARON SAID THIS (SYSTEM SHOWED INSENSITIVITY) SOMETIME AFTER THE MASSACRE, BUT WE DON'T KNOW WHEN.

PAGE 3   JERU/3/NYK   12 FEB 83
PARA 18: SAGUY'S FIRST NAME IS YEHOSHUA.

PARA 19: TECHNICALLY, SAGUY IS CHIEF (NOT DIRECTOR) OF MILITARY INTELLIGENCE.

SAME PARA: LET'S SAY THAT "HE HAD BEEN OVERRULED BY SHARON, WHO HAD PREFERRED TO TAKE THE ADVICE OF THE MOSSAD"—MAKES THE POINT A BIT MORE CLEAR, WE THINK.

PARA 25: THE QUESTION: WHY DID THE COMMISSION APPARENTLY MAKE NO EFFORT TO INTERVIEW PHALANGIST COMMANDERS REALLY OUGHT TO BE CHANGED. THOSE COMMANDERS WERE INDEED (EMPHASIS) ASKED BY THE COMMISSION TO APPEAR, BUT THEY REFUSED.

IN FILE, PLEASE NOTE GENERAL DRORI, WHO HAD BEEN UNCOMFORTABLE WITH THE LEBANESE GOING IN, DID ASK THE LEBANESE ARMY TO ENTER THE CAMPS. THE LEBANESE SAID NO, ACCORDING TO THE COMMISSION REPORT.

THE LAST QUESTION AS TO THE COMMISSION AND MOTIVES FOR ATTRIBUTING CONTRADICTORY TESTIMONY ETC. IS IRRELEVANT TO US, SINCE THE COMMISSION SOMETIMES IN CASES OF CONTRADICTION DID EXPRESS AN OPINION ON WHICH VERSION THEY BELIEVED TO BE CORRECT. IN THE CASE OF THE LT. COL WHO WAS SUPPOSED TO HAVE RECEIVED COMPLAINTS FROM IDF SOLDIERS OF A MASSACRE, BUT DID NOT PASS IT ON, COMMISSION RECOMMENDED THAT THE IDF CONDUCT AN INVESTIGATION.

Appendix L
The Parker Press Release
(February 13, 1983)

For release:
3 p.m. Eastern Time
Sunday, February 13, 1983

Contact: Brian Brown
(212) 841-4923
Sunday: Robert Parker
(212) 841-4923
Radio/TV: Marilyn Sahner
(212) 841-2783

SHARON SAID TO HAVE URGED LEBANESE TO SEND PHALANGISTS INTO CAMPS

An unpublished passage in the report of the Israeli commission on the Beirut Massacre discloses that Israeli Defense Minister Sharon met with the Gemayel family on the day after Lebanon's President-elect Bashir Gemayel was assassinated, Time magazine reports this week.

Time says: "Sharon reportedly told the Gemayels that the Israeli army would be moving into West Beirut and that he expected the Christian forces to go into the Palestinian refugee camps. Sharon also reportedly discussed with the Gemayels the need for the Phalangists to take revenge for the assassination of Bashir, but the details of the conversation are not known."

The Israeli commission recommended the removal of Sharon as defense minister. Sharon later resigned his position, though Time speculates that he may remain in the cabinet as a minister without portfolio.

Time says that the Commission's report "was hailed in the U.S. and Western Europe as a remarkable example of self-criticism by a democratic society." The New York Times commented: "How rare the nation that seeks salvation by revealing such shame." In France, Interior Minister Gaston Deferre remarked, "This report is the honor of Israel. It gives the world a new lesson in democracy." The Italian Communist newspaper L'Unita called the report "a turning point for Israel," while Italian Journalist Arrigo Levi commented in Turin's La Stampa: "It would be difficult to find any other nation at war that would let itself be subject to such an open and hard self-criticism."

Reaction to the report in the Arab world was much more critical. The Jordan Times said that the purpose of the report was "to protect the Israeli version of justice and self-rightiousness," and one Cairo editor described the report as an attempt "to find scapegoats to save the Israeli defense establishment."

Says Time: "It was unfortunate that the Arab reaction so demeaned their case. Arabs were at a loss to respond cogently to the results of the Israeli inquiry precisely because no government in the Arab world would dream of subjecting itself to the scrutiny of an independent commission."

Kelly's "Cheers" Memorandum to Duncan

February 15, 1983)

STM: JERU/1 NYK   15 FEB 83   MSG: ADM
TO: NEWS DESK   FOR: DUNCAN
FROM: JERUSALEM   BY: KELLY
SLUG: INQUIRY   EOH:

THAT MUST HAVE BEEN ONE HECK OF A NEWS RELEASE ON THE INQUIRY COVER, SPECIFICALLY ON THAT FAIRLY INNOCUOUSLY WORDED "TIME HAS LEARNED" GRAPH ABOUT SHARON'S MEETING WITH THE GEMAYEL FAMILY.

IT WAS ON PAGE ONE IN THE PAPERS MONDAY. SOMEBODY AT THE DEFENSE MINISTRY WAS COMMENTING IT WAS ALL LIES. THEN THE PRESS OFFICE PUT OUT A STATEMENT THAT THE DEFENSE MINISTRY RESPONSE WAS "NOT AN OFFICIAL DENIAL." THEN LATER IN THE KNESSET MONDAY BEGIN CALLED IT "BALD LIES AND SLANDER" AND CALLED ON TIME'S EDITORS TO APOLOGIZE TO SHARON AND THE STATE OF ISRAEL "FOR DISSEMINATING THIS LIBEL."

AND I DON'T THINK ANYBODY'S HAD A CHANCE TO READ THE STORY YET: AT LEAST OUR COPY HASN'T ARRIVED. WE MUST HAVE STRUCK A NERVE. CHEERS.

Appendix N

"Personal & Confidential" Letter
From Halevy to Duncan
(May 17, 1984)

Personal and Confidential

To: Dick Duncan
Frm: David Halevy

whenever i feel like writing or even when i am forced to write, i seem to have some kind of problem with the opening lines. so, in order to make it simple, basically there are two reasons for this note: one, i felt like writing to you and sharing some of my personal feelings and two, there are practical reasons.

i have to admit that the last weeks have taught me a lesson. apparently journalistic "victories" only leave a sour taste. almost four years after publishing the story on the jewish terror network, after telling the story of Begin halting the investigation, etc. the facts are finally proving the accuracy of the story published by the Washington Star on August 7, 1980.

and while saying this i don't mean Time. being right or wrong in our profession has little meaning. it is the personal professionalism, self-integrity and self-confidence that counts. the rest is actually irrelevant and this includes all the rough times—you know—i went through, the names and the suspicion.

aside from the personal point of view, there are some developments—to which jewish terrorism should be attached—that seem to me to be very worrying. these are the actual vindication of arik sharon, the cabinet minister's statement justifying the bombing of the west bank mayors (professor yuval ne'eman) and other signs of mysticism, fascism and radicalism. i don't want to draw historical analogies but it seems to me that the difficulty in recording these trends is as complicated as it was in the twenties and thirties in europe and mainly germany. one thing is clear and this is that the deteriorating economic fabric, which will only become really clear after the general elections on july 23, will only add to the frightening reality.

the involvement of IDF soldiers and officers is another factor leading to a general feeling that someone has pulled the rug from under my feet. as far as i know the facts, i wonder whether the investigation will actually dig to the end. a few days ago, when harry interviewed amos oz, the writer, he said that he does not feel an exile in his own land. the fact that he used this phrase speaks for itself. yet, i cannot share his feelings. the gap between my generation's dreams and the day to day reality is too big.

strange as it may sound, the result of all this is boredom. there is nothing here to cause enthusiasm, nothing rates as a challange anymore. the political developments are running in a pattern that is easy to predict. the military-defense establishment is taking a route that at best will lead nowhere. and the intelligentzia [sic] is taking such a non-ideological approach that no sparks are lighting up the darkness that is engulfing us all.

if these statements lead you to believe that i have lost my senses, am pessimistic or have lost the ability to analyse, you will be wrong. i know this country and its people. i was once part of it and them. this tunnel is going nowhere and there is no light at the end. i might be wrong from A to Z, but i may also be right.

whatever the case my own personal point of view is irrelevant. someone else has to sort it out. harry and others should find the answers and make the judgement.

i managed to survive mrs. meir and mr. begin. i have done
it all. i had my victorious moments and weeks. i had my first
rate stories and i had a bigger share of suffering for being
first, for spelling it all out. i have established my reputation
from here and whatever is here i have already done it. i want
to spend some time in a place where the level of my personal
involvement will be less acute.

    i can no longer become enthusiastic over here and i
will not regret what i have written, nor have i said it all
because i am in a bad mood. i will not change my
decision, when the weather improves or when shimon
peres will (if at all) become prime minister. cutting a long
story short, i'll stay as long it [sic] suits you, harry and
the magazine. i would love to hear from you about the
timing of my next assignment.

David /s/

PS: an isreali [sic] publisher and also an american agent
have approached me and asked me to write a book on
jewish terrorism. harry—and i share his view—thinks it
is a bit too much to handle for us and myself right now.
please let me know your feelings.

Appendix O
Letter From Duncan to Halevy
(May 23, 1984)

Personal and Confidential

Dear Dudu:

Thanks for your letter. I can certainly see how you must feel let down that justification doesn't really come in kind, for the story that got you into so much trouble. On the other hand, I have always felt that the trouble you were in was not so much a matter of truth or falsehood; plenty of stories can be wrong or half-wrong. The heart of the trouble was politics.

And even when the facts now tend to vindicate you, the politics are the same. Perhaps not quite the same in the Begin sense, but the politico-cultural atmosphere which makes an outcast—or worse—of those who dare to criticize the Central Myths of Israel (some of them the finest myths in the west, some pretty damn debased and self-serving recently); that atmosphere is unchanged and seems to be stifling you. As it most [sic] stifle many.

Your German analogies frighten me. I know what you mean, I think, but I hope you are not proved right.

My timetable for your departure is still the same. I'll have word for you by late summer, at the latest, of a move to be initiated late this year. There are a few things I want to clear up first. But I'm quite clear in my own mind, and I think you are, that this is the right way.

Perhaps you could come to the states and rub elbows with all the nice liberal, intelligent, devout jews here and pick up a little much-needed rosy nostalgia for Israel. You know, singing songs together down on the Kibbutz, that sort of thing.

In a funny way there is an American parallel. The

Moral Majority is fighting for a return to the rural and
small-town Protestant cultural (into which I was born)
which is lost forever, except in Ronald Reagan's speeches.

Please cover the elections for us and get us through
the formation of a government, and then we'll get you a
mover for your furniture.

Also please do not do any books on terrorism,
especially Israeli. And lie low on Sharon. You will be
rewarded, although I'm not sure I'll ----- another Bureau
Chief as good as Kelly. Love to Nikki.

                                        Dick

Steimatzky Books of Special Interest

Buy them at local bookstores or use this convenient coupon for ordering.
MAIL ORDER BONUS: No shipping charges.
EXTRA MAIL ORDER BONUS: No tax will be charged on this special offer. We will pay it for you!

☐ **THE LEBANON WAR,** *by David Eshel, Lt. Col. (IDF ret.).* Softcover (8¼"x10½"). 80 pp. With maps and photographs. $14.95.
An in-depth and illustrated account of this wrenching Mideast conflict.

☐ **OUR MAN IN DAMASCUS: ELIE COHEN,** *by Eli Ben-Hanan.* Paperback. 143 pp. $5.95.
The thrilling, shocking, true story of Israel's most daring spy. Reads like a Le Carre or Fleming novel.

☐ **PILLAR OF FIRE** *by Yigal Lossin.* Hardcover (8½"x11"). 545 pp. Illustrated. $40.00.
Adapted from the renowned Israeli television series, this powerful book chronicles the dramatic history of Zionism from 1917 through the creation of the State of Israel in 1948, using vivid photographs and accompanying text.

☐ **THE WESTERN WALL (HAKOTEL),** *by Meir Ben-Dov, Mordechai Naor and Zeev Aner.* Hardcover (8½"x11"). 245 pp. Illustrated $29.95.
The story of the most important national and religious monument in Israel. Illustrated with hundreds of magnificent photographs and works of art by some of the world's great artists.

☐ **THE JERUSALEM I LOVE,** *by Joan Comay.* Hardcover (8½"x11"). 155 pp. 548 full color and 78 b&w illustrations. $14.95.
This book captures in vivid prose and pictures the 4,000-year saga of this wondrous city.

Many more books available in English and in Hebrew.

Send your check or money order to:
Steimatzky Publishing Inc., 152 E. 65th Street, NY, NY 10021

Please send the books in the quantities marked above to:

Name

Address

Enclosed is my check for $_____ . I understand that Steimatzky will pay all shipping and handling costs, as well as all taxes on the orders.

☐ Please send your English catalog.   ☐ Please send your Hebrew catalog.

Steimatzky Books of Special Interest

Buy them at local bookstores or use this convenient coupon for ordering.
MAIL ORDER BONUS: No shipping charges.
EXTRA MAIL ORDER BONUS: No tax will be charged on this special offer. We will pay it for you!

☐ **MASADA** by Yigal Yadin. Softcover (5"x7½"). Illustrated 256 pp. $12.50
Newly-published softcover edition of Yigal Yadin's popular account of Herod's fortress and the Zealot's last stand. (Also available in hardcover.)

☐ **ISRAEL AIR FORCE, 1984.** Softcover. (8¼"x10½"). Approx. 80 pp. Illustrated. $14.95
Updated, illustrated history of this modern Air Force and its combats. More than 130 photos highlighting the F-16, F-15, F-4, Kfir, A-4 and Lavi.

☐ **JERUSALEM: Sacred City of Mankind.** By Teddy Kollek and Moshe Pearlman. Hardcover (7¼"x10"). 284 pp. 64 full color and 140 b&w illusrations. $35.00.
Captures the drama and flavor of the story of Jerusalem from earliest times to the present day. Co-authored by Teddy Kollek — not only the present Mayor of Jerusalem but also the first Mayor of the City reunited.

☐ **THE REVOLT,** by Menachem Begin. Hardcover (5½"x8½"). 166 pp. Illustrated. $14.95.
The inside story of the revolt of the underground army, the Irgun Zvai Leumi, against the British forces in Palestine.

☐ **WHITE NIGHTS: The Story of a Prisoner in Russia.** by Menachem Begin. Hardcover (6"x8½"). 240 pp. $14.95.
The story of Menachem Begin's grueling experience as a prisoner in a Siberian hard labor camp in the 1940's.

Many more books available in English and in Hebrew.

Send your check or money order to:
Steimatzky Publishing Inc., 152 E. 65th Street, NY, NY 10021

Please send the books in the quantities marked above to:

Name _____

Address _____

Enclosed is my check for $_____. I understand that Steimatzky will pay all shipping and handling costs, as well as all taxes on the orders.

☐ Please send your English catalog.   ☐ Please send your Hebrew catalog.

ii. General Ariel Sharon (left) with Don Aharoni, the book's author.

i. Ariel Sharon and wife Lily enjoy a front page *New York Post Story*:
   "Sharon Jury Blasts Time."